LENT

LENT

*Reflections and Stories
on the Daily Readings*

Megan McKenna

ORBIS BOOKS

Maryknoll, New York 10545

The Catholic Foreign Mission Society of America (Maryknoll) recruits and trains people for overseas missionary service. Through Orbis Books, Maryknoll aims to foster the international dialogue that is essential to mission. The books published, however, reflect the opinions of their authors and are not meant to represent the official position of the society.

Copyright © 1996 by Megan McKenna

All rights reserved. No part of this publication may be reproduced or transmitted in any form or by any means, electronic or mechanical, including photocopying, recording or any information storage or retrieval system, without prior permission in writing from the publishers.

Queries regarding rights and permissions should be addressed to: Orbis Books, P. O. Box 308, Maryknoll, New York 10545-0308.

"In the Land There Is a Hunger" by Michael Lynch, copyright © 1981, 1986 by C & M Productions. Published by Oregon Catholic Press, Portland, OR.

Published by Orbis Books, Maryknoll, NY 10545-0308
Manufactured in the United States of America

ORBIS/ISBN 1-57075-045-9

For Christopher McCoy
gypsy moth, missionary, ardent lover of maps, geography,
Peru and all strange lands, Early Fathers of the Church,
and the poor, especially of Villa Salvador, Lima.
Dedicated passionately to the Mystery,
the Kingdom's enduring justice, peace and truth.
My home in Liverpool, web connection to Wales
and England and anywhere else we can go,
who feeds me images, books and unfinished stories,
gleefully corrects my English and translates for me.
Best at laughing as he disappears right before my eyes!
Mil gracias, mi amigo, de mi corazón.

"Growth does not come from putting on any spiritual clothing. Growth comes from removing and removing, ceasing, undoing, and letting ourselves drop down or even fall into the core of our living being."

—Linda Hogan
Chickasaw poet
quoted in *Listening to the Land*

Contents

Monday of the Third Week of Lent   89
Tuesday of the Third Week of Lent   93
Wednesday of the Third Week of Lent   97
Thursday of the Third Week of Lent   102
Friday of the Third Week of Lent   106
Saturday of the Third Week of Lent   109

THE FOURTH WEEK OF LENT

Sunday of the Fourth Week of Lent   113
Monday of the Fourth Week of Lent   122
Feast of St. Joseph   126
Wednesday of the Fourth Week of Lent   130
Thursday of the Fourth Week of Lent   133
Friday of the Fourth Week of Lent   136
Saturday of the Fourth Week of Lent   141

THE FIFTH WEEK OF LENT

Sunday of the Fifth Week of Lent   146
Feast of the Annunciation   155
Tuesday of the Fifth Week of Lent   159
Wednesday of the Fifth Week of Lent   162
Thursday of the Fifth Week of Lent   166
Friday of the Fifth Week of Lent   169
Saturday of the Fifth Week of Lent   174

HOLY WEEK

Passion Sunday/Palm Sunday   178
Monday of Holy Week   185
Tuesday of Holy Week   190
Wednesday of Holy Week   195
Holy Thursday   199
Good Friday   205
The Easter Vigil   212

Works Cited   223

Introduction

✠ Once upon a time there was a storyteller who loved words: the sound and feel of them, the way they flowed, eddied about, returned, and spiraled down in little currents. Better, he loved stories: any kind really, but especially the ones that caught folks and carried them, casting them forth in a place distant from where they were when the story began. Best of all, he loved telling the stories. He was compelled into it by some power deeper than any force that moved rivers and stirred the seas in their depths. He was most himself in the telling: graceful, free, light, and truthful, obedient to Another, whom he liked to think of as the Word, the Story that all others could only serve and imitate.

He lived simply and faithfully and told stories whenever he could. Then, one day, he began to notice things changing, or to be more precise—disappearing. First, it was little things: his keys, glasses, notes to himself, pages off the calendar, socks, spoons. Nothing disappeared that was of any import really, but it was annoying. He thought of himself as forgetful, and he chalked it up to short-term memory loss and laughed about mid-life.

But the problem grew worse, and it became harder to laugh at. More began to disappear: hours of the day, sleep and dreams at night, acquaintances, even friends. Then pages of his manuscripts disappeared, also notes for classes or talks, his suitcase. None was ever returned or found. He wondered if he might be ill, or losing his mind, or becoming senile. And then he began to notice connections, disconcerting connections. He carefully kept records until he was absolutely sure of his findings, which disturbed him greatly. Everything that had disappeared was closely connected to a story he had told.

He tried not telling stories, but that didn't work. He tried to monitor the stories and figure out ahead of time what he'd lose. Sometimes that worked, but the logic was not always immediately apparent. There seemed to be another structure of logic and symbolism at work. He tried being detached, unattached, even practicing the virtue of poverty, and he soon realized that this was hard. He grew fearful and apprehensive. When and where would it all stop?

This predicament became the backdrop of his life. Stories continued to enchant him, and there seemed more of them. He found them in books, peoples' conversations, his mind, observing situations and relationships on the street, traveling. There was suddenly a surfeit of stories. They couldn't have come (or were they presented to him as choices?) at a worst time in his life. He took them in, gingerly, greedily, like a man hungry for food, insight, wisdom, and hope.

Then he began to lose pieces of himself! First, he lost his hair, fingernails, toenails: replaceable pieces. One day he told a story— enthralled by it himself as the words flowed from him—and he lost a finger. The next day it was another on the same hand. It was time to make some major decisions. He just couldn't go on like this, at least not without consciously knowing what would happen every time he was caught in a story. Still, he was bound to the stories and to the telling.

Soon he noticed another side-effect. As he disappeared he became more and more adept as a teller. The stories acquired more power, breadth, and influence. In fact, they began to come true in reality. He began to hope that in losing himself perhaps there was a larger design, a whole that he was contributing to and literally creating out of his own flesh.

That thought sustained him at times, but he kept losing himself and disappearing—legs, hands, arms, feet, shoulders, hips. Not much of his torso was left. He clung to his face, eyes, and mouth, his memory and mind, his ears and lungs, and, of course, his heart. It was all that he had left. Was any story worth losing his sight for? or his memory? or his heart? or his very soul? Was the Story insatiable? Did it really want everything, all of him, down to the last shreds of his body and soul? More to the point: could he and would he give it all up, in trust? Could he?

That is the question. Can we and will we give ourselves up, in trust to others, to the Other? Where is the end, the limit? How much are we willing to lose? How much of ourselves must be emptied out so that the Word, the Story, can come through us?

This book is about Lent, a book of reflections, stories, and questions for forty days based on the daily lectionary readings for the season. Its context is this story. What if this story came true in each of our lives, all of our lives in the community of the Word? What if every day of Lent we lost something of ourselves so that the Teller, the Word, might flow through us more surely and freely? At the end of the forty days, what would be left? Can we, will we consent to the story? to the diminishment? to the loss? to the mystery of the ending? to total trust in the Word? What if there is no end until all time disappears into eternity in the incarnation and the wording of the Story in our flesh now?

Supposedly, after giving a talk in the Far East, Thomas Merton left the room with the words: "I think I'll just disappear." They were his last words. Soon he was dead, electrocuted by an electric fan, and shipped home to the Kentucky hills in an army transport plane. Did this monk, who spent twenty-seven years seeking the face and the mystery of God, know something? Did he just disappear with a twinkle in his eye? This Lent, let us just disappear back into the arms of the One who created earth to be a garden, a dwellingplace secure for all peoples, a haven for the least among us.

Long before Jesus, a disturber of structures and souls, disappeared into the tomb he was intent on vanishing into the reverence of God, the shadow of the Spirit, the will of his Father, the service and obedience of his human companions, and the depths of history and time. Let us disappear with him and into him. As we go to die with him, losing ourselves in obedience and trust, so too we will rise with him on the first day of the week, before dawn . . .

The Sunday readings vary each year on a three-year rotation—cycles A, B, and C. The readings are carefully chosen to form a complete unit that best illustrates the church's understanding of the Lent-Easter season. An important theme in all the cycles, shown most clearly perhaps in the cycle A readings, is preparation for baptism. By presenting the major passages from the gospels, for example, catechumens are introduced to the faith and the faith of believers is deepened. The Sunday reflections in *Lent* are based primarily on the readings for cycle A. Scripture references for years in the B and C cycles appear as footnotes on the "Sunday" pages of each week. Daily readings are the same in all three cycles.

LENT BEGINS

—— ✛ ——

Ash Wednesday

Joel 2:12-18
2 Corinthians 5:20-6:2
Matthew 6:1-6, 16-18

The season of disappearing begins with intimations of impending disaster, oncoming doom, the approaching day of Yahweh, a day of judgment and reckoning and justice for all the nations and the peoples. This day will be "exceedingly great, terrible and dreadful—who can endure it?" (Joel 2:11).

The prophet Joel, in the company of all prophets, knows the transitory nature of all life, of governments and structures and reigns of power. One day they will all disappear. Judged by God's enduring standards, there will be a separating of the just and the saved from the unjust and lost.

The reading begins with the words of Yahweh:

> Yet even now, return to me with your whole heart, with fasting, weeping and mourning. Rend your heart, not your garment. Return to Yahweh, your God—gracious and compassionate.

The invitation/exhortation is announced. It sounds as if God is pleading with us to come home, to turn from the directions we are headed. The words are proclaimed with the power of a trumpet blast. This summons is a warning for the soul, an alarm set off to jolt the heart of the people and set it back on its natural rhythm. It is for repentance, a pulling back of the people so that they are one in communion, obedient, belonging to God. All are to be drawn back into the heart of the community, in our case, to the body of Christ, the church. Martin Luther King, Jr., called the church the "gathering of sinners." Everyone—infants nursing, newlyweds, priests, ancients, children, and those who have no rank in the nations—is to come home. It is time to be gathered together, to be sanctified, to bring together the disparate, the lost, the separated, and the exiled.

It is a proclamation about Yahweh, our God who is gracious and compassionate, slow to anger, full of kindness. And who knows? God probably will relent once more and spare some part of the harvest to be given as sacred offerings. But it is not just food that Yahweh is interested in sparing, it is we, God's people, who are spared so that we too might become sacred offerings given wholeheartedly to God. It is we who are to become a blessing that God leaves behind for all the nations to take heart from and to marvel at the presence of God among us. This God of ours, we are assured, will be stirred to concern, even for the land, and will take pity on us all. It is time to heed the summons.

God is a reconciler, pleading our case, begging on our behalf, intervening between us and ways of life that are dangerous and selfish and inhuman. This season is about returning to the image of God that we were fashioned to reflect. It is time to work again at being reconcilers, peacemakers, ambassadors for Christ.

This season is not just for us but for the reconciliation and communion of the whole world. These forty days are for becoming the very holiness of God, for radical alterations in the society and life we dwell within. We all become fellow workers receiving grace and the power to reconstitute human life and the universe. Our response must be immediate. We must bend our wills and grab hold of one another and walk together again as we usher one another into the presence of God.

How do we do this? By disappearing! We must be on our guard against performing religious acts for people to see and instead learn to be invisible, sly, crafty, ingenious, secretly aiding and abetting the kingdom's coming into the world. We must be creative and imaginative in fasting and performing acts of mercy and compassion—imitating God, who dwells among us and delights in giving solace and help anonymously, borrowing the flesh of believers for God's work in the world.

And we must pray: in secret, with stealth, behind closed doors, humbly, privately, intimately. When we fast, we should work at looking good so no one suspects the radical change within us and so within the world. No one is supposed to know what we are doing individually although we have all been summoned to do this with one heart and spirit together. Our actions are to seep into the world like the scent of perfume distilled in the air or, as a Japanese proverb says, The scent of the flowers remains on the hands of the one who gives them away as gift.

Why all the secrecy? At root, our God is a secret, hidden in mystery, hidden in all the earth and its creatures. Nothing is as it seems to be. God lurks in the most unlikely places, waiting to be uncovered, found, and embraced. The ancient practices of Lent—prayer, fasting, almsgiving, and the works of mercy—remind us of these truths, which form the core and heart of our practice of belief in God.

Peter Chrysologus, a fifth-century bishop, tells us that fasting is the soul of prayer and that mercy is the lifeblood of fasting. So, if we pray, fast; if we fast, show mercy; if we want our petition to be heard, hear the petition of others. If we do not close our ear to others, we open God's ear to us. God hides among us. Now is the time to learn lowliness, obedience, and turning again toward God without fanfare. The whole community is doing it; it is something we are doing in common.

THE RITUAL OF THE ASHES

The ancient tradition of ashes weaves together the glory of the past year's Palm Sunday and unfaithfulness with today's steadfast intent to turn toward the cross and our baptism once again. The ashes were once palm branches waved gloriously before the coming of the Lord, loudly proclaiming joy and belief as Jesus rode on the back of an ass into the city of Jerusalem. Now they are a symbol, not just for today but for the season. They are a marking out, a signing in memory of our baptismal signing with oil and water. They are also connected to death, the cross, and suffering—the suffering and our share of the burden of the cross that is a necessary response to the unnecessary suffering, death, and injustice rampant in our world. This is a time to acknowledge the sin, evil, and injustice in us and our collusion with it in the world. It is the time to undo it, to repair the world and restore the reign of God on earth, now, here, beginning with our bodies and relationships. It is sobering yet hopeful to hear the words: "Remember . . . that you are dust and unto dust you will return."

There is a story about a Zen teacher named Fengxue (Wind Cave), who said to his monks: "If you raise a speck of dust, the nation flourishes, but the elders furrow their brows. If you don't raise a speck of dust, the nation perishes, but the elders relax their brows." A speck of dust—what is that? What kind of power lies in a speck of dust? Talk to anyone with dust in his or her computer or digital sound system, or even on a contact lens or in the eye! To raise a speck of dust is to stir up goodness, struggle for justice, speak up for those who stutter or do not speak the languages of power, to band together to stand resolutely and nonviolently before evil and refuse to be absorbed into it or intimidated by it. Do this and the powers furrow their brows in consternation. Neglect the dust specks and the elders in charge breathe easy, relax their brows—and the people perish.

The Zen story sounds like Joel's call to stir the Spirit, to practice compassion, and thus to confound the horrors of inhuman living. Lent is about making sure that the people flourish. Lent is about encouraging and giving fresh heart to those around us, strengthening the bonds of community, reminding everyone that no one resists evil alone, and recalling that we are already reconciled to God in the cross of Jesus. Now it is up to us to accept that gift, dedicate ourselves to that reality in gratitude, and extend that gift to all in need. The ashes, mixed with the waters of our baptism, make good fertilizer; it will help the seeds of the gospel take deeper root in us and bring forth the fruits, the harvest of justice, peace, and generosity, as well as return us to true worship of God—knowing that our God will return the gift by leaving behind a blessing for us.

This is a day of dedication, consecration, and purity of heart. God again and again relents and does not deal with us as our sins deserve. It is time for us to become relenting children, to humbly beg for mercy and give mercy to others by what we do with our weeks of Lent. Perhaps each family, each religious community, each parish, diocese, and national church needs to do the same thing together for Lent— something that draws us outside ourselves and turns us toward others with joy, fresh faces, and gladness.

We are called to fast in the ways the prophets describe—to fast from injustice and insensitivity to the poor and the suffering and needy around us; to fast from selfishness and indulgence; to fast from concentration on our own sinfulness and to turn toward others, as God always turns toward us and hears our cry in our need. Then we can be assured that we will be different at the end of this season of greening hope and purpled flowers of intense attentiveness to God. Let us pray together for one another.

Lord our God, you make known the true life. You cut away corruption and strengthen faith, you build up hope and foster love. In the name of your beloved Son, our Lord Jesus Christ, and in the power of the Holy Spirit, we ask you to remove from your servants all unbelief and hesitation in faith, the love of money and lawless passions, enmity and quarrelling, and every manner of evil. And because you have called us to be holy and sinless in your sight, create in us a spirit of faith and reverence, of patience and hope, of temperance and purity, and of charity and peace. We ask this through Christ, our Lord. Amen. (Exorcism prayer #97, RCIA)

Thursday after Ash Wednesday

Deuteronomy 30:15-20
Luke 9:22-25

These readings in the first days of Lent are previews of all that is to come. They articulate the foundations of what will be asked of us daily in the weeks ahead. In the first reading it is Moses who confronts the people:

Today I have set before you life and prosperity, death and doom . . . I have set before you life and death, the blessing and the curse. Choose life, then, that you and your descendants may live, by loving the Lord, your God, heeding his voice, and holding fast to him.

Choose! It is an imperative. It is crucial to survival, to salvation, and to the quality of our lives now and far into the future.

Moses' exhortation to the people echoes the belief of many Native American tribes: when decisions are made, the people sit upon the earth, their mother, and upon the bodies of the children to be born of her flesh, and they choose, reckoning the consequences on the next seven generations of children. Nothing is just individual or personal; everything is communal and interpersonal.

Moses approaches the people prior to their entrance into the promised land. They have endured the desert together, and a generation has perished in the sojourn. They have come far from their attachment to Egypt and the place of their bondage. Indeed, they have begun the process of becoming the people of Yahweh, belonging to God, to each other, and to the land given them as an inheritance.

They have learned something of faithfulness and of sticking together and trusting both God and one another. They are more than the ragtag bands of people who escaped into the Sinai wilderness. They have entered into a covenant and are tied intimately through the Law and the power of God in Moses and Joshua and their ancestors before them. They have learned about justice, lived through fear, and experienced the need for responsibility for one another and accountability for their words and actions. There are memories of what God has done for them and continues to do. They know that their personal beliefs and actions mark the community, either slowing it down, detouring it, or contributing to its slow movement to the promised land. They are close, and it is a time of danger and a time of testing out their sense of obedience. What they do will reveal their God. By their choices, their obedience or disobedience to the Law, they will bring forth life or court death and destruction. Without God's presence, support, power, and closeness they will be left helpless before all they will soon face in this place of promise, already occupied by others. They are not just entering the land of Canaan, they are entering a new level of intimacy and knowledge of God. It is time to choose. It is time for all of them to choose as one heart, with one mind and one intent.

There is a prayer from the Laguna Pueblo that is a call to communion and joint action:

> I add my breath to your breath, that our days may be long on the Earth, that the days of our people may be long, that we shall be as one person, that we may finish our road together.

The gospel from Luke extends the command to choose life, demanding more from those who enter a covenant now with the Son of Man. This Son of Man faces a time of suffering inflicted by others; rejection by his own followers and the leaders of the people; and the sentence of death by crucifixion. And then he is raised up on the third day. It is sobering and harsh, terrifying in its implications. Jesus goes first, precedes us, but if we are to follow behind him then we must begin by denying our very selves, taking up our cross each day, and following in his steps. Whoever would save or cling to life will lose it, and whoever loses their life—lets go and lets it slip away—will save it, if it is done for the sake of the Son of Man. Choose! Choose life and blessing or choose death and cursing!

Superimposed on Jesus' cross we often see a rendering of *ixthūs*, the Greek word for "fish," the sign of the early Christian community; or a depiction of the lamb, the Passover sacrifice, carrying aloft a banner of triumph and glory. These are basic symbols of our faith. The sign of the cross is a way of dedicating ourselves to prayer, of blessing one another, or of being blessed as a group. It is ritual expression of belief, a public acknowledgment of who we are: believers in Jesus, the crucified One.

For Jesus' immediate contemporaries and companions, the sentence Jesus was to face was horrifying, yet a constant reality in a country held under the grip of domination and oppression by occupying forces. This rejection, this cross, this legal death was inhuman suffering inflicted by those with power and might upon those without power. It was violence, controlled and intended to instill terror into masses of people in order to keep them in line and compliant, even though despairing and angry, poor and enraged by their future and lack of hope for any life of freedom. Gerard Sloyan quotes an Easter sermon by Melito of Sardis, given around 170 C.E., which offers a graphic description:

> Listen while you tremble before him on whose account the earth trembles: He that suspended the earth was himself suspended. He that fixed the heavens was fixed [with nails.] He that supported the earth was supported on a tree. The Master was exposed to shame, God put to death.

The early rituals of baptism often called for the catechumens to kneel on the floor before immersion and before their profession of faith, reminding them, "You are saved, but on your knees and under the sign of the cross." This initiation into the daily life of the Christian believer was founded on acceptance of this command to deny oneself, to be emptied out, to disappear, to bend to God's will and the needs of others. Profit in this religion is not about gaining the whole world but rather about losing one's hold on the things of this world and using them to serve another kingdom.

Prayer, fasting, and almsgiving were the basis of this practice of denial of self and taking up the cross daily. Christians were called daily to let go of goods and services that were necessary for the survival of others in the community. Ambrose, bishop of Milan in the fourth century, the teacher and confessor of Augustine, preached in Lent:

> How could it not be evil to alone possess the Lord's goods, to alone enjoy what belongs to everyone? Therefore, if we can call our own the goods that belong to the Lord of all, they also belong to everybody else, just as do we his servants. For the Lord's things belong to all.

Choosing life—accepting baptism and inclusion in this group that follows the Son of Man—has serious consequences and implies obligations and responsibilities. This call to life is as ancient as the prophets, recorded in the books of Sirach and Wisdom.

> My child, if you have decided to serve the Lord,
>   prepare yourself for trials.
> Keep your heart upright and remain resolute:
>   do not be upset in the time of adversity.
> Hold fast to the Lord,
>   do not separate yourself from him so that you may
>   be successful to the end of your days.
> Accept all that happens to you,
>   be patient when you are humbled,
> for as gold is tested in the fire
>   so those acceptable to God are tested in the crucible
>   of humiliation.
> Have confidence in him and he will take care of you;
>   follow the right path and hope in him.
>   (Sirach 2:1-6)

This second day of Lent we are told that this will be a daily discipline and choice for life—for a life in common, for a life that cares for others, for a life that trusts God in the face of hardship and trials, for a life that will be redeemed and restored and will become a life of abundance beyond any of our present hopes. It is time to choose life and blessing and to choose to hang on for a dearer life, a life flowing with milk and honey for all peoples, a life of justice and holiness that endures faithfully. Even in the beginning it can seem overwhelming, but we follow in another's steps and many have gone before us in faith.

John Henry Cardinal Newman (1801-90), a member of the Oratory and a convert to Catholicism, wrote a prayer during his own struggle to grow as a Christian:

> *May Christ support us all the day long, till the shadows lengthen and evening comes, and the busy world is hushed, and the fever of life is over and our work is done. Then in His mercy may he grant us safe lodging and holy rest and peace at the last. Amen.*

Friday after Ash Wednesday

Isaiah 58:1-9
Matthew 9:14-15

This day is about fasting, abstaining, doing without, emptying out our storehouses, and giving to others as we have received from God. It's about fasting from food, from excess, from greed and avarice, from collecting and hoarding material possessions.

But it goes deeper and moves into more personal areas of our lives as well. It's about fasting from selfishness and obsession with self-knowledge, security, and peace, peace of the kind the world worships and encourages—devoid of grief and mourning for those who lack the basic necessities of life or suffer because of the violence and insensitivity of others. It's about fasting from comfort, from ease, from the route of least resistance, from the herd mentality, from pleasure for the sake of pleasure. Most important, it's about fasting from power and self-gratification and glory.

Isaiah is the prophet of power, and the prophet of the servant who suffers on behalf of the truth and the cause of hope for those without hope in this world. He begins with the words of God resounding, shattering our eardrums: "Cry out full-throated and unsparingly, lift up your voice like a trumpet blast: tell my people their wickedness." God is appalled by the people's lack of understanding, arrogance, and self-righteousness. They fast and religiously obey the laws and decrees. They afflict themselves, and they are insulted and upset that God takes no note of them.

God tells the people about their fasting—it insults God. On fast days the people continue to go about their own pursuits. It's business as usual and, worse, they continue to act unjustly, practicing all sorts of legal violence, driving their laborers without respite or rest. The day of fast ends in bitterness, quarrelling, and fighting, "striking with wicked claw." The image is that of a bird of prey, a hunter intent on raw meat, death, and destruction, of carrion, of uncleanliness and foul decay. All the expressions of the fast that are practiced are external: bowed heads, sackcloth and ashes, self-posturing. This is not acceptable to God.

What kind of fast does God want? What kind of fast does God long for and desire?

> This is the fasting that I wish:
>> releasing those bound unjustly,
>> untying the thongs of the yoke;
> setting free the oppressed,
>> breaking every yoke;
> sharing your bread with the hungry,
>> sheltering the oppressed and the homeless;
> clothing the naked when you see them,
>> and not turning your back on your own.

This is fasting from selfishness and insensitivity and inhumanity. This is fasting from competition and profit at the expense of others; from the ways of the world and the kingdoms built on accumulation of goods in isolation from the massive needs of all those who dwell upon the earth. It is the hard work of breaking bounds that are unholy and destructive, that feed off unnecessary suffering and death. It is the work of shattering the yoke of slavery, of nationalism, of one group holding another in bondage, servitude, and misery, so that one group becomes bloated and satiated while the other is starved and impoverished.

This is the work of bridging the gap between rich and poor, between those who control access to services and life and those who wait for what is leftover, discarded, or rejected. This is the work of confronting unholy differences created by sin, both personal and structural. This is the naming and acknowledging of wrong, of evil beginning with the seven deadly sins on an individual level—pride, anger, covetousness, lust, sloth, envy, and gluttony—and the structural and collective sins named by Gandhi as equally deadly: politics without principles, wealth without work, pleasure without conscience, knowledge without character, commerce without morality, worship without sacrifice, and science and technology without humanity.

This kind of fasting begins with an examination of conscience and an intent to turn from these practices and, in the presence of the community, to be held accountable for our word, our firm purpose of amending our ways. It is the work of fasting from individualism and turning into communion and solidarity with others, especially the *anawim*, the poor, the oppressed, those who in their lack and need hide the presence of God incarnated still.

Do we want results? Do we want to be noticed by God? Do we want a reward for our labors and conversion? In a lyrical and impassioned response God tells the people through the mouth of Isaiah his prophet what will happen:

> Then your light shall break forth like the dawn,
>   and your wound shall quickly be healed.
> Your vindication shall go before you,
>   and the glory of the Lord shall be your rear guard.
> Then shall you call, and the Lord will answer,
>   you shall cry for help and he will say: Here I am!
> If you remove from your midst oppression
>   false accusation and malicious speech.

This is fasting that is acceptable and desired by the Lord: fasting from oppression, from false accusation, and from malicious speech.

This kind of fasting is public, political, and economic as well as religious and personally virtuous. In the early church it was seen as essential to the ongoing conversion of baptism among those who belong to God. Basil, the bishop of Caesarea in the fourth century, reminds his congregation:

> The rich declare themselves the masters of the common goods they usurped because they are the first to claim them. If people kept only what is required for their daily needs and if the surplus were given to the poor, both riches and poverty would be abolished.

This is fasting from power that is self-serving and based on violence, from structuring society so that some have too much and most have little or nothing. This is not just devotional but subversive. It means hearing the word of the Lord.

The scene in Matthew's gospel is a set-up by those who decree the rules and rituals of fasting in religious circles and those who consider themselves the followers of John the Baptizer. They query Jesus: "Why is it that while we and the Pharisees fast, your disciples do not?" They are questioning Jesus about the rituals of food and drink, sackcloth, ashes, all the public expressions of doing without.

Jesus' reply might strike us as surprising: "How can wedding guests go in mourning so long as the groom is with them? When the day comes that the groom is taken away, then they will fast." Jesus is describing himself as the groom at a wedding feast, the image of the banquet feast of justice and peace that will usher in the messianic reign of God's power for all the just and the poor who depend on God for their sustenance and survival. *Now* is the time when the groom is being taken away from us.

Along with Jesus, his followers and friends, we are turning toward Jerusalem and picking up our cross daily and denying ourselves. We have known the presence of joy, of the bridegroom, of celebration, of shared company, of the gift of God in Jesus and the gifts of the Spirit and community. Now we share those gifts, give over what has been given into our hands, and fast from taking more, from clinging to the sense of security.

The groom is to be taken from us. His life is to be taken brutally, cold-bloodedly, and with the intent to stop this kind of fast, this kind of almsgiving, this kind of worship of God. This is the way of Lent. This is the story of liberation from oppression and the yoke that weighs down human beings, making them beasts of burden, expendable workers, sources of endless profit. This is what our God wants stopped. This is what God wants us to abstain and fast from wholeheartedly. The book of Sirach puts it succinctly:

> My child, do not deny the poor his food
>   and do not make the man who looks at you with
>   pleading eyes wait.
> Do not sadden the hungry person
>   nor annoy anyone who is in need.
> Do not exasperate an angry man
>   nor withhold alms from the beggar.
> Do not drive away the beggar who is weighed down
>   with afflictions,
>   nor turn away your face from the poor;
> do not snub the needy
>   nor give anyone a reason to curse you. . . .
> Make yourself acceptable to the community. . . .
> Listen to the poor man
>   and reply to him with kind words and with peace.
> Deliver the oppressed from the hands of the oppressor.
>   Do not be weak when you administer justice. . . .
> Then you will be like a child of the Most High
>   and he will love you more than your mother.
>   (Sirach 4:1-10)

The reflection of Etty Hillesum in *An Interrupted Life* reminds us of this kind of fasting and work:

> Whether you are truly attached to life in the raw, in whatever form it may come, is something the years alone will be able to tell. There is energy enough inside you. There is also this: "whether you spend your life laughing or crying, it is still your life." But I am still attached to Western notions of the good life: being healthy, growing wiser and stronger, learning to stand on one's own two feet. But now to work.

"Now to work" at the fasting God wants. We pray in the words of the psalm this day:

For you are not pleased with sacrifices;
    should I offer a holocaust, you would not accept it.
My sacrifice, O God, is a contrite spirit;
a heart contrite and humbled, O God, you will not spurn.
                                                (Psalm 51:18-19)

Saturday after Ash Wednesday

Isaiah 58:9-14
Luke 5:27-32

These are the last of the preparations for long-term involvement
in Lent. The reading from Isaiah is repeated in part and extended
into the arena of worship—how to make holy the day of the sabbath.
In so doing Isaiah reminds and reveals to the people new and strong
faces of their God. And Jesus, in Luke's gospel, reminds the people at
Levi's grand reception (to celebrate his being accepted as a follower
of Jesus) of who he is and why he has come. He has come for sinners,
not the healthy or the self-righteous. It is a stunning declaration of
intent. Thus he is revealed as the one Isaiah describes as beloved of
God, a true believer, and worshiper, the Repairer of the breach, the
Restorer of ruined homesteads. Jesus will add to this description that
a follower of his is also a doctor of souls.

Along with the call to examine our consciences and our ways in
the world, along with the call to repentance and holiness, come promises of delight, strength, nourishment, light, and plenty from the hand
of God. There are reiterations of the promise, reminders of grace to
come. We recall the extravagance of God whenever we stop, turn,
and move once again closer to God by moving closer to one another
in compassion and reverence for all that God has created.

The text from Isaiah picks up the closing line from yesterday:

If you remove from your midst oppression,
    false accusation and malicious speech;
If you bestow your bread on the hungry
    and satisfy the afflicted;

> Then light will rise for you in the darkness,
>   and the gloom shall become for you like midday;
> Then the Lord will guide you always
>   and give you plenty even on the parched land.

This is the work of Israel, of the people bound in covenant with Yahweh. This is what faithfulness looks like on the outside to others watching them to see if God resides with them.

The images of what the people will become are lush: a watered garden, a spring whose water never fails, and even ancient ruins rebuilt and foundations from the past raised up—all this in a country whose deserts are legendary for their harshness. All this will be a reality, a logical outcome of true worship, of offering one day, the sabbath, to God, instead of pursuing our own interests.

Worship begins with the words of prayer on the sabbath in the presence of God and publicly among other believers, but it continues in the words of commerce and politics when we practice courtesy and kindness in our dealings with other human beings. What rises as prayer in synagogue and church must daily be offered to one another. Our words must be consistent. We must stand on our words, for they reveal our own inner recesses. Albert Camus, in a speech given at a Dominican monastery in France in 1948, said:

> What the world expects of Christians is that Christians should speak out, loud and clear, and that they should voice their condemnation in such a way that never a doubt, never the slightest doubt, could rise in the heart of the simplest . . . that they should get away from abstraction and confront the bloodstained face history has taken on today.

Our words uttered before God as we pray are a prelude to the words we will utter to the world. We must become our words so that our witness to the world is true. There can be no gap between our liturgy and our commitment to life in our work and neighborhoods and world. Our Lenten intensity and repentance are as much for the salvation and the healing of the world as for our small communities of believers. In being truthful publicly we are strengthened within our small churches.

Matthew's account of Jesus' call to Levi, a small-town tax collector, probably begins with this emphasis on integrity. Most tax collectors worked ostensibly for the Roman occupation forces, collecting tithes, penalties, and taxes, but in fact they worked primarily for their own self-interests. There were only a few people who knew precisely what the taxes and tithes were on herbs, spices, services, and goods, and the collector pocketed any "extra." Tax collectors were not easily tolerated in a community that was oppressed by a hated foreign army and even further oppressed by its own greedy and faithless members. Tax collectors were considered idolaters, worshipers of other gods.

Levi was called, interrupted while he sat at his customs post. Matthew describes his response to Jesus in stark terms: "Leaving everything behind, Levi stood up and became his follower." He stood up, aligned himself with Jesus and a life of resurrection, and left everything behind for the company of Jesus and the other disciples. Levi joined another community.

Levi reacts with joy to his call and throws a party, a great reception for Jesus at his house. Just as he has entertained others in the past, now his resources, his house, and the life he is leaving behind are laid at Jesus' feet. He introduces Jesus to his friends—a large crowd of tax collectors and other guests.

Interestingly enough, the Pharisees and the scribes find all this difficult to accept, but they don't address their concerns to Jesus. Instead, they approach the other disciples, who will soon welcome Levi as one of their own. Their question is as much an accusation as inquiry: "Why do you eat and drink with tax collectors and non-observers of the law?" This is sometimes known as guilt by association. In the Jewish religion, as well as the Christian one, and many others as well, who you eat with is an absolutely crucial indicator of what you believe and where you stand on economic, social, political, and religious issues.

But Jesus responds: "The healthy do not need a doctor; sick people do. I have not come to invite the self-righteous to a change of heart, but sinners." The answer is devastatingly truthful and puts those who question in jeopardy, for now there are only two categories: the self-righteous or the sinners.

There are people who think there is nothing really wrong with them, and people who know there is much that is not well with them. There are people who think that what is wrong with the world is rooted in other people, and those who know they themselves are part of the problem. There are people who worship and pray with integrity, without self-interest, and those who confuse worship with just one more way to further their agenda and confirm their place in the world.

A holy person once put it to me bluntly: "If you're praying or doing worship, really praying, then you are constantly changing and making others very uncomfortable, because they never know exactly what you will do in response to the Spirit. If you aren't changing noticeably, becoming more sensitive to others' needs and difficulties and less tolerant of injustice, then you simply aren't praying."

The Dutch writer and philosopher Abel Herzberg tells a story that echoes this sentiment:

✤   A rabbi, upon entering a room, saw his son deep in prayer. In the corner stood a cradle with a crying child. The rabbi asked his son, "Can't you hear?" The son said, "Father, I was lost in God." And the rabbi said, "One who is lost in God can see the very fly crawling up the wall."

True prayer and worship sensitize us and extend our perceptions through the eye and heart of God.

Henri Nouwen, in *Love in a Fearful Land*, says it this way: "Praying is letting one's own heart become the place where the tears of God and the tears of God's children can merge and become tears of hope."

Today we hear what our work is about in Lent: we are to become repairers of breaches and restorers of ruined homesteads and call sinners to another life and hope. Our prayer and worship instill in us the attitude of humility and service that is necessary if we are to do this work. In the words of the psalm:

> For you, O Lord, are good and forgiving,
>   abounding in kindness to all who call upon you.
> Hearken, O Lord, to my prayer
>   and attend to the sound of my pleading.
> Teach me your way, O Lord,
>   that I may be faithful in your sight.
>   (Psalm 86:5-6, 11)

THE FIRST WEEK OF LENT

✛

Sunday of the First Week of Lent

Genesis 2:7-9, 3:1-7
Romans 5:12-19
Matthew 4:1-11

For this first Sunday of Lent we go back to our beginnings, our roots in a garden, and we are exhorted to remember who we are, where we came from, how it was originally meant to be, and how we changed the story. The story begins with God forming the first human being, Adam, out of the ground itself and bending to breathe into Adam the life of God. And Adam became alive, with breath! Life is shared, passed on. We are born with the exhalation and inspiration of God close to us. Home is a garden full of plants and trees, two especially that are gifts of presence, pleasing to the eye like the others, but not necessarily good to eat. These are the tree of life and the tree of the knowledge of good and evil. It is a good beginning.

But the story moves off to a serpent, not God, but still created by God. This one approaches the woman and insinuates, questions her: "Did God really say you must not eat from any tree in the garden?" The question posits a Creator who baits those with whom Divine life was shared. It insults God. The woman answers, logically and truthfully, that it's only of the tree in the middle of the garden that they are not supposed to eat, because if they do they will die.

The serpent is cunning. He begins by separating the two, questioning only one, so that they cannot rely on one another. Then he

B Cycle: Gn 9:8-15; 1 Pt 3:18-22; Mk 1:12-15
C Cycle: Dt 26:4-10; Rom 10:8-13; Lk 4:1-13

lies, twisting the words so that they sound reasonable and are partially correct—disfiguring and maiming the very words of God. Now the serpent contradicts God, adding to the insult, insinuating that God is a liar. "You won't die. God knows that the day you eat it, you'll both be like gods yourself." Humanity will know good and evil both; know how to be human, made in the image of God, and how to be inhuman, marring and scarring that image beyond recognition.

She looks, sees, eats, and then shares the fruit of the tree with her husband, who now joins her in the endeavor. Their eyes are opened, and they do see. The first thing they see is that they are naked—self-conscious, aware of separation, difference, distance. They have listened to words not of God and acted on them—and the story goes off kilter, careening out of control. From here on the Creator will have to be more and more imaginative and inventive in order to keep the story full of life, for now death has taken root in the story.

What's done is done. The consequences will seep through the history of the garden, exile, and all the earth. The trees are still there— the tree of life and the tree of the knowledge of good and evil. Our heritage is both good and evil, and we are passionately exhorted that no matter how much we now know of evil, we must choose good. It is imperative for humanity that we choose the good.

The segment of Paul's letter to the Romans couches this primeval story in legalistic terms of sin, death, law, disobedience, fault and compensation for sin, condemnation of the sinners, transgression, and the sentence of death. It's rather depressing. But the language is alternated with the theology of grace and gift, which is pardon that ever more abounds in the face of sin.

The comparison is between the first human being, Adam the transgressor, and Jesus Christ, who is righteous and holy and just before God and who makes us friends of God once again. But, basically, it reminds us that grace is stronger than death, that God is more gracious than anything we could hope for, and that God is generous in gifting us with the presence of Jesus Christ, who brings forgiveness for sin into the story and so makes possible another ending besides condemnation and death for all sinners, for all human beings. In Jesus, and the reign of God that comes with his presence in the world, comes life. The reign of death is broken. Now what does the story say? What marvelous possibilities and choices lie ahead for those who grasp hold of their freedom as the sons and daughters of God?

Traditionally the readings for the first Sunday of Lent are accounts of Jesus in the desert struggling with Satan. After the struggle he sets his face toward Jerusalem and chooses the way that will lead invariably to the cross and resurrection. We are to listen to Jesus with ears open to the truth—as opposed to listening to the serpent, Satan. We are told again to choose, but now we have a story to hear and attend to: the story of the One who chooses rightly, freely, gracefully, and so redeems the tale.

This story of Jesus being tested in the desert is a model for all Christians who will more consciously deal with temptations, sin, and evil—and choices in regard to these issues—in the next six weeks. It is an example of behavior that shows us how to resist, how to chose rightly, how to become again the children of God.

Sin is the temptation not to act as sons and daughters of God, the temptation not to obey the Word and not to respond to the commands of God. Jesus is seen in the desert, alone with Satan, and Satan is trying to find out who Jesus is—is he the Son of God? The answer is revealed not just in words but in Jesus' obedience to the word of the Lord in the scriptures.

Jesus and Satan interpret scripture in vastly different ways. Satan—the word means "the hinderer"—is anyone, anything, any interpretation of reality, or religion, any relationship or situation or philosophy that hinders us from being the children of God, from sharing in the breath of God, life itself, or hinders others from recognizing that life within us.

Satan interprets scripture in bits and pieces, out of context, trying to use the word for his own benefit or knowledge. Jesus, on the other hand, sees all of scripture as one piece, a holistic call to integrity that defends the honor of God and situates all choices in a balanced framework that calls us to obedience and humility.

In Matthew's account the first temptation is to make bread from stones. The second is to jump from the top of the Temple, thus baiting God to prove the Divine love by saving us from being human, from suffering and death. The last temptation is to use the ways of the world, where power and authority belong to Satan and those with whom he chooses to share his kingdoms, as the way to bring the kingdom of God on earth.

The passage is layered with meaning and includes basic reminders of how to deal with life's temptations and inclinations toward evil. The scriptures tell us how to live if they are interpreted correctly, meaning if they are used to inspire us to respond as Jesus did. First, we live as Christians, on every word that comes forth from the mouth of God. Second, we do not put the Lord our God to the test. Rather, it is God who tests our faithfulness, our righteousness in the daily situations of life, history, society, family, and church. There is suffering, pain, and death to contend with. Our relationship with God as our Father, Jesus as our Brother, and the Spirit as our strength and guide protects us, but it does not save us from pain. It does, however, reveal God's will in every situation, especially in pain, injustice, suffering, and death. God does take care of us in hard times, during persecution and the ordinary course of human life and death, but not in superhuman ways; rather, God cares for us by companionship, hope, faith, and sustaining grace. Our religion teaches us to obey God and bend before God alone, to live humanly in the face of consequences that reek of death and despair. Jesus obeyed even in the face of rejection, the cross, and death.

The third temptation is about worship, where we surrender to and submit to power. There is only One to surrender to if you are a child of God. Homage is for God alone and not to the world's ways of money, power, prestige, security, fortune, fame, authority, a place in society at the cost of others, selfishness, or violence.

The three encounters between Satan and Jesus are a three-pronged attack on evil as it creeps into our lives. They reveal the three things most helpful in repelling evil: the study and practice of the scriptures; faithfulness in the midst of suffering and death (including penance and fasting and almsgiving); and the true worship of God that is integral to government, family, church, society, and personal lives. God must be served in every area of life—that is the kingdom of God and how it comes.

Lent is a time to take back the pieces of our lives that have been given over to authorities other than God. It is a time to do homage to God alone, and it is a time, too, when angels will come and wait on us, a time of challenge, choices, failures, promises, change, small victories, and a deepened awareness of how much we must grow still in the Christian life. It is a time of trust, with the season of the cross shadowing us.

The cross is the symbol of salvation, of the gifts of mercy and justice, of the truth of how much we are loved and trusted by God. It is in these days that we turn toward the cross in hope and begin to obey Jesus' call to discipleship more intently and wholeheartedly. Our cross is our share in both the practice of injustice and evil of the world and our share in the sufferings of Christ to restore the world and weave all of creation back into an integral body that worships God and lives in thanksgiving. Lent is for putting the world back together again; we are joined with Jesus as he pulls the world back into relationship with God in his own flesh and blood and bone and we share in that work in our bodies too.

These stories of Genesis and the beginning of Matthew's gospel tell the truth of why the world is the way it is, why evil is among us and laced seemingly in the very bones and patterns of our mind, why disobedience seems stronger than goodness, why we do evil, why we affect one another so strongly, why we sense this terrible separation from God and one another, why the world seems to be falling apart, and, lastly, why God created us. They obviously cover a lot.

Sometimes Genesis and other fragments of the gospel are called myth. Theologians and storytellers say that a myth never happened because it is still in process. It is not finished; it is still happening now. So, these stories are not just about beginnings but about the present, now, in our lives and inconsistencies and disobediences, our broken relationships and separations, our searches for wisdom, eternal life, and a relationship with God and one another that is whole and life sustaining. We have all sinned, and we all do sin and encourage others to sin—all in varying degrees. We are human and responsible for the earth and one another. The stories are not just about individuals: Adam and Eve or Jesus. They are stories about all human beings and the roots that we share in common.

We have all shared in the sting of the serpent. In ancient and medieval times this sting of sin, lies, and death was symbolized by a scorpion. In 1 Corinthians 15:54-55 we read: "Death is swallowed up in victory, Where, O death, is your victory? Where, O death, is your sting?" In many Spanish countries and neighborhoods there is the custom of making a large papier-mâché scorpion (with six legs and a stinger) to signify the sting of death. Each week, one leg is hacked off. The stinger is cut off in Holy Week. On Easter Eve, fire from the Easter fire is brought home and the scorpion is set on fire and destroyed, as in the life, death, and resurrection of Jesus. Lent is about stopping the sting, about destroying death, and about uncrucifying the world.

The telling of the desert temptations is a good place to begin our testing, to see where we are weak, or need help or strengthening. This examination of conscience can be used in conjunction with the three temptations and with the readings that follow in this first week of Lent.

- What feeds me (that is not the Word of God)?
- What do I use to avoid conflict?
- How do I avoid being vulnerable (hungry) in my life?
- Do I take care of my needs and feelings first?
- In times of hardship or depression do I remember to look to scripture for help, comfort, directions, remedies?
- Do I use the things of the earth wisely, for what they were created for, or do I use them for what I want?
- Do I violently try to change others or situations for my immediate needs?
- Do I try to prove to others who I am by what I do in public?
- Do I worship the ways of the world instead of God, or besides God?
- Do I use money, reputation, or power to change things instead of changing myself?
- Do I look for answers to my life in society's values and morals rather than trying to live up to the demands of the gospel?
- Do I "sell my soul" to get what I want?
- Do I rely on my privileged relationship with God (as son or daughter) to protect me from harm, from being human, from suffering and dying?
- Do I use God to reassure myself that I'm okay?
- Do I act like I'm a god with others?
- Do I obey God's commands, remembering that I am human and need to learn discipline and practice if I am to be a follower?
- Am I always trying to get ahead and move up in society?
- Do I trust God to take care of me and my family and so spend time working for the kingdom and taking care of the people who are poor and less fortunate than I?

Lent is a time to look at our weaknesses and failures and work on changing so that we can help others. It is a time of mutual encouragement and strengthening. This exercise of freedom, of making choices, is a gift of God. We can bring hope to the story, to others' stories, and to the story of the universe too. The following story—sometimes called "Is the King Ready Yet?"—may help us to go through this week with courage, daring to take risks for the truth and life.

✛ Once upon a time there was a king, a good and just man, who struggled to bring peace to his land. One day as he stood listening to a master preaching he resolved to leave his kingdom behind him and become the master's follower. Soon after, he presented himself before the master and asked to become his disciple. The master looked hard at him and finally spoke, "You were once a king. It is not going to be easy for you to become a disciple, a servant of all." The king stood silent.

The master looked at him again and spoke again, "However, I will take you on a probationary basis. I will assign tasks to you, and when I think you are ready I will make you a disciple. Are you willing to obey me and learn how to be a disciple by unlearning how to be a king?" The king heartily agreed, for this was to be his life from now on.

With that, the king was welcomed into the group. Immediately, the master assigned him to the most lowly, humiliating task of collecting the garbage and slop pails three times a day.

The king, now a follower, joined the daily round of work and prayer, study and lessons, discipline and assigned tasks. He did his onerous job faithfully, without complaining. And as the days passed many of the other disciples began to be bothered by the daily ritual of seeing this man, once their king, now reduced to such work. Finally a group of them approached the master on his behalf. "Master," they asked, "isn't the king ready yet? After all, he has been obedient and never once complained about his role."

The master simply responded, "No, he's not ready yet."

But they pleaded his case and finally the master said that he would send his number one disciple to test him and see if he was ready truly to enter into discipleship. The disciple was summoned and commanded to test the king.

Obediently the disciple set off to look for the former king. He found him walking across the marble floors of the main hall, carefully carrying his slop pails. The disciple waited for him to come closer. When the two men stood facing one another, the disciple shoved the king hard, causing him to drop the pails and spill the slops all over the clean and waxed floor. There was a long silence, and then the king looked hard at the man, his face red and the veins pulsing in his neck. He barely withheld the fury inside as he spoke: "You are lucky that I am no longer a king or else I would have had you severely punished. But I am not, so you can get away with this." With that, he went about the task of cleaning up the mess and then went back to cleaning the hall. The disciple returned to the master and reported what had happened. The master turned to the others and said: "See, I told you he wasn't ready."

Weeks and months went by, and the other disciples watched the king day after day clean up the slops and garbage and empty the chamber pots, and they respected him for his faithfulness. After all, they had only been poor and their lot had been bettered by joining the master, but he had been king and had sunk so low.

Finally, they again approached the master—the group interceding on the king's behalf having grown much larger. They pointed out to the master that he *must* be ready now. The master looked calmly at them and said—"He isn't ready yet." They pleaded to have the disciple test him again. And so a second time the disciple went to the main hall and waited for the king.

They met in the same place as before and eyed one another. The disciple moved quickly and once again shoved the king, causing him to drop the buckets again. This time the king looked at him, the anger burning in his eyes, but he held his tongue—though his feelings showed in the tenseness of his face and body. The disciple reported back to the master, and the master turned to the others saying, "See, I told you he wasn't ready yet."

Months passed and the other disciples grew to know and admire the king and to become friends with him. He was courteous, reflective, honest, and patient. He never spoke of his humiliating tasks or the treatment he had received at the hands of the head disciple or the fact that the master seemed to ignore him completely. Many new recruits had come to the group and had been welcomed without any stipulations. No one was asked to dump the slop pots or take the king's job.

Again, the group approached the master. This time they didn't ask. They were adamant: "Send the disciple and test him. We know he's ready." So once again the disciple went to the hall and waited for the king to come with his daily burden. They stood face to face again, and the disciple shoved him, hard, and the pots went flying off, spilling all over the floor. There was silence and the king looked mildly at the disciple and said and did nothing. Then the disciple shoved him again, almost causing him to lose his balance. And this time the king smiled and bowed respectfully to the disciple.

The disciple returned and reported it to the master. The master looked at the other disciples and said, "Now he's ready." They rejoiced.

But then the master turned and looked hard at his head disciple and spoke. "Go," he said, "and return to the hall. Find the man who once was king and tell him to come to me. You take over his job, for now you are on probation and he is now the head disciple!" Stunned, the long-time disciple moved to obey, his heart and mind in a turmoil about the turn of events.

The story is one of testing and discipleship, of learning to follow and to obey, and especially of discerning who and what we are, in all circumstances. The time is Lent. It is time to find out: Are we ready yet? Are we disciples of the Master who has gone before us into the desert, into life, death, and resurrection?

Monday of the First Week of Lent

Leviticus 19:1-2, 11-18
Matthew 25:31-46

This is the first full week of Lent, and so the readings will remind us of basics, of the groundwork that must be laid in our lives as disciples, as a people that belongs to God publicly in this world. Our behavior individually and as groups must show our priorities and values and reveal the God that we serve. The first reading is an account of the Law given by God to Moses. The first line is the basic commandment: "Be holy, for I, the Lord, your God, am holy." This is really the only commandment. All the others are about how to express this commandment externally and to cultivate internally the attitude of holiness.

The commands listed in Leviticus are more to the point and more specific about behavior than the broader-based Ten Commandments. The "thou shalt nots" relate to economic and social relations—how we are to treat workers, the poor, and our neighbors in speech, common decency, respect, and actions. In some ways they reflect good business practices and common courtesy in relational skills. But they are also excellent to use to examine our attitudes and practice because they are *not* the accepted rules of conduct in a society founded on materialism, individualism and capitalism.

The usual rules are there: do not speak falsely, steal, swear falsely by the name of God, rob, or defraud. But what follows is more revelatory, perhaps, of who we are to be to one another. Do not withhold overnight the wages of your day laborers, curse the deaf, or put a stumbling block in front of the blind. Rather, fear your God. These admonitions look to the least, to those disadvantaged among the community, to those who cause the group aggravation and grief. They reveal whether a community appreciates human life, and they offer dignity to those lacking in specific areas of employment, sight, or hearing. They also reveal underlying attitudes of pettiness, meanness, and superiority or the tendency of strong human beings to take advantage of those who are not as adept.

Do not act dishonestly when rendering judgment. Show neither partiality to the weak nor deference to the mighty but judge your neighbors justly. Do not spread slander among your kinsmen or stand idle when your neighbor's life is at stake. These commands probe deeper into the heart and soul of what it means to be human in community. Any group that is bound to God, who is Justice, must be bound to one another in justice, justice for all, justice not based on the position of others, but the virtue, practice and appreciation of justice itself. Justice is based on truth and the defense of truth in the face of evil. We are not allowed to excuse ourselves or rationalize our lack of opposition to injustice. Not to act upon our beliefs or to allow injustice a foothold destroys the integrity of the community and the individual at its root-soul. Not to act when we see injustice is to participate in evil as a willing observer, and thus to be equally guilty before God.

Do not bear hatred in your heart. Reprove others when they sin, and do not incur sin because of others. Take no revenge; cherish no grudge. If all these things are foremost in our mind and practice, then we know that we love our neighbor as ourself. The law of the covenant is not just rules to follow but a public confession and affirmation of belief in the Lord. This is the reason for obedience; for the practice of the letter, the spirit, and soul of the Law. This is what makes community and sustains it—the cherishing of one another. This is the beginning of understanding how God cherishes all people. This is the first law, the first testament between God and God's people.

Matthew's story of the judgment of the nations extends this earlier testament beyond the confines of the Israelite community. "Whatever we do to the least of our brothers and sisters, we do unto God." Specifically, the corporal, bodily works of mercy reveal us to be believers, Christians, human beings who are followers of Jesus, the Son of Man. The necessities of food, drink, shelter, health care, clothing, and the realities of forgiveness and repentance—another chance after failure and breaking of the laws—must be afforded *all* people, not just specifically chosen groups. This judgment will be rendered upon nations as well as upon individuals. This is the essence of being human: careful treatment of all those formed in the image and likeness of the Maker of heaven and earth.

What makes this a startling religious precept is that the least of the earth's children are the privileged presence of God among us. What we neglect to do in our care and appreciation of them, we neglect in our worship and attentiveness to God. The two cannot be dissociated; they are as tightly bound together as flesh on bones. This is the staggering proclamation of Jesus' good news. We are revealed as true believers and worshipers of God by the way we treat those among us who are the most without resources or power in the kingdoms of the world. Our very souls depend on our relationships with them.

The truth is part of the long tradition of the church, begun early and connected to the practice of eucharist and community. Basil, an early church father, writes:

> The bread which you do not use is the bread of the hungry. The garment hanging in your wardrobe is the garment of the one who is naked. The shoes that you do not wear are the shoes of the one who is barefoot. The money you keep locked away is the money of the poor. The acts of charity you do not perform are so much injustices you commit.

These words are intended to serve as slaps, as a Zen master sometimes slaps a disciple or bats him with a stick. They are meant to startle, shock, and shake the disciple into awareness, into a sense of the intimate interconnectedness of every human being and each created thing. If we are to be human, then we must learn the attitude and the compassion of Buddha or of Jesus, of one willing to let go of even life to give life to others. This attitude of reverence toward all life begins with the simple practice of charity. To neglect this practice is to practice instead the ways of injustice and selfishness that result in isolation and the distortion of our relationships with other human beings.

We are the children of God, the brothers and sisters of the Son of Man. We are the bracing Spirit of God present in history. These commandments are the word of God to those who belong to God. They are imperatives, not options. They reveal the attitude of Christ, and this attitude makes us Christians. Perhaps today is the time to shift base so that the words of G. K. Chesterton (writing about Thomas Aquinas) might one day be used to describe many more of us:

> He had from the first that full and final test of truly orthodox Catholicity: the impetuous, impatient, intolerable passion for the poor; and even that readiness to be rather a nuisance to the rich, out of a hunger to feed the hungry.

Tuesday of the First Week of Lent

Isaiah 55:10-11
Matthew 6:7-15

Charles de Foucauld has a famous prayer that is devastatingly simple, as simple as fire which consumes all in its path, growing hotter in intensity, feeding on any air that fans the flames. Prayer, any prayer, is supposed to consume us, hand us over in sacrifice, and transform us from mere recitation of words and formula into the reality of the words. Prayer makes us come true. So this is what Charles de Foucauld prayed:

> Father, I abandon myself into your hands.
>   Do with me what you will.
> Whatever you may do, I thank you:

I am ready for all, I accept all.
Let only your will be done in me, and in all your
   creatures.
I wish no more than this, O Lord.
Into your hands I commend my soul;
   I offer it to you with all the love of my heart,
   for I love you, Lord,
   and so need to give myself,
   to surrender myself into your hands, without reserve,
      and with boundless confidence,
   for you are my father. Amen.

Prayers are not just words, nor are they just the fundamental meaning of the words. They are invitations, commands even, to alter reality radically, beginning with the only reality we have a good deal of control over: ourselves. They are doors left wide open so that the Divine can slip in at any time, move the furniture around, or empty out the house so that there is space inside us for God. Prayers are eviction notices rendered on our priorities and agendas, displacing all else but God and God's agenda: the coming of the kingdom into the world with justice and peace.

When we speak words, especially words of God, we set something awesome in motion; it can soon be uncontrollable because these words do not just come from us. This concept is often hard for modern men and women to grasp, for too many of us play with words as though they are one commodity among others, there simply for our use. But this idea should be alien to anyone who is born of the tradition of the word of the Lord in the Jewish, Christian, or Muslim communities, or in any tradition where the spoken word has priority over the written word.

This power of words, let alone the word of the Lord, is the subject of two lines from Isaiah the prophet, a man who certainly knew the power of the word of God in his own mouth and the massive ramifications that issued forth in politics, economics, and society as he uttered them. He spoke in the first person, but they were not his words. They were God's words, and he only handed over his voice and lungs and body to express them to others. Even as he spoke them, they made and remade him, destroyed and recreated him; they set him in the maelstrom where history and God's time collided.

The text starts out lyrically describing God's word that leaves his mouth likened to rain and snow that fall from the skies. Once they fall they do not return until they have watered the earth, making it fertile and fruitful. The moisture sinks into its new home, and nurtures the seed for the one who sows and yields bread to one who eats the harvest. This rain and snow returns to the sky utterly transformed; it is usually invisible to those who are enchanted by the falling snowflakes and pelting rain but unaware of moisture and air. This process, this pattern, is shared by the word that falls from the mouth of God. It goes forth, and it does not return to God void. It does only God's will, achieving the end for which it was sent. It sinks deep into the ground of hearts and into history itself, and it will give seed to those who sow it and bread to those who eat it and harvest it, sharing it with others. It will eventually return, but not until the work is finished.

This is the word of the Law on Sinai, which every Jew believes was uttered in his or her own heart and still hangs in the atmosphere of the world, waiting to be heard by those with open hearts. This is the word of the prophets, detailing injustice and threatening retaliation, a reversal of fortune on those who have and those who do not have because of the thievery and lies of others. It is the word of the prophets, promising, seeding hope, and making remnants of those who are faithful. And it is the Word of God, spoken in Jesus, who became human and dwells among us, sent to echo in our bones and settle in our hearts until we understand how to praise God and make the Divine will a reality on earth in history.

In the gospel today this Word Jesus exhorts his disciples not to rattle on like unbelievers who think that by the numbers of their words they'll get a hearing. Prayer to Jesus' Father is a different experience altogether, for God knows what we need before we ask. So, we don't have to ask. We start in another place, in God's place, and ask for what God wants for each of us and all of us.

It begins with remembering that this is not just a connection between "me and God," but it is a connection among Jesus and us, all of us, and Jesus' Father, who is graciously shared with us. We don't chatter—"parakeet prayer" as Don Lito of El Salvador calls it—but we slip into the prayer of Jesus as we slip into consciousness after sleeping and dreaming, becoming more and more conscious of who we are, who is God, and how close we are intended to be, all of us in Jesus.

The Our Father, the Lord's Prayer, is about universal, incarnational, everlasting things all dear to the heart of God. We pray that God's name is hallowed; God's kingdom comes; God's will is done, on earth, in us, right now. We pray, "Give us today our daily bread"—enough for everyone. We ask God to forgive us the wrongs we have done as we forgive those who wrong us, so that we live freely in relation to one another with open hands and hearts, sharing bread as sustenance and forgiveness as freedom. Finally, we pray, "Subject us not to the trial and deliver us from the evil one"—rescue us from all death, especially the death that is most to be feared, the death to hope, to life, to grace, to community and everlasting communion; deliver us from the hinderer, wherever evil is found. If we knew how to pray this prayer, if we knew how to be drawn into the grid that overlays reality as it is spoken aloud or sighed in silence, we would need no other words, no other prayer. The power and the word would be set in motion and carry us along.

What stops us? Sunk deep in us, like rocks in the soil or saline water that destroys seeds, is our lack of forgiveness, hard-heartedness, cold-bloodedness, refusal to embrace or respect others. We expect, demand even, that God treat us kindly and with unlimited forgiveness. But we do not return the favor to others. Our hard-heartedness short-circuits the words in our hearts, twists and makes them hollow and without meaning, turns them into idle twaddle and nonsense. Jesus is blunt: if we do not forgive others, neither will the Father forgive us. If we truly attempt to pray, then we will begin to experience a shifting of "tectonic plates" deep within us, for, as Søren Kierkegaard says, "The prayer does not change God, but it changes the one who offers it." Prayer makes us disappear into God. Lent is time for serious practice!

Wednesday of the First Week of Lent

Jonah 3:1-10
Luke 11:29-32

There is a fable by Gellert I found in a collection of great tales in English and Chinese. It is called *The Land of the Halt*. As I remember, it goes something like this.

✛ Once upon a time in a very small country all the inhabitants were struck by two maladies: everyone stuttered and everyone was halt in walking. But what was surprising, at least to outsiders, was that both of these defects were considered accomplishments, a mark of belonging. Stuttering and limping were considered normal.

One day a stranger passing through noticed that this was a strange country indeed. He did not stutter and was not lame. And so he walked, straight and proud, through the villages and city streets, sure that they would notice and would not only appreciate his gracefulness but be converted to walking the way he walked. He was noticed, but he was not appreciated! The people pointed at him, stared, and talked about him behind their hands. Soon even the adults were laughing rudely at him while one or another of them yelled: "Somebody take pity on the man and teach him how to walk properly!"

The stranger was taken aback. How could they not know or want to walk straight and true? And so, he defended himself and confronted them boldly, pointing out that it was they who were lacking in grace, awkward, and shuffling. They listened to him as he spoke and then started laughing all the harder—the man didn't stutter. His words flowed, rose and fell like liquid, moving along with ease—similar to the way he walked. They were bent over double with laughter, the tears running from their eyes. He was so hard to understand. Not only did he need to be taught how to walk correctly, but he needed someone to teach him how to speak or he'd never be able to survive in the world. After the laughter subsided, they pitied the man. He would never know

what it meant to walk or talk as other human beings did. It was
so sad.

There are many ways to express the same thing, but if we are intent on ours being the only correct way, then we tend to laugh and
insult whatever is not like us, especially if we see it as attempting to
correct or change us. This is a reality shared by individuals and countries alike.

In the readings from the prophet Jonah and from Luke, which
describe the same experience but with vastly different responses, this
moral is brought home again and again. Jonah is a reluctant prophet.
He hates the Ninevites. They are the enemies of Israel, and he most
certainly doesn't want to go to them and call them to conversion!
After all, that's a dangerous business—being a prophet and accusing
people publicly of being sinners.

Worse still, what if they repent? Then his enemies will escape the
wrath of condemnation and punishment that he believes they so aptly
deserve; they will live in peace with God. He does not want to take
the chance of that happening! But God is compelling, annoying really,
and Jonah is pushed kicking and screaming into the sea by his companions when he tries to escape the command of the Lord. After his
sojourn in the belly of a big fish—indigestion for the fish, who spews
him out—he obeys, but still grudgingly.

Nineveh is a huge city; it takes three days to go through it. Like
Los Angeles today, it is spread out. After a day's walk, Jonah is one
third of the way through, yelling out the call to repentance and
change: "Forty days more and Nineveh shall be destroyed." And his
worst fear is realized. They repent! They believe him; take his message to heart. The people of Nineveh declare a fast and put on sackcloth and ashes from the greatest to the least.

The word finally comes to the king of Nineveh, and he responds
as his people have before him. He rises from his throne and lays aside
his power and authority and outward manifestation of kingship, and,
like the rest of his subjects, repents. He makes it official and binding
on all in the kingdom declaring:

Neither man nor beast, neither cattle nor sheep, shall taste
anything; they shall not eat, nor shall they drink water. Man
and beast shall be covered with sackcloth and call loudly to
God; every one shall turn from their evil way and from the vio-

lence he has in hand. Who knows, God may relent and forgive, and withhold his blazing wrath, so that we shall not perish.

This is total reversal, immediate response, acknowledgment of sin, confession, and a firm purpose of amendment. The decree names what they will refrain from doing: evil and violence. They will cry loudly to God, as much to encourage one another in their conversion as in their fasting and their intent to live differently from now on. The words of the prophet, thus heeded, compel God to obey his own decree. Because of their actions and hearts, God repents of the threatened destruction. They are saved—the whole city! Poor Jonah! God has used the people of Nineveh to catch him in his own hate and reluctance to let God be God for everyone, and so save everyone!

Jonah's prophetic admonition is simple: forty days or else! Forty days to look at ourselves as a people and turn from our evil and violence. Forty days to repent and fast and cry out loudly with one voice. Forty days for all the earth—creatures and humans in each city, parish, and community—to heed the word of the Lord in the mouth of the prophet. It doesn't matter whether the prophet is reluctant, half-hearted or even our enemy. Anyone who calls us from evil, injustice, and violence and calls us back to being human and submissive to God is the word of God given to us as a gift, necessary for our very life, survival, and salvation. The book of Jonah is marvelous because a pagan city hears the word of the Lord in the mouth of a not-very-faithful Israelite prophet. The Ninevites put the prophet and the chosen people to shame by their overwhelmingly wholehearted response to God's call to conversion.

Jesus doesn't seem to fare as well. He too comes among the people and preaches the same call to conversion. Jesus, in Luke's gospel especially, is the prophet, the one with the word of God in his mouth; in fact, he is the Word enfleshed, and he sounds the call to the people clearly: This is an evil age. It seeks a sign. But no sign will be given it except the sign of Jonah.

Just as Jonah was a sign for the Ninevites, so is the Son of Man a sign for the present age. Jesus is intent on the salvation of the people, especially his own people who are dearest to his heart. They are his kin and country, yet they refuse to listen. They want a sign that says who he is and whether or not his words are worth listening to. And so Jesus presents a riddle: the only sign will be the sign of Jonah.

What sign is that? That Jonah spent days and nights in the whale underwater and then was spewed forth onto the land to walk it and preach to those who were open to repentance and the news of God's care for them and God's intended judgment of them? Jesus, the Son of Man, will spend days and nights in the tomb, buried by hate and violence and the evil ways of human beings. But the very earth will not be able to contain him; it will spit him forth into the world again, so that he can walk among those who are willing to listen and change their hearts in response to his life, death, and resurrection.

Jesus mentions a stranger, the queen of the south who came to listen and learn from Solomon, accusing them of being blind to who is among them now. Jesus is caught in the same dilemma as the stranger in the fable of the land of the halt. He is laughed at, scorned, and rejected by people who are halt and stuttering in their practice of faith. Even more, they are blind and violent in their treatment of him. In the tradition of the prophets Jesus condemns their choice. He reminds them of Nineveh's repentance and salvation, not the chosen people but foreigners who hearkened to the word of the God in the prophet Jonah's mouth. He declares that the people of Nineveh, as well as the queen of the south, will rise along with the citizens of this present generation to condemn it.

There is a choice here: repent or else. They are in the presence of one much greater than Jonah, and they refuse to repent, to open their ears and hearts. They will be judged and condemned. If they do not change, what didn't happen to Nineveh could happen to them. Jesus' presence in the world is the only sign necessary or given. Jesus is the word come to us. Our choice is to go the way of the halt and the stutterers or to go the way of the Ninevites.

Thursday of the First Week of Lent

Esther 12:14-16, 23-25
Matthew 7:7-12

The book of Esther is unusual in many ways. First, it is entirely devoted to the story of a woman who saves her people who are in mortal danger. Enemies within the king's court are intent on destroying the Jewish people. This segment of the story is Esther's prayer, in anguish and fear, to the One who alone can help her. Her position in the king's harem, as his most beautiful and therefore influential wife makes her a possible savior for her persecuted people. She prays for herself, but for herself as part of her nation, her people, and her ancestors. She remembers her childhood and her first understandings of God, who chose Israel as God's own nation and people and made them a lasting heritage, promising them strength and safety even in times of distress. Esther calls on this God of her people, this God of promises, to be mindful of her people once again and mindful of her. She prays for the courage to act on behalf of her people.

She needs the courage, strength, and power of God, beginning with the right words in her mouth, to charm the king, "the lion," as she describes him. She must walk into the lion's den, stand in his presence, and turn his heart from hatred of her people to hatred of the enemy who seeks to destroy them. Her prayer is for what needs to be done on behalf of her people. She is going to practice civil disobedience on behalf of her people, for she intends after her prayer to disobey the law of the king and go unannounced into his presence and with craft and holy seduction get him to see who is seeking to destroy the Jewish community.

Esther is bound to her people more than to her own life, and her prayer is forthright: "Save us by your power, and help me, who am alone and have no one but you, O Lord. You know all things." She will be heard, answered, and accompanied in her work for her people. She will be ruthlessly just in the sense of "an eye for an eye and a tooth for a tooth" when her enemies are caught out. The plotters had intended to hang the Jews, but now the sentence will be executed on them and the ones in league with them, those who would benefit from the destruction of the Jews. Esther is a model for her community in strict justice, especially in time of desperate need.

In the gospel reading Jesus speaks about prayer, about our attitude in approaching God. Our attitude toward God must be confidant, faithful, and hopeful, because of who God is and whom we profess to believe in. Our God too is the God of promises, of strength, of care for the people, of presence in time of need. Like Esther, we are to ask, to seek, to knock, and God will give, will uncover a way and will open wide to us. We will receive, find, and be opened too.

Jesus explains more about God's care for us in our need. He tells of a father who hands his son a stone when he asks for bread or gives his child a poisonous snake when he asks for a fish. This is, of course, unheard of. The relationship of father and child, even on earth, does not admit of such horror. Even we sinners, selfish and violent toward others, give to our own what they need and what is good. So, is it surprising that God, who is Goodness itself, who is Father of all, will give good things to all who ask?

Our prayer reveals our relationships to those we love here on earth. These relationships of love are weak intimations of how God loves. And although we stumble even in our intense love relationships on occasion, God never does. If we entreat on behalf of others, as Esther did, if we make intercessions for others and call out to God to care for others as he has cared for us, God will respond. God responded to Esther and saved her people. God used her to show the divine care and protection for God's people, once again fulfilling the promise to the chosen people.

There is a tag-on line that is crucial, for it puts into perspective our relationship with God in prayer: "Treat others the way you would have them treat you: this sums up the law and the prophets." When we treat others in this way, God treats us as God's own children, own people, own beloved ones.

Prayer is integral to being holy, to being a disciple and a follower of Jesus. Jesus' entire life was a prayer of intercession on behalf of the people, on our behalf. This is also our calling as disciples: to pray for the world and all peoples. This is not just a teaching about prayer for persons who are dear to us: family, friends, or acquaintances. This is about the salvation of the world. Walter Wink, in *Engaging the Powers*, puts this across well:

> No doubt our intercessions sometimes change us as we open ourselves to new possibilities we had not guessed. No doubt our prayers to God reflect back upon us as a divine command to become the answer to our prayer. But if we are to take the biblical understanding seriously at all, intercession is more than that. It changes the world, and it changes what is possible to God. It creates an island of relative freedom in a world gripped by an unholy necessity. A new force field appears that hitherto was only potential; the entire configuration changes as the result of the changes of a single part. An aperture opens in the

praying person, permitting God to act without violating human freedom. The change in even one person thus changes what God can thereby do in that world.

What kind of possibilities are there when a whole community, a parish, or a nation prays, interceding for those in need, for strangers, and even for enemies? Esther learned to do justice, strict justice, and her prayer stopped the escalation of violence. Perhaps we, who are called the followers of Jesus and call God Father, can learn more than justice. Perhaps we need to pray to learn mercy and nonviolent responses to the evil of the world. It is in the cross of Christ that mercy and justice meet.

The traditional prayer before each station of the cross is a good starting place: "We adore you, O Christ, and we praise you, because by your holy cross you have redeemed the world." And on our knees we can pray together to take up our cross and go after Jesus, walking in his footsteps, remembering the words and prayer of the psalmist from today's liturgy:

> Lord, on the day I called for help, you answered me.
> Because of your kindness and your truth;
> > for you have made great above all things
> > your name and your promise.
> When I called, you answered me;
> > you built up strength within me.
> > Your right hand saves me.
> The Lord will complete what he has done for me;
> > your kindness, O Lord, endures forever;
> > forsake not the work of your hands.
> Lord, on the day I called for help, you answered me.
> > > > > > (Psalm 138)

Then pray this psalm a second time in the plural, aware that we belong to one another in the Lord, who saves us.

Friday of the First Week of Lent

Ezekiel 18:21-28
Matthew 5:20-26

It seems from the reading of the prophet Ezekiel that there are basically only two kinds of people in the world: those who turn from evil to do good and so have life and God rejoices; and those who turn from good to do evil and so die in their sins and God mourns their loss. There are two paths to trod: the path of good and virtuous deeds, and the path of those who have broken faith. One leads to life, and the other to death.

Ezekiel expresses our reaction; the response remains the same across generations and borders. We say, "'The Lord's way is not fair!' Hear now, house of Israel: Is it my way that is unfair, or rather, are not your ways unfair?" We, like the people of Ezekiel's time, fall easily into the rationalization that we can flip flop back and forth in our lives, doing good, then doing evil, then doing good. But in reality we must have a sense of single-heartedness, much like the path an arrow takes once it leaves the bow. For those who belong to the people of God, who have made covenant with God, like the Israelites and those of us who have been baptized into Christ and now live "hidden with Christ in God," there is only one direction to take: the path that leads toward home and communion with God and one another. To choose other things is to break faith, to insult God, and to defy our own words of commitment to the One who beckons to us.

It's an either/or choice. It cannot be sometimes yes and sometimes no, or worse still, Do I have to choose now? To be in relationship with God along with others who seek his presence is to be single-mindedly intent and pure in our choice for life. This blunt language and seemingly harsh reminder of the prophet questions us on how faithful we really are. Are we faithful only when it is convenient? When it is easy and there are no obstacles? When the rest of the world, or at least our circle of friends, is in concert with us? When we can just drift along? Or is our faithfulness intent, passionate, devoted, constant, encompassing more and more daily, spreading out as patterns made in water when a stone drops into the depths? Another way to look at these questions is to change the word faithfulness to holiness. In the gospel Jesus tells his disciples—us—that our holiness must surpass that of the scribes and Pharisees or else we shall not enter the kingdom of God. Jesus sounds just as blunt and unnerving as any previous prophet!

Jesus acknowledges that the scribes and Pharisees practice a certain kind of holiness based on obedience to the law. And Jesus takes a number of these laws that are universally accepted in his religious community and extends their meaning. He begins with life and death issues, as Ezekiel did:

> You have heard the commandment imposed on your forefathers, "You shall not commit murder; every murderer shall be liable to judgment." What I say to you is: everyone who grows angry with another shall be liable to judgment, anyone who uses abusive language toward another shall be answerable to the Sanhedrin, and if you hold another in contempt you risk the fires of Gehenna.

Jesus pushes the boundaries of what is considered murder. It is, of course, physical destruction of life, but it is also anger, hate, or rage, expressed in words, stance, and public attitude as well as inner thoughts of destruction and separation. Jesus keeps using the term brother—to imply that *everyone* among his followers is related intimately in his family and all human beings are as closely knit as siblings with him as older brother and God as Father. The demands of association with Jesus change at the root our relationship and responsibilities to others.

The quality of our being with one another must be examined carefully before offering our gifts at the altar, for if we recall that anyone has anything against us, then we are to leave our gift at the altar and go immediately to be reconciled. We are to waste no time. Reconciliation takes precedence over worship. In fact, we are incapable of worship, of prayer, of standing in the presence of God or the community if any of us is at odds with another human being. The prelude to all worship and adoration is reconciliation. The word for reconciliation in Greek means "to walk together again," and we are commanded to be at one before we come before God.

Jesus continues outlining the process of reconciliation that all of us must follow. First, we go to the one we must be reconciled with and lose no time doing it. This is a priority of life—to live in communion, at peace, justly with one another. We need to seek reconciliation before we go to a court. In this escalating series of judgments and punishments leading to condemnation we realize Jesus is not just speaking about our ways here on earth, but he is also speaking about our relationships with God. Settle on the way to court otherwise your opponent may hand you over to the guard, who will throw you into prison. "I warn you, you will not be released until you have paid the last penny."

These words in Jesus' mouth sound brutal, threatening, and accusatory, and they are, especially for those who call themselves Christians, followers of the light, bearers of the good news of forgiveness in the world. Where others stand in relation to us must be of crucial importance, for it reveals more than anything else whether or not we are holy and virtuous according to Jesus' standards of judgment. This is about holiness, about faithfulness, and Jesus' words begin with the order to "surpass" those intent on being holy according to the law. All holiness begins with life, protection of it, appreciation for it, and nurturing of it. Anger, contempt, abusive language, expressions of violence, deliberate separation from others and our lack of humanness sever the bonds of Jesus' family where all are entitled to forgiveness, mercy, and reconciliation.

The command has both a renouncing side and a positive appropriation to it. William Penn, the founder of the Quakers, said: "If there is any kindness I can show, or any good thing I can do to any fellow being, let me do it now, and not deter or neglect it, as I shall not pass this way again." It is an attitude of concern for others' well-being, for living in peace with one another. Henry Wadsworth Longfellow said: "If we would read the secret history of our enemies, we would find in each one's life a sorrow and a suffering enough to disarm all hostility." Murder, rage, hate, contempt, and abuse are founded on seeing others as so distinct from us that we make them unrecognizable as human beings.

In Jesus' kingdom, to dehumanize others is a sin against holiness, against a life of faithful virtue. These people whom we hate, murder in our hearts, and hold in contempt are mirrors as much as swords in our souls. André Gide spoke of this: "I owe much to my friends, but . . . even more to my enemies. The real person springs to life under a sting even better than under a caress."

Jesus is interested in making us responsible for our actions, but even more, responsible for everyone else on a daily basis. We are not allowed to stand alone before God and expect to be heard if we refuse to acknowledge and stand together with others. "We are all responsible for everything to everyone else," Fyodor Dostoevski wrote.

This business of holiness entails more than virtuous acts. It is built on an attitude of intertwining worship of God and compassion for one another. We are called to treat one another with the same respect that we offer to God. Obedience to the law is assumed. But we are asked to be attentive to anything that might lead to breaking the Law or ignoring the Law or missing the lowest rung of people that the Law was designed to protect. We are not released from the Law by adherence to Jesus' way, but we are drawn deeper into its heart so that the Law shines with spirit and reveals the depth or hollowness of our own holiness before God and the world.

The responsorial psalm puts our relationship to both God and to other human beings in perspective from God's point of view: "If you, O Lord, laid bare our guilt, who could endure it?" This acknowledgment and confession stands as both prayer and insight into our own place at the altar before God and makes us remember anyone who might have good cause to be at odds with us. The only response is to waste no time, but to go and be reconciled with God, whom we have pushed to the far limits of our life, and return together to the altar.

Saturday of the First Week of Lent

Deuteronomy 26:16-19
Matthew 5:43-48

The first reading has Moses speaking to the people. It is full of promise and hope, for it tells us who we are, giving us an identity that can sustain us in all situations and experiences. The people are reminded that there is an agreement being made between God and us, that we are to walk in God's ways and hearken to the voice of God first and foremost. We are now God's possession, a people particularly belonging to God. If we follow God's ways, we will be raised up high in praise and renown and glory before all other peoples, and we will be a people sacred to the Lord.

This reading is not talking about nationalism but about sacredness and intimacy. God, we are reminded, made all peoples, all nations, but chose one to make this agreement with. God's choice must be remembered and honored with great attention to obey the statutes and commandments. God's promises far outstrip anything we are asked to do in God's name. To live justly and to be in relationship with God bring joy and abundance of life. The people of God were chosen to model for the other nations the possibilities of life that God offers to all peoples. The people consecrated to God are set apart for hope, imagination, and creativity, for proclaiming the possibilities of being human in history, and for the fullness of life, thankfulness, and depth of identity.

The beginnings of this consecration, the place where learning and initiation into a relationship of privilege with God are found, is seeking to know God with all our hearts by walking in the way of the Lord. Diligence, firmness of purpose, uprightness, thankfulness, a life that is blameless, are sure indicators that God is close to us and that others will see the presence of God among us.

Jesus, like Moses the liberator and leader of his newly chosen people, is intent on making sure that his disciples know what he will ask of them. Jesus begins with the existing law: "You shall love your countryman but hate your enemy." Initially that may sound like a terrible commandment, but it specifically narrowed and pointed out to the people whom they were responsible for—their own people, their nation, bound in covenant with the Almighty. But now Jesus breaks the boundaries: "My command to you is: love your enemies, pray for your persecutors." There are to be no limits to love; there is no one we are not required to pray for or intercede for before God. In fact, the new criterion is not our own country or nation or people but our very enemy, both collectively and individually.

If we do obey Jesus' commandment we prove without a doubt that we are children of our Father, for God's sun rises on both the bad and the good. God's rain falls on the just and the unjust. If we love only those who love us, what merit is there in that? The world does as much. In fact, sinners and people we think very little of—tax collectors, politicians, corrupt business corporations, or our enemies—do as much. If we are going to imitate God we are to be as perfect as God is perfect! It sounds impossible, outrageous, even naive. In some translations of this famous line the words *compassionate* or *holy* are used instead of the word *perfect*. Perhaps in our society, which sees the word *perfect* as a negative way of being in the world, the other words are closer to what Jesus is telling us we must try to express in our lives. When I was much younger this reading evoked in me an image that was strong and powerful. I would walk around in the bright sunshine in a parking lot or playground or shopping mall and look at the people: some were basking in rays of sunlight, dancing in sunbeams; others carried dark shadows or had black clouds trailing along behind them. I thought what a terrible place the world would be if we knew at every minute where we stood before God, whether we were bad or good! In the rain, which I dearly loved to walk in for hours, I thought again of this passage. What if it only rained on us when we were just? We would have no moisture, no respite from the dust and sand and grit unless we were just in the eyes of God. I couldn't think of a worse way to go through life—exposed, judged, and experiencing the condemnation publicly. There would be no leeway, no breathing space, no kindness or place of sanctuary to reevaluate our position and move toward another. Thankfully, we have instead God's kindness, pity, mercy, hospitality, simple courtesy, and gentle invitation to come home—to the sun and the rain and to God. We are to make sure that everyone else knows that invitation is always there, the door always open. God is like this; we have to do as much once we have known such kindness and care. We must extend such courtesy and openhandedness to all others.

Exclusion, the making of enemies, the decision to treat any human being with disrespect, or refuse them forgiveness is a curse. It is contempt for God. It is a terrible sin. Loving one's enemies is as natural as God loving us, but it is only with awareness of God's tenderness that this phenomena becomes utterly apparent. This experience of God, as Simone Weil says, "is not consolation, it is light." Perhaps it is both realities: light that makes us see others with God's gentle eyes, and consolation that the only way we can respond to that love in our own experience of God is to look with such eyes upon all human beings, especially our enemies.

There is a whimsical poem that my grandmother once gave me that recalls this fact.

A Dream

I dreamed I died and Heaven's gates swung wide,
A smiling angel gently ushered me inside.
There, to my great amazement, were hundreds
    of people I had known down on earth.
Some, I judged as unfit and of very little worth.
Immediately angry words came to my lips,
    but never were set free.
For as I looked around, not one expected me.

—Anonymous

Perhaps St. Augustine prayed to this compassionate, perfect Father when he finally came to his senses and turned toward a life he could not have imagined or borne before. It is the life of one who has accepted discipleship and so become a son or daughter of God. Niall O'Brien in *Island of Tears, Island of Hope* describes the experience in just one line: "Prayer is contact with God, and when it is authentic the mercy of God touches the searchers and flows out on their fellows, radiating God's mercy and love to them."

This experience in prayer is not a one-time thing, though the first time it can seem to have a magnitude that dwarfs anything previous. But once there has been this contact with Jesus' Father —Compassion, Perfect, Wholeness—there begins both a hunger for it in the soul and a fresh awareness of its lack in our lives. Prayer is about that experience, but it is ultimately about sharing that experience with others who are as desperate for its taste as we are. We are not allowed to take from such Compassion without passing it on to another, especially anyone we think of as our enemy. In fact, spiritual writers are quick to remind us that if we truly pray and know God, there is no way we can think of another as an enemy.

Teresa of Avila writes:

Prayer is not just spending time with the Lord. It is partly that—but if it ends there, it is fruitless. No, prayer is dynamic. Authentic prayer changes us—unmasks us, strips us, indicates where growth is needed. Authentic prayer never leads to complacency, but needles us, makes us uneasy at times. It leads us to true self-knowledge, to true humility.

Prayer makes us see clearly that there are no enemies. There are only others just like us, and the rain falls on us all, just and unjust alike; the sun warms us all, the good and the bad. Even the horrible, according to our standards, are invited into God's love. Luckily our standards are not the ones used by Jesus' Father. Prayer is the place for learning new standards, ones that are based on God's unutterable kindness for all of us, beginning with our enemies and extending even to us.

THE SECOND WEEK OF LENT

✛

Sunday of the Second Week of Lent

Genesis 12:1-4
2 Timothy 1:8-10
Matthew 17:1-9

"Abraham was seventy-five years old when he left Haran." This seems like an add-on, a detail tagged onto the promise of the covenant that sets in motion the driving force of God's history in the world. But it is crucial. This reading notes Abraham's obedience to the command to "go forth from his own house," the house of his ancestors and his past, and it records his birth into another reality. His name changes from Abram to Abraham. His future will be built on words and dreams, the vision of humanity redeemed and once again living together with God, as it was meant in the beginning.

Abram begins to live at seventy-five. Everything up to this time was preparation. I used to take heart from the life of St. Teresa of Avila, telling myself not to worry because nothing of real significance happened in Teresa's spiritual life apparently until after she was fifty years old. Now Abram's life and the life of a people in faith begins at seventy-five. Obviously, time with Yahweh is a different thing altogether than just consecutive years or an accumulation of experiences. Something else is seeded in history, and faith draws it forth on its own schedule. There is always something else going on besides, in, through, over, and under historical time. There is another perspective to life for one who believes in the words of God.

B Cycle: Gn 22:1-2, 9, 10-13, 15-18; Rom 8:31-34; Mk 9:2-10
C Cycle: Gn 15:5-12, 17-18; Phil 3:17-41; Lk 9:28-36

These words are the future of the human race, of the meaning between God and Abram—and so between all those who come after, who stake their lives on something as intangible as a covenant, a promise for their children and their children's children, willing themselves to be bound to a future of hope. These people become a blessing for all the peoples of the earth, people who live in community, with shared possibilities and pasts held in common. It seems, as with Abraham at seventy-five, that it is never too late to begin something earth-shattering and momentous with this God of ours!

The word *blessing* is repeated, as though it is a mantra, a word fraught with power in itself. It is something that God speaks, both sets in motion and accomplishes. It is also a reality already in existence that seems to have a life of its own. It is what God does and what we become and what all others on earth will recognize and take heart from, finding in this new creation humanity's redemption and the grasping of once-lost possibilities. We will be the blessing. We are re-created by the word of God. We become the blessing of God, a sigh that drifts over the world and seeps into all things and time. Eventually it will take us all home.

This Sunday, the Sunday of Transfiguration, is a day of blessing, hope, and promises made and remembered and perceived now in a person who is the blessing of God on the human race: Jesus, beloved of God. On the second Sunday of Lent we are blessed with an experience of God's continuing meaning of blessing. As Daniel Berrigan, says: "Religious experience is at its root an experience of an unconditional and unrestrained being in love." The covenant says that God is unrestrainedly and unconditionally in love with us, and all of time is for us to learn its patterns in our flesh and blood so the world can breathe easier and live in hope.

Lent is for learning that we are one in Christ, that our communities are blessings for others when we believe and obey like Abram, no matter what age we begin.

Counterpoint to age and the past is Paul's letter to young Timothy and its exhortation to the future and all it holds for us. "Bear your share of the hardship which the gospel entails." This is our response, like Abram's obedience to the command to leave behind his former life, and it is based on a promise of God. Timothy and all of us are reminded that we are called to a "holy life" according to God's own design—the grace of God held out to us in Christ Jesus. This is the heart of today's readings and the meaning, the depth charge, of the story of the transfiguration: in the appearance of Christ Jesus, our Savior, not just on the mount where they go to pray together, but in history, God has robbed death of its power and has brought life and immortality.

All the words of God are about life, not bound only by time and history but by love revealed in everlasting life for all. The gospel is the covenant in flesh and blood, the person and abiding power of Jesus, who shatters history with his appearance. We live now in the shadow of Jesus, in the same Spirit that gave life to creation and reanimates all life with outrageous hope. We are saved by hope, by joyfully bearing our share of the hardships that this gospel entails. The word *bear* is core to the meaning of what Timothy and all of us as disciples are being told to grasp hold of. A woman bears a child, bringing it forth in hard labor, carrying it to its fullness and readiness to emerge into history. That bearing stops time momentarily. All that is possible is to bear the pain in hopes of a child's cry bursting forth with the pushing forth of life into history, from one world to another.

The gospel entails hardship, hard work, labor that will end in glory, in birthing a new life, a new world of hope. The message of this Sunday of Lent is not easy, but it has all the wild possibilities of Abram being told he and Sarai will have children out of time and of Jesus being raised from the dead, shattering the pattern of birth, life and death forever. Thomas Traherne, in *Centuries of Meditations*, puts it poetically, teasing out the endless possibilities we are to bear in mind as we go through time, especially these forty days:

> The cross is the abyss of wonders,
> the center of desires, the school of virtues,
> the house of wisdom, the throne of love,
> the theatre of joys and the place of sorrows;
> It is the root of happiness, and the gate of heaven.

When dealing with God we must remember that we never get just what we are expecting, we always get more than we bargained for. Although God lives in "no time," we join the presence of God in time through our share in the life of Christ Jesus, given to us in baptism. Our hardships are not vague but usually very specific: obeying the laws of the church consistently; defending all life, not just the life of chosen ones that are deemed deserving; instilling Christian values into our communities and children and practicing them our-

selves in the face of contradictory values of American society; sup-
porting the church; critiquing society; defending belief; being faithful; facing suffering and hardships with trust in God and without
bitterness and blame; reconciling and forgiving and clinging to forgiveness as God's gracious presence; being truthful and without rancor when the church and members of the church fail personally and
collectively; and often doing penance that atones for our own and
other's lack of obedience to the gospel and to the needs of those
clamoring to us in history as believers in Jesus' good news to the
poor.

Jesus, in the gospel, is intent on sharing this time, this experience
of God, with his friends. It is a traditional account of glory and resurrection, out of time, prior to the experience of the cross. It is the
story of the saved, the redeemed, inserted as hope into the season of
Lent, the season of springing forth into newness of life, into the saving grace of believers' time. It is a reminder of hardship and the reality of death that is laced through the reality of resurrection. We are
saved. The resurrection is a reality in our lives now, because the cross
and resurrection and continual life of Jesus are with us still. It is a
bolstering of spirits for the next five weeks. It is a scene of glory, awe,
and reverence, a glimpse of who Jesus really is, human and obeying
God, preaching the gospel, caring for the poor, bringing others back
from the dead, unraveling history's hold, even if he is hidden from
view for now. Our lives—our efforts and repentance and emptying
out of our old life—are hidden from view as well.

God reveals Jesus in this account witnessed by Peter, James, and
John, his disciples and friends. It encourages them and gives them
heart. It is given to us, his disciples and friends, as well. Jesus announces to his disciples the reality of what time and history will do
to him and all of us—seek to destroy us—yet God the Father will
raise the Son of Man from the dead and will repay each according to
his or her deeds. The Son of Man will come in glory in the kingdom
of God. This is a promise.

Jesus is seen in this glory, as radiant as light, as the sun of justice,
along with Moses and Elijah. These men have transcended history as
hope for their people: liberator of slaves, giver of the law, prophet,
words of God in the mouth of human beings. Both have deaths that
seemingly defy time. No one knows when Moses died or where he
was buried. God and the angels buried him, and the grave is kept
secret. Elijah disappeared in a fiery chariot, borne to heaven. He is to

reappear when the world is ready for the Messiah to fill time and history so completely that all the earth will know that justice and peace dwells with a people and that God visits the people once again. All history comes together in this one person, Jesus.

Peter wants to stay in this moment and place and not face the promise of the cross and suffering and death. He does not really believe in the future. He wants to stay in the present. He wants to build booths, create monuments. He is already figuring out how to use this, keep this, as we often do with experiences of God, rather than let it escort him into the future transformed. But the voice that spoke at Jesus' baptism interrupts Peter, and us, trying to get us back on track—the track of hope and promise, the track of obedience and worship. "This is my beloved son on whom my favor rests. Listen to him."

It's that simple: Listen to him and no one else in history. The disciples fall forward on their faces, flat on the ground, overcome with fear and awe, out of time, in the presence of the Holy. Then Jesus comes forward again into their lives and ordinary time and lays a hand on them saying: "Get up, do not be afraid." These few words are the essence of resurrection life: Arise and live without fear of death, the end of time, hate, injustice, suffering. We have been given the life of the Son of Man to sustain us in this history that serves God's time and promises.

When they look up again, they see only Jesus. That's the core, the heart of all history and of all life, only Jesus and what he brings into this world. On the way down the mountain Jesus commands them, in the same vein as Abram was commanded to leave his past behind, "Do not tell anyone of the vision until the Son of Man rises from the dead," that is, until the seemingly impossible becomes reality.

This account is an intimation of Easter five weeks from now. We are weak-hearted and basically timid and fearful folk and oftentimes, even by the second week of Lent, we're ready to give up. This Sunday is for courage, blessing, encouragement, and a moment of prayer, an experience of the glory of the Lord, of revelation for all us faint-hearted folk. It is for us when we act like Peter, wanting it easy, wanting to stay with glory, wanting to stay with our limited and oftentimes off-base assumptions about what is going on. It is a time for God to interrupt and once again tell us: "This is my beloved on whom my favor rests—the favor of grace, spirit, justice, care for the poor, obedience. *Listen* to him and not to anyone else."

We are called to redirect attention to Jesus, the central point of everything—the Law; the prophets; Old Testament hopes, covenants, stories, and history. All is pinned on him, his life and his response to God. His life and death and resurrection are the result of his trust and belief in God and his obedience.

The resurrected Jesus is with us as we journey. Lent has its moments of glory as well as its hard uphill climbs. Lent has its joys and mystical experiences and intimacies with Jesus and with the community of believers as well as its penance, almsgiving, fasting, and repenting. Lent has its revelations as well as its acknowledgments of sin and the need for forgiveness. Lent has its moments of fear and the beginnings of true worship, when we see ourselves as we truly are before God, and yet stay. Lent has its inadequacies and failures, like Peter's and the others' response to Jesus' crucifixion, as well as the times when Jesus invites us to come and pray with him alone, off apart from others. Lent is for looking up and seeing only Jesus, human and with us, as well as divine and beloved of God. He shares that beloved status with us freely and generously, even as we fall on our faces, sin, and get stuck in our old ways of being, believing, and not living up to the promises of our baptism.

Transfiguration is the glory of God shining through the body, through Jesus' flesh, his person. This glory of God is connected to us through his body: the person Jesus, eucharist, the community of believers, the church. Jesus' body is a bridge that we cross to meet God face to face. Our baptisms transfigure us individually as children of God and collectively as the body of Christ so that we can become that transfiguration, that bridge of glory, for a sinful world that needs to see God face to face.

Eventually evil and those who align themselves with evil take Jesus into their hands and seek to destroy him, to kill hope incarnate. We will need to rely on this vision of transfiguration and tell the story again and again to each other in the times ahead. In the weeks to come we will be asked to side with Jesus and so go to the cross or to stand aside and refuse, standing instead with Satan the hinderer. There are only two choices: the cross or a life that has no glory, no hope, no meaning, no future of redemption, no possibility, and no redeeming grace.

Jesus is the Light for all of us. We are to be light for the catechumens just as Jesus was light for his friends Peter, James, and John.

Today is about proclaiming the glory of God in spite of the suffering that will precede it. The glory will be there. The cross too will be there. Both are reality. We have to face the challenge squarely. We must struggle to be true, to disappear so that the presence of God can be revealed, so that history can be altered to accommodate the nearness of God in our flesh and blood.

There is a children's story from the traditions of the Lenape Indian Nation, which was originally from the Pennsylvania area. It is called "Rainbow Crow," and it is a story of transfiguration that mirrors much of today's gospel.*

✢   Once upon a time, long ago, before any two-leggeds walked this earth, earth was at peace. It was warm, summer always, and the animals wanted for nothing. They roamed the earth and blessed the Great Spirit. Then one night, as some slept and others came out to play and hunt, there was a new thing. Things began to fall from the sky. They had seen rain before, but this was different. It was lovely, soft, very cold, and it didn't immediately disappear into the ground like rain. It stuck to the ground, to trees, branches, even fur and feathers. It stayed, growing harder and colder as it lingered. But it was lovely too. And so, when the first snowfall came, the animals were delighted that the Great Spirit was still making such grand things for earth's pleasures and needs.

But it kept snowing, long after the first night and the next day. It didn't stop, and the smaller creatures had great trouble getting around. They were trapped in their burrows, disappearing under the drifts, and exhausted from the daily need to find food. First Mouse disappeared; only a tail stuck up out of the snow. Then Rabbit and Possum and Fox. Even Coyote, sly and wily, was panting with exertion and grumpy. He was much too tired to play tricks on the others.

Some of the animals, though, were having a grand time. Otter and Seal loved the cold and snow, but eventually they had trouble diving under the ice to get home. Moose and Elk, and even Bear, began to wonder how they'd keep their young ones strong and how long this would last. One never knew with the Great Spirit.

---

*This is my adaptation of the legend. A version for young readers has also been published by Nancy Van Laan.

One day they all gathered in a rocky clearing in the forest to talk about the weather and what could be done. They quickly decided that someone had to visit the Great Spirit, to inform the Great One what was happening on earth, and ask for the snow to cease. But who was to go? Some suggested Owl, but he had trouble seeing in the light and the sun seemed so glaring with the snow on the ground. (Amazingly it snowed in darkness, with gray, thick clouds, and in bright, shining day.) Others thought of Raccoon, but he was always scavenging for food and forgetful of important things. Even Coyote was put forward, but it was pretty clear most didn't think that was wise. Coyote was a thief, a trickster—it was his nature and no one was sure exactly what he'd do on a journey to the Great Spirit, and they had enough trouble to deal with already. They were stymied. They made a terrible racket as they wailed and worried about what to do. In the meantime, the snow kept on, steady and sure, getting deeper all the time. Finally, the animals resorted to standing on top of each other in silly looking and very uncomfortable pyramids, with the largest animals on the bottom, others on top of them, and the tiniest animals at the very top. This was getting ridiculous and dangerous. How long could they keep this up?

Then from high in the pine trees came the sound of Rainbow Crow, the most beautiful of all the birds. Crow sang out: "I'll go. I'll stop the snow." And in gratitude the animals sang a song of praise and thanksgiving. Off went Crow, up and up, above the clouds and falling snow, past the winds and stars, disappearing into the darkness beyond night. Finally Crow flew right into the presence of the Great Spirit, singing and crying of the animals' plight down on earth. He sang a prayer of praise of the Creator and Maker of all things: of birds and animals, earth itself and weather, things of water and small flowers, and of the wonders that never cease, even new ones. And then the song of praise, the psalm, turned into a lullaby for the Great Spirit. Crow knew how much all the birds and animals loved to be sung to sleep and lulled by music, and since the Great Spirit made them all, why, maybe the Great Spirit would like to be sung to also! The Great Spirit listened attentively to Crow's song.

The Great Spirit delighted in Crow's lullaby, and in response Crow was told to choose any gift. Immediately Crow asked the Great Spirit to stop the snow down on earth, because all the animals and birds were disappearing under it, lost and cold. But surprisingly, the Great Spirit refused, saying, "I can't!" This surprised Crow. After all, this was the Great Spirit. Then the Great Spirit explained that Snow had a spirit and power of its own, and whenever Snow went to visit with his friend the Wind, then the snow would stop down below. But as long as Snow stayed with the Clouds, snow would continue unabated. Even when the snow stopped, there would still be cold.

So Crow asked the Great Spirit to stop the cold. Again, Great Spirit said: "I can't. I'm sorry. But I can give you another gift—the gift of Fire. It's another new thing, and it will keep you warm and melt the snow. It's very useful, a balance to Cold." And so the Great Spirit picked up a stick, put fire on the end of it, handed it to Crow, and told Crow to fly as fast as possible back down to earth. Off Crow went as fast as wings could fly, for the Great Spirit had said that the gift could only be given once. Crow had been commanded: "Go. Fly to earth before Fire disappears altogether."

Down Crow went. On the first night there were showering sparks that sprayed out as he flew fast and furious, and they darkened his tail feathers. The next day the fire crept down the stick, getting closer to Crow. It grew hotter as it ate the stick, and poor Crow was blanketed with soot as thick as the snow down below. That night the stick was a stub, and the smoke choked Crow, filling his lungs and making him cough and gag. Finally, with morning, Crow flew into the gathering, but there were no animals left to greet him on his return. They'd all disappeared under the snow! Only the highest tops of the tallest trees, very thin and sticking up like blades of grass out of the mounds of snow, remained.

Crow landed on the snow, his feet moving numbly in circles, and his voice hoarse with the cold. And soon, at first very slowly, the snow began to melt. Then it melted faster and faster. Air fed the fire; Wind stirred it up. It became Grandfather Fire, sure and hot, a beacon of hope. Finally, Crow was once again standing on firm ground, and all the animals and birds danced in a circle and sang praises of gratitude to him for saving them. But their song also sang of loss and change, for now beautiful Rainbow Crow, who once had carried all the colors in his feathers and wings, was black as a night without a moon.

When the rejoicing was over, Crow was left alone. Off he flew to his old soggy wet nest high in the pines, and he wept. He was cold and ugly. His feathers were soaked and thick, and he shook in the cold and the wind. And when he tried to sing, to soothe himself with the lullabies of old, all that came out was this terrible "caw caw caw."

Next morning Snow must have gone to visit his friend Wind, because it stopped snowing. But it was crisp and bitter cold. And still Crow cried. Finally, his cawing was noticed even by the Great Spirit, who came down in pity to hear and see what happened to poor, forlorn Crow. Great Spirit told Crow: "Soon there will be others upon the earth—two-legged creatures, very different from all the birds and animals. They will claim Fire for their own, take and use its power. In fact, they will have power over all the birds of the air and fishes of the sea and all animals—all except you, dear Crow. Because you were kind and gave me your gift of song, singing lullabies to me, and because you were so unselfish in asking for Snow to stop, no two-legged will ever have dominion over you! They won't think you're that important because you don't sing—you croak and caw and jar their ears. They won't think of eating you because your flesh is raw and sinewy and tough, like charred meat. You'd taste like smoke and ashes to them and remind them of fire's touch and destruction. And they won't even want your feathers that are as black as night and as common. But there will be a few who see clearly, as I do, and, at certain angles in the light of day or the sheen of the moon they will see the rainbows hidden in the commonness. But they'll have to get close and care and look at you kindly; others will be blind to the loveliness you carry with you always."

Crow looked, and as the sun glinted across his eyes the rainbows came and went, and he was content with the Great Spirit's blessing. The Great Spirit knew and some of the two-leggeds, the ones who saw as the Creator and Maker of all things did, would know too. And so Crow returned to his friends and crowed—"caw caw caw"—night and day, afraid of no one, not even the two-leggeds to come. He sang loudly, proclaiming rainbows that cry out concern for friends who disappear in the snow, great and small alike. And even though the two-leggeds stole fire for themselves, it is Crow who really knows fire and what it does. They say it is so to this day.

Listen to Crow's voice. It interrupts. It's insistent, loud, jarring, never-ending. There are so many of them, as black as night, as rude and bold as they can be. But they know. Listen and learn of the Great Spirit's gifts to those beloved and most like the Great Spirit who gives, never takes back, and has always something hidden away that saves the day. Caw. Caw.Caw.

The gospel is direct: "Listen to him, to the beloved of God, Jesus, only Jesus." There is a song that is good for this season of Lent, called "In the Land There Is a Hunger." It goes:

> In the land there is a hunger
> In the land there is a need
> Not for the taste of water.
> Not for the taste of bread.
> In the land there is a hunger
> In the land there is a need
> For the sound of the word of God
> upon ev'ry word we feed. (Refrain)
>
> Hear, O Lord, my cry.
> Day and night I call
> My soul is thirsting for you, my God.
>
> Your word, O Lord, is spirit and life.
> You have the words, Lord of everlasting life.

Monday of the Second Week of Lent

Daniel 9:4-10
Luke 6:36-38

This week we move closer to Jerusalem in the company of Jesus. We watch more closely and see what the reactions are to the words, stories, and actions of the Word made flesh and how they rub and chafe with the histories and powers of the world. We have been told to "listen to him," for Jesus is the beloved of God, filled with grace and favor, filled with the Holy Spirit. We will hear the stories and words of others from the past who listened to this same Spirit, how they confronted the world and sought to bring hope to people wearied by evil and injustice. We will hear how they sought also to worship in spirit and truth a God wearied by the people's unfaithfulness. Both are part and parcel of our history and our past. Both must be faced sincerely and embraced or atoned for, singularly and in community, if the world is to catch glimmers of the rainbows hidden in the history of those who believe in God's promises.

In some sense we are all called to be crows—unselfish, brave, caring about the least among us, those who disappear under the burdens laid upon them by others. We are to praise God and sing lullabies to the Great Spirit and then return to our homes with the fire of the Spirit kindled by the Word of the Lord. We may lose much that is precious to us, but God is always more creative and gracious than the world's harshness and destructiveness. Lent is a time of greening, of leaping up in faith, of restoring hope, and of repairing earth in order to create a place where promises can thrive.

We begin with Daniel, who is the first to receive visions of the coming of the Son of Man. Daniel, who is a prophet, is also a pray-er, one who beseeches God on behalf of his people. The prayer is the same for all prophets and all those who do penance for others; it is a sad litany of failure, unfaithfulness, and forgetfulness in the presence of the enduring mercy of God. It is an acknowledgment of shame, loss, and being scattered among the nations, of being broken in pieces by our sin and of treachery toward God and one another. But always the cry comes back to God, to the essence of the covenant: "But yours, O Lord, our God, are compassion and forgiveness! Yet we rebelled against you and paid no heed to your command, O Lord, our God, to live by the law you gave us through your servants the prophets." It is a short summation of history. The remedy? Reiteration of the age-old command: be holy.

The good news of Luke from the sermon on the plain is Jesus' clear command to the disciples, to us, "to be compassionate as our Father is compassionate." These two lines of scripture could be the meditation for all of life. As we do to one another, so it shall be done to us—and more when we resemble God even a little: "Give, and it shall be given to you. Good measure pressed down, shaken together, running over, will they pour into the fold of your garment. For the measure you measure with will be measured back to you."

This endeavor we are about in Lent is not small or merely singular. It is about salvation and the re-creation of earth, about God's compassion being let loose on earth so it covers us, like a quilt that brings peace and the sleep of the just, where children can be safe and all can dwell secure. It is about the coming of the Kingdom of God into history, transforming everything, undercutting evil, and shaking sin and death to their foundations.

The commands are straightforward: be compassionate as your Father is compassionate. Do not judge and you will not be judged. Do not condemn, and you will not be condemned. Pardon and you shall be pardoned. Give and it shall be given to you. All these are predicated on community, on the reality of our being connected to all the beloved of God.

Thomas Merton once said that "The distance between God and me kills me." Anyone struck by God—by vision, scripture stories of faithfulness, blessings of the covenant, the presence of Jesus—is torn by this sense of distance and the overwhelming need to bridge the gulf. This is our essential work; all else is laid aside. We deny our very self before attempting to pick up our cross to come after Jesus. Positively, the gulf is bridged by compassion, almsgiving, the corporal works of mercy, charity, work for justice. These are necessary, not simply options for believers, for the ones covenanted to God. We, like Daniel, learn to pray on behalf of all the people, to atone for the past and what is lacking in the present in relation to God.

Our experience of God is usually and primarily through other people. God's epiphanies are more often than not in the human experiences of poverty, rejection, violence and unnecessary suffering. Christian life is about transforming the ordinary into the dazzling, about transfiguring the broken flesh of others into the resurrected flesh of the body of Christ. And this is a fight, a resistance to the world. In 1993, after years of struggle in South Africa for freedom and human dignity for all, Allan Boesak wrote: "We will go before God to be judged, and God will ask us, 'Where are your wounds?' And we will say, 'We have no wounds.' And God will ask, 'Was nothing worth fighting for?'"

Martin of Tours, a soldier who became a Christian, said, "I am a soldier of Christ now and may not fight with a weapon in my hand."

We must stand without external weapons, with empty hands and open hearts, attentive to the needs of those in our midst.

This is hard and demanding work, daily picking up of our cross and also learning to carry others' crosses momentarily so they can just breathe easier. Lanza del Vasto, in *Principles and Precepts of a Return to the Obvious*, explains what this might look like in practical everyday actions.

> Learn that virile charity has severe words for those who flatter, serene words for those who fight you, warm words for the weary, strong for the suffering, clear for the blind, crushing for the proud, and a bucketful of water and a stick for those who sleep.

Once we have the words, they teach us the accompanying actions and introduce us to those who will be in our company: those who will support us and encourage us in this kind of daily struggle to contain despair and stem the spread of callousness and insensitivity. Being compassionate as Jesus' Father is compassionate takes all the power and force of the Spirit. It is useful to remember that in the religion of Islam, sometimes thought of as a militant religion, Allah means "most compassionate one." This is the God we are revealing in attending to others with delicate touch, strong arm, and a glance that says we see only Jesus in our world—everywhere, in everyone.

Tuesday of the Second Week of Lent

Isaiah 1:10, 16-20
Matthew 23:1-12

Some of the imagery of battle is continued in the reading from Isaiah the prophet. "Make justice your aim"—the image evoked is a target. There is the stance of readiness, concentration and attentiveness, letting nothing distract from the center, the heart of the target to be hit. Success entails strategy, daily practice, and a love for the work itself.

There is an English story told about a king who was obsessed with the sport of archery.

✛   The king wanted more than anything else to hit the bull's-eye every time. It might have seemed like an impossible goal to others, but it was what kept him practicing every spare moment that he had. He was king, but what fueled his life was his archery practice and his dream of perfection. He scheduled his whole day around what had to be done so that he could once again get back to his beloved practice sessions. And he was good—he could hit the bull's-eye nearly 75 percent of the time, no mean feat for one in his twenties. His reputation and fame spread. But it wasn't enough.

The king finally found a teacher, renowned in the discipline called Zen, who claimed that he could teach him to hit the bull's-eye more often, and do it most of the time with his eyes closed! The king was a bit skeptical, but he became the man's apprentice, beginning once again at the beginning, humbled before one who was master of the craft. And amazingly, within a few years it was true. He could hit the target more than 90 percent of the time, and usually with his eyes closed! Now he knew that there was more than skill, practice, or luck involved. His craft demanded inner discipline, concentration, and detachment (freedom from the need to hit the target).

For years the king stayed at the level he had mastered, but went no further. And it pained him. One day as he was visiting one of the small villages of the kingdom he rode by barn after barn filled with targets. Each had a single arrow dead center! He was excited. There was a master hidden in this tiny, out-of-the-way place. This was what he had waited for all his life. He was startled to learn that the master was a young boy, no more than a dozen years of age. How could one so young be so skilled? Humbly, he sought out the young boy.

At first the boy was awed in the presence of his king, but when he realized that the king was serious about learning and that he loved archery, always searching for that 100 percent accuracy, he was delighted to show the king what he knew. Off they went to a barn to practice. First, they covered the routine of any teacher: attitude, care for the bow and arrow, stance, eye, the feel of the instruments. The boy was a master. He stood easily, pulled the bow taut, and the arrow flew. He had demonstrated his technique, and he asked the king to do the same. The king obliged, and the boy nodded approvingly. But then came the hard learning.

The boy left the king's side and approached the side of the barn. He grabbed a bucket and paint to draw the bull's-eye, the target that would prove or disprove the skill of each. And to the king's absolute disbelief, the boy drew the target around the arrows that were just for practice. The boy turned, grinning from ear to ear, and said: "King, that's how I do it all the time, 100 percent. I just paint the target on afterward!" Needless to say the king was stunned and humiliated, then angry and speechless, and finally, he burst out laughing himself.*

The story says much to us about being perfect and compassionate, and about making justice our aim, as well as about following the master, Jesus, to the cross. We start where we are and with what is around us. We launch our arrow and we paint the target around it afterward. As odd as it sounds, that is what obedience, compassion, and justice are all about. The prophet goes on to specifics: redress the wronged, hear the orphan's plea, defend the widow, cease doing evil, learn to do good. It's that simple and clear-cut. We start by doing something that pulls us outside of ourself and makes us attentive to another, for there are always others, so many others in dire need. And whatever is done for them with kindness, in justice, will center them—and us in relation to them.

Isaiah continues with the words of God: "Come now, let us set things right. Though your sins be like scarlet they may become white as snow. . . . If you are willing and obey, you shall eat the good things of the land; but if you refuse and resist, the sword shall consume you: for the mouth of the Lord has spoken!" "Let us set things right"—it is as surefire as painting the bull's-eye around the arrow after its flight. God is at least as concerned as the young boy that we are forgiven and called back to justice and righteousness—all 100 percent of us in all cases and circumstances. Like the king, we are dubious. But like the king, we can learn to laugh at the wonder of a God who cares

---

*I've used a slightly different version of this story in *Parables: Arrows of God* to make a quite different point. Good stories lend themselves well to multiple interpretations.

more for justice in the land than skill or personal attainment of goals. Humbly, we begin again, as the king before his master, the boy of no more than a dozen years.

Jesus' words in Matthew's gospel are about some teachers, supposedly models of behavior and learning. His words go to the heart of the issue: "Do everything and observe everything they tell you. But do not follow their example. Their words are bold but their deeds are few. They bind up heavy loads, hard to carry, to lay on other men's shoulders, while they themselves will not lift a finger to budge them." It is a devastatingly blunt indictment of hypocrisy. The image that Jesus uses is the reverse image of picking up our cross or bearing our share of the burden of the gospel. Instead, it is an image of those who lay the cross on the shoulders of those condemned to death—most innocent of any crime except poverty, a dream, and a desperate hope for freedom and a better life. The teachers who have succeeded Moses must be listened to with care and obeyed, but they are not to be imitated in their callousness, lack of compassion, disregard for justice, and hypocrisy. They disobey the prophets and do not make justice their aim; they do not share the king's or the young boy's love of the skill of hitting the mark 100 percent. They do not even respect the target—the poor, the widow, the orphan, or the outcast.

Jesus is harshest on those who think of themselves and put themselves forth as God-fearing and law-abiding, yet live only for show and for others' good impression of them. They have no kindness, no courtesy, no justice toward others.

Jesus is clear about the criteria for being a true teacher in his company: "The greatest among you will be the one who serves the rest. Whoever exalts himself shall be humbled, but whoever humbles himself shall be exalted." We become skilled in making justice our aim by bending to serve others, by closing our eyes to what others may think about our actions and choices of company, and by concentrating on the one thing necessary: setting things right in the world and thus letting God make things right between us and God. Let the arrow fly! "Come, now, let us set things right," says the Lord.

Wednesday of the Second Week of Lent

Jeremiah 18:18-20
Matthew 20:17-28

The readings of this week are full of stories, almost unbelievable stories of dedication, deceit, power, reputation, and repudiation. They are meant to dazzle us into openness to the experience that Jesus had with God as his Father.

The portion from Jeremiah is especially hard to take to heart because it is so brutal and cold-blooded. It is plotted by the citizens of Jerusalem and the people of Judah, those who live in the land of the covenant, at its very heart. They intend to destroy the prophet Jeremiah, and they are very rational about what they will do and the effect it will have on them and others:

> Let us contrive a plot against Jeremiah. It will not mean the loss of instruction from the priests, nor of counsel from the wise, nor of messages from the prophets. And so, let us destroy him by his own tongue; let us carefully note his every word.

These people consider themselves religious. They are sure of where they stand in the structures of religion, yet at the same time they are torturers and murderers, backed up by those who have the power.

Jeremiah cries out in anguish to God to heed him in his need. He begs God to listen, perhaps just as carefully to what his adversaries say, and he questions God in the tradition of all those passionate about justice. He has become a voice on behalf of the victims of sin. He is expendable if not problematic to existing structures of society and life.

Jeremiah questions God: "Must good be repaid with evil that they should dig a pit to take my life? Remember that I stood before you to speak in their behalf, to turn away your wrath from them."

Jeremiah prays for a sinful nation and hard-hearted people. He pleads in their behalf. Now he stands in jeopardy of his own life because of their hate and rejection of him. They are heartless, unremorseful, and steeped in their own self-righteousness and sin.

The only protection from people like that is God. They cannot be reasoned with or converted. They have made their decisions and are entrenched where they stand. They have moved into active persecution of good and cannot long tolerate the presence of the truth or the presence of those who speak of justice and conversion and forgiveness before God and with one another. Jeremiah's position is, of course, the position that Jesus will find himself in with the leaders and teachers of his own society and religious structures. It is a sad and lamentable reality that the most dangerous people are those who, sure of their own rightness, do evil.

In the gospel, Jesus is sure of his own position and the effect his presence is having on the structures and powers of his own nation and Temple. He tries to teach his disciples not to be naive, to be aware of the vehemence with which evil confronts pure goodness and the lengths to which human beings will go to avoid facing the truth and changing their ways, let alone atoning for their evil. Jesus is direct, brutal in his description of what they will do to him:

> We are going up to Jerusalem now. There the Son of Man will be handed over to the chief priests and scribes, who will condemn him to death. They will turn him over to the Gentiles, to be made sport of and flogged and crucified. But on the third day he will be raised up.

This is also a theological description of the early church's belief about Jesus, the Son of Man, who, like Jeremiah, stands always before the Holy One and speaks in behalf of the human race, turning away the just wrath of God. This is the One who will come in glory, the One whom we glimpsed Sunday at the transfiguration, shining and powerful in the holiness of God, who will come to judge all peoples on the basis of their conduct, their belief, and their prayer.

But the disciples do not want to hear. They are following the Messiah, whom they expect to be a political and military figure, one who will make Jerusalem a strong nation and overthrow the Romans, expelling these hated and despised oppressors from their land. They do not want to hear Jesus' understanding of who he is—not a military or political leader at all, but a prophet intent on saving the people from their blindness, their self-righteousness, and their sins. His own disciples share in that blindness, self-righteousness, and sin! They do not want Jesus the prophet any more than the people wanted

Jeremiah's truth. They want Jesus' power; they hope their association with him will benefit their selfish aspirations.

And so there is the story of the mother of James and John, Jesus' cousins, coming to him to ask a favor. She is well-intentioned but totally unaware of either the immediate or long-term consequences of her request. She—and, one must suspect, James and John—wants power, the power she thinks will come from close affiliation with the one who will be king in Israel. They all are deaf to the reason they go now to Jerusalem. She asks the favor: "Promise me that these sons of mine will sit, one at your right hand and the other at your left in your kingdom."

One can only imagine the sadness that Jesus feels at the stubborn refusal to listen to him. (After all, we were counseled by the voice of God at the transfiguration to *listen* to him, not to the other voices within us and all around us.) Jesus tries once again to tell her and his disciples that they do not know what it is they are asking. He uses the image of the cup, querying them as to their willingness to drink the cup that he will drink—the cup of suffering, rejection, torture, crucifixion, and death. They are quick to say they can. However, they have another cup in mind—more banal and apt in the world of power—a cup that toasts power, achievement, status, hierarchy, and oppression of one group by another, a simple reversal of who is on top.

But Jesus will not commit himself or promise her, for he is clear that some things are not his to give. They belong to his Father. It seems power, the power of close association that comes with sharing intimately in the sufferings of the Son of Man and thus the sharing of the judgment seat of the prophets comes not from the choice of the individual or even delegation from Jesus, but from the Spirit and the Father whom Jesus obeys. There are reserved seats and places of suffering and rejoicing that are given out by the Father.

Of course the rest of the disciples are indignant and go after James and John, causing dissension, rancor, and division among themselves. They are *all* vying for power, acting like a group of irate and petty hirelings rather than disciples of Jesus, who preaches servanthood and care for the least among them. They have not been listening to him. Instead, they have been planning their own rise to power and influence.

So Jesus patiently calls them all together to remind them yet again of how things work in his kingdom. "You know how those who exercise authority among the Gentiles lord it over them; their great ones make their importance felt. It cannot be like that with you." There is a radical break, a gulf between whatever authority and greatness is in the world and in Jesus' domain, and he will spend the rest of his life trying to get them to see it and even embrace it gladly in behalf of others, as he did.

In his community authority and power are primarily used in behalf of others, of those who have no voice in the dominant cultures and structures of the world. Jesus is subversive. He is intent on grasping hold of the ones no one wants and protecting all those who fall into the clutches of the selfish, the self-righteous, and the pseudo-religious.

> Anyone among you who aspires to greatness [and who among us doesn't in our heart of hearts?] must serve the rest, and whoever wants to rank first among you, must serve the needs of all. Such is the case with the Son of Man who has come, not to be served by others but to serve, to give his own life as a ransom for the many.

These words are the bull's-eye that Jesus is intent that his followers work at hitting 100 percent of the time. It is the only goal worth aiming for: being a servant filled with the power of the Spirit, intent upon ransoming the many sinners, the many who do evil, and the many more who are the victims of injustice, systemic evil, and the backwash of personal sin. This goes against everything they had hoped for, staked their following of Jesus on. This is not the way they had hoped for or wanted. It is time now for the disciples to decide. Do they go now into Jerusalem, the place of the confrontation with power and the death of the prophets? Or do they subtly and even unconsciously begin to withdraw and renege on their commitment to being his disciples and friends?

They—we—must learn to pray to God from the position of Jesus, who serves God alone and so suffers in this world because of that single-hearted choice. The prayer of the psalmist today is a good place to start, to remember our priorities and absolute need for God as the only power worth serving with all our heart and soul and mind and strength.

> *You will free me from the snare they set for me,*

for you are my refuge.
Into your hands I commend my spirit;
   you will redeem me, O Lord, O faithful God.
Save me, O Lord, in your steadfast love.

I hear the whispers of the crowd, that frighten me from
     every side,
  as they consult together against me, plotting to take my
     life.
Save me, O Lord, in your steadfast love.

But my trust is in you, O Lord;
   I say, "You are my God."
In your hands is my destiny; rescue me
   from the clutches of my enemies and my persecutors.
Save me, O Lord, in your steadfast love.
                (Psalm 31:4-5, 13-15)

There are some things that we can only learn from God. The Spirit teaches us to pray and to know the steadfast love of God, which allows us to pray for our enemies and to do good to those who persecute us. That is power and authority in Jesus' company.

Thursday of the Second Week of Lent

Jeremiah 17:5-10
Luke 16:19-31

Today's readings are heart-wrenching. It is a day of deciding where our hearts are rooted, whom we court, and where our loyalties lie.

The images of the prophet are diametrically opposed: the first is a barren bush in the desert. It stands in a lava waste, in a salted and empty earth—dead already. The second is a tree planted beside water. It stretches out its roots to the stream and so is unafraid of heat or drought. It is fresh and green, and it bears fruit for others. The bush is disconnected; the tree is bound to a source of nourishment and life.

Which mirrors our state of soul and quality of faith and behavior? Usually we know, but all we have to do is ask others if we give shade, a place of rest, abundant fruit, life, and hope, or if we are tied up and shrunken inside ourselves, with no stretching out toward others.

The words of God that follow are jarring and full of rueful truthfulness. God says:

> More tortuous than all else is the human heart,
> beyond remedy; who can understand it?
> I, the Lord, alone probe the mind
> and test the heart,
> To reward everyone according to his ways,
> according to the merit of his deeds.

God knows us and knows why we live as we do, regardless of false impressions or a sinful lack of awareness on our part.

God's reminder is fleshed out in the story of two men: a rich man, traditionally named Dives, a man who does not honor God with his trust but puts his faith in the strength of the flesh and in other human beings. He lives without consciousness of what it means to be human. The other man is a beggar who lives at Dives's gate, covered with sores, desperate for the scraps that fall from the table. The dogs lick his sores, and this is the only kindness he knows, for he receives none from other human beings. His name is Lazarus. Dives had more than he could ever use, and Lazarus lay at the gate of his house and was ignored. Lazarus's trust was in God. No one else was trustworthy.

But that is only the prelude. The beggar dies, and the angels carry him home—to the bosom of Abraham, the one who fed God and his angels at his table as they passed by on their way to Sodom and Gomorrah to judge those people for their inhospitality and violence. The rich man dies, too, is buried, and finds himself in the abode of torment. He lifts his eyes and sees Abraham afar off, with Lazarus resting like a child clasped close to his heart. This is torment and pain indeed. He sees what he is without, and he yearns for it. Dives has become the beggar at the gate of paradise.

Dives calls out to Abraham to have pity on him, asking that Lazarus dip the tip of his finger in water to refresh his tongue, for he is tortured in the flames. It's interesting that Dives recognizes Lazarus. Though he ignored Lazarus when the man would have settled for table scraps, he now begs that Lazarus give him a drop of water to ease his thirst.

But Lazarus is not the one who makes the choices in paradise. Abraham, the patriarch, makes the judgment call and is careful to make sure that Dives knows what the decision is and why it was made:

> "Remember that you were well off in your lifetime, while Lazarus was in misery. Now he has found consolation here, but you have found torment. And that is not all. Between you and us there is fixed a great abyss, so that those who might wish to cross from here to you cannot do so, nor can anyone cross from your side to us."

The abyss was once a gate that could be opened easily, but with recurring choices to ignore the need of others the gate separates us and becomes uncrossable.

Dives accepts the judgment for himself, but he asks Abraham to send Lazarus to his house to warn his five brothers of what lies ahead—judgment, and then eternal life or withering death. But again, Abraham is adamant. They have all they need: Moses and the Law and the prophets' words. When there is justice in the land, and care for those in need of the basic necessities of food, clothing, shelter and dignity, then the covenant is honored.

Jesus tells this story to the Pharisees, who know exactly what he is saying. He continues to an unbelievable ending. When Abraham tells Dives that his family should listen to the prophets and to the Law, the rich man says, "If only someone would go to them from the dead, then they would repent." A sign that breaks into history, that shatters the pattern of normality, of being human; this would be a sign that would demand response. Then they would practice justice and human kindness toward others. But Abraham retorts: "If they do not listen to Moses and the prophets, they will not be convinced *even if one should rise from the dead.*"

Signs, miracles, and disruption of what is human will not quicken life in the hearts of those already dead through selfishness, greed, and distance from those they could have helped. This is the parable of Dives and Lazarus. The reversal of fortunes reveals what was reality long before the judgment: one was already dead, without heart or worship or faith; the other was demeaned by the world but should have been cared for like a child by those faithful to God's covenant.

Abraham models for the Pharisees what Dives should have done: cradled the body and life of Lazarus, the beggar, in their own hearts and lives as true worship of God, true faithfulness. Jesus is prophetically trying to alert them to their own refusal to be faithful and to follow in Abraham, Moses, and the prophets' footsteps. But because they are already so distanced from the covenant and the people around them, nothing will get through to them—not even one who comes back from the dead, as Jesus will.

The parable is stark. It demands that we do some serious reflection. We need to begin by looking at our gates, the entrances and exits to our own life—work, church, friendships, organizations, hobbies—and see if we suffer from the same inhospitality and insensitivity. Any relationship with God begins here. If we do not obey the laws that make us good members of the community, then we will not hear the words of the prophets calling us to justice and human freedom and dignity for all. We will be deaf and disbelieving of one who preaches the kingdom of God, the presence of God among the least of our brothers and sisters. The resurrection will mean nothing to us.

Today we are reminded to look to the gates in our lives and see who waits for us, for it is God who sits there begging for us to notice. God is the masses of poor and needy outside our gates, and we are judged already.

Friday of the Second Week of Lent

Genesis 37:3-4, 12-13, 17-28
Matthew 21:33-43, 45-46

Today we have two stories about sons. One is from the book of Genesis. It tells of Joseph and his brothers, the sons of Israel (Jacob) by Leah and Rachel. The other is the parable that Jesus told to the chief priests and elders of the people about a property owner who sends his son, as a last resort, to obtain his share of the vintage from those who work in his vineyard. The workers kill him, with the odd rationalization that they will then get the vineyard. Note that tomorrow's gospel reading is the story that Jesus tells to the Pharisees about the lost son. These two days of readings overlap, and there are many connections when we read them together that we wouldn't necessarily notice otherwise.

The story of Joseph begins with tenderness and the kind of unequal love that can destroy families.

Israel loved Joseph best of all his sons, for he was the child of his old age; and he had made him a long tunic. When his brothers saw that their father loved him best of all his sons, they hated him so much that they would not even greet him.

The tone of what will come is set ominously at the very start—love that is singular among many and made obvious by special gifts and treatment. Of course, we know from earlier in the story that Joseph doesn't make it easy for his brothers to live with this favoritism; he flaunts the dreams he is given that further separate him from the others, putting the others in a position of having to bow to him. So they refuse to speak to him, to acknowledge his presence in their midst.

Israel sends Joseph out to his older brothers, who are pasturing the flocks at Shechem. Joseph goes in obedience and catches up to them in Dothan. They notice him from a distance—probably from his tunic—and they plot to kill him. They mock him with the name "master dreamer" and throw him into a cistern, intending to tell their father that a wild beast devoured him. Their real anger is about his dreams, which include them, but only as lesser than he is, without power: "We shall then see what comes of his dreams."

Joseph's older brother Reuben tries to save him. He offers the brothers an alternative: Instead of killing him outright, he suggests they just throw him into the cistern and leave him there. (Reuben intends to come back and rescue him.) So they seize Joseph as he approaches and throw him into the well. But Reuben cannot act on his plan, for while they are eating their meal a caravan of Ishmaelites (the descendants of Hagar's child by Abraham) come from Gilead on their way to Egypt. Another brother, Judah, suggests that they sell Joseph into slavery: "Instead of killing him ourselves and concealing his blood, let us sell him—after all, he is our brother, our own flesh."

It is agreed, and they sell Joseph for twenty pieces of silver—the blood price of the next to the youngest brother.

This turn of events sets in motion the long history that will form Joseph and teach him faithfulness. One day the brothers will come in need, all the way to Egypt, to bow before their brother. But the path also leads to forgiveness, reconciliation, and the reuniting of the family in celebration and great joy, especially for Israel, the father of all of the brothers.

In the second reading Jesus tells a parable to the leaders. He sets the scene: a property owner plants a vineyard, puts a hedge around it, digs out a vat, erects a tower, rents it out to tenant farmers and goes away on a journey. Then the time comes for the vintage to be harvested, and the owner promptly dispatches his slaves to obtain his share of the grapes. But the tenants respond by seizing the slaves. They beat one, stone one, and kill another. The owner sends another group of slaves, trying again to get his share of the grapes. But they are treated the same way.

Now the owner decides to send his son, thinking, "They will respect my son." But when they saw the son, they plotted among themselves to kill him. Their flawed logic is that the son was to inherit everything, and if there is no son, they will inherit it instead! They have no concept of justice, of vindication, of judgment rendered on them as murderers unworthy of receiving any property because of their treachery and deceit, let alone the murders they have committed. And so, they seize the son, drag him outside the vineyard, and kill him. The deed is done and the story told. There is an old saying among storytellers that "the story begins when the teller stops talking"—and Jesus must know that, for he questions his listeners: "Now what do you suppose the owner of the vineyard will do to those tenants when he comes?" Jesus is intent on getting the chief priests and elders of the people to deal with the situation and to make a judgment.

Jesus knows, as does everyone in the Jewish community, that the image of the vineyard symbolizes the land of Israel, and that the covenant is the arrangement between the property owner and the tenants. He knows that the covenant demands that God receive a just share of the vintage at each harvest. When God is denied, the servants of God, the prophets, are sent to the leaders and the people to remind them of their promises and the nature of their relationship to God.

This vintage is the quality of relationship among his people: justice for the *anawim*—the poor of the land. How the "least of these" are treated is the criterion for how faithful the nation is in fulfilling the commands given it in the desert. The people of God are never to forget that they were once slaves in Egypt, and they are never to treat others as their oppressors treated them. Instead, they are to be known by their hospitality and care for the least among them, for Yahweh cared for them, who were the least and the most burdened, as a father cares for his firstborn, as a mother cares for the child she has brought forth in labor and pain. The prophets are sent by Yahweh with the word of the Lord in their mouths only when the vintage is not cared for and God is not being honored and worshiped in life as well as ritual.

Jesus' words tell the story, in abbreviated form, of the history of Israel: the long litany of unfaithfulness by the leaders and the people and the long chain of prophets who are rejected, killed, or exiled. The twist at the end is the owner sending his own son to them and the tenants' distorted logic that they will be able to take for themselves what belongs by right to the son and the father if they kill the son. The reasoning is sick, violent. It is full of hate, selfishness, and the violence the human heart is capable of. It reminds us of Joseph's brothers killing him without care for their aging father or awareness of the effect their crime will have on them for the rest of their lives.

Jesus is the son of the property owner, but he is also the brother of the elders and chief priests of the people of Israel. Jesus is in the same position as the master-dreamer, the best-loved of all the children of God. His dreams of the kingdom of peace and justice will lead many to react with murder in their hearts.

The stories are meant for our hearts. That same lack of understanding of how God can love the least among us and the reaction of murderous treachery to the presence of God among us are kept deep inside our own minds and hearts and revealed often in our lack of care of the poorest, our lack of justice, and our shallow and dishonest worship of God.

So how will the father react to his son's death? The elders answer: "He will bring that wicked crowd to a bad end and lease his vineyard out to others who will see to it that he has grapes at vintage time." They make the judgment. They know, as elders of the people, about the human justice of the story as well as the religious imagery that Jesus is employing. He wants them to see themselves in relation to him and his mission, for he is the son sent to them as a last resort. Perhaps they will respect him. But, of course, they do not, and often neither do we. Jesus quotes to them, "The stone which the builders rejected has become the keystone of the structure. It was the Lord who did this and we find it marvelous to behold." Joseph's brothers rejected him and sought to kill him, and God slipped into history redeeming their evil and hate, leading Joseph so that he could one day call his brothers to take responsibility for their actions and to forgive them. Jesus is doing the same for those who intend to kill him.

But Jesus has entered into our history and is intent on only one thing: getting us to take responsibility for our actions, our murderous and hateful actions, and to repent and to be forgiven—or else the "kingdom of God will be taken away from us and given to a nation that will yield a rich harvest." Jesus' listeners realize that he is speaking about them, and they want to arrest him, but they fear the crowds who regard Jesus as a prophet. They are foiled and their anger and hatred grow.

Do we realize that Jesus is speaking about us? And what is our reaction, as individuals and as communities? Are we jealous of the love of God revealed in others besides ourselves and hateful of others struggling to be faithful under harsh conditions? Are we acting often without regard to the consequences of our behavior and without thought of justice and judgment? When dealing with a prophet there are only two choices: repent and atone for past deeds by caring for the least among us, or stubbornly refuse to accept responsibility for our actions and refuse to hear the Word of the Lord in the presence of the poor, who confront us with our unfaithfulness to the covenant of the kingdom of God. Do we hear Jesus' question in our hearts today: "What do you suppose the owner of the vineyard will do to those tenants when he comes?"

Saturday of the Second Week of Lent

Micah 7:14-15, 18-20
Luke 15:1-3, 11-32

This portion of the prophet Micah's words is lyrical, describing Yahweh as a shepherd with a staff, herding the flock of his inheritance, drawing them apart so that they can dwell secure and feed in freedom in the fields of peace. This outward bounty is nothing in comparison to the pardon, clemency, and compassion that God lavishes on us, again and again treading underfoot our guilt and casting away our sins. This is God's usual practice. Although God is angered by our sins and lack of faithfulness, God is more intent on our living in the divine presence. If only we would be faithful once again, as we swore an oath as partakers of the covenant! God's oath to us is old and reliable. Ours is not, but God's patience and endurance can perhaps one day teach us to appreciate the meaning of a word given in trust.

Jesus is the Word spoken again in peace, reconciliation, and hope that we will hear, remember, and turn again to God. This Word tells fabulous stories of the Father and what God is waiting to do for us, if we just offer the chance. Just as of old, when Yahweh shepherded the people and gave marvelous signs to them and removed their guilt from them, God wants again to forgive us, to take us back, to reconcile us to each other.

So Jesus is seated at table with tax collectors and public sinners who are hungry for his words. He is publicly eating with them. This is scandalous behavior to the eyes of the Pharisees and scribes, who murmur: "This man welcomes sinners and eats with them." If only they remembered that God acts like this all the time, seizing upon any opportunity to draw together those willing to feed upon pardon and clemency. These self-righteous religious people sound more like those who murmured in the desert against God rather than those who see and rejoice in the return of the people to the words and the ways of the covenant. So Jesus tells them this story, the third in the trilogy of the lost sheep, the lost coin, and now, the lost son.

The story is so familiar to us that sometimes it's hard to hear. We need to keep in mind that it was told at a meal where some were eating with Jesus and some refused to join them, judging "that man who welcomes sinners and eats with them." Jesus' story will end with a meal, the feast of the fatted calf, with one son eating with his friends and the father out in the field, pleading with the other one to come in and be seated at the table with his brother. But the story starts out with a man who has two sons—two very unloving sons—who must each cause him great heartache.

One son wants his inheritance now. Traditionally the elder son could expect to inherit the bulk of the estate and property. He would decide upon the portions the others would receive. It was his right and his responsibility as elder son and brother to provide for his younger siblings and to assume the role of father in the family. But obviously there is friction between these two brothers already, and the younger son wants what he can get now—and he can get more out of his father than he can out of his brother.

What is unusual and unheard of is the father acquiescing to his younger son's wishes. Perhaps he favored his younger son over his older, as Israel did with Joseph over the rest of his brothers. For whatever reason, the inheritance is transferred and the younger son is off to seek his way in the world—the world outside the Jewish law and community. He has betrayed his father, family, covenant, and nation, and squandered his money on dissolute living. He has lost his portion of the inheritance of Israel as well as his place in his family. He ends up as a servant among the pigs and the slops and garbage. For a Jew this is the depths of misery and horror. He lives among unclean animals as one of them, thinking only to fill his belly with leftovers—but nobody even offers him that.

But then he comes to his senses! He begins to plot a way to go back home, where even the hired hands eat better than he. This is not conversion or remorse or a sense of shame for what he has done. He is not thinking of the humiliation he has caused his father or the anger he caused his brother or the scandal of the community; he is thinking only of his stomach. He already knows his father is an easy touch and probably will take him back in some capacity, so he comes up with a speech. He breaks away from the pigpen and goes home, memorizing the "line" he's going to use on his father so that he can eat, get paid, and live on his father's and brother's property. He's desperate, but he's still as selfish as ever.

The father is remarkable, to say the least. He sees the younger son coming from afar off (this phrase is in the reading about Joseph and his brothers and in the parable of the son and the tenants also). And he's ready for him, running out to greet him (as Joseph's brothers and his own brother won't do). He cuts off the son's apology, however sincere or insincere, wraps his arms around his neck, kisses him in public, and summons the servants to bring a robe (a tunic for the best-loved son) and shoes and a ring (traditionally the signet ring of the family, reserved for the elder brother!). He throws a feast for the whole village, ignoring whatever they might feel about his unfaithful, rude, insensitive son who broke every law of family, tribe, nation, and religion. The father only cares about one thing: he's back! This has nothing to do with the son, or his "coming to his senses," but with the wild, unbounded, and unquestionable love of the father for his child.

Still the plot thickens. The elder brother is out in the fields—what's left of the original estate after a share was given to the younger son, who squandered it. He hears music and dancing, and when he inquires of a servant what's going on, he hears that his father has killed the fatted calf that was saved for glorious occasions because his brother is back in good health. And the elder brother is furious. There is hatred, perhaps even murder in his heart (like the brothers of Joseph and the tenants of the vineyard). He refuses to go in, refuses to share in the feasting, and humiliates his father just as his younger brother did, by his lack of respect and disobedience. Besides, as elder brother he was responsible for his younger sibling. He has done nothing to fulfill his responsibility. He should have gone out after him.

Instead, it seems that the father waited daily, like a watchman keeping vigil (or a prophet) on the edge of the town so that just in case he came back, he could walk with him again (the meaning of the term "reconciliation") back through the village and into the safety of the house. The son has been unfaithful not only to the family but to the religious and national tradition of the people. He could have been pelted with garbage, and would certainly have been mocked and insulted, maybe even stoned as he came back. Now the father has to come out again, leaving the feasting behind, to beg his other son to come in.

The son is vicious in his response to his father, telling him bitterly that he "has slaved for him all his life" and he has nothing to show for it, not even a kid to celebrate with his friends! He reveals the way he feels about his father—master/slave, hateful, and ungrateful. He is more like the tenants in the previous parable than child to father. And he thinks he's the rightful one to inherit! He even refuses to acknowledge his brother. His brother is dead to him, murdered in his own heart if not in fact; he refers only to "that son of yours."

But the father will not stand for that. He will take unfaithfulness to himself and rudeness and disobedience, but he will not tolerate what his children do to each other. Jesus wants this story to turn out like Joseph and his brothers—with responsibility taken by the elder brother, with forgiveness on both sides and reconciliation that can be celebrated in the midst of all the community—with communion all around. There is the gentle reminder of what the elder brother has never accepted: "My son, you are with me always and everything

I have is yours. But we must celebrate and rejoice! This brother of yours was dead, and has come back to life. He was lost, and is found." Remember. Remember.

In doing so, the father puts the relationships—family, community, and nation—back together again. Forgiveness and compassion are based on the pardon, clemency, and compassion of the father, not on anything else, and that pardon, clemency, and compassion have always been there for those who have not been exiled, rejected, murdered, or excluded. The story abruptly ends. Once again, Jesus is waiting for a reply from the listeners: the Pharisees and scribes, the "elder brothers."

In reality, the majority didn't come to the feast of forgiveness that Jesus' presence announced and inaugurated. They remained lost, dead and severed from their younger brothers and sisters, refusing to take responsibility for their own actions or to allow the father to forgive them and change his relationship to them and share in the wondrous joy of communion. And so, as in the other parable, the tunic, the ring, the relationship, and the inheritance are given to the other son, to other children who will bring in a rich harvest for their father.

We must wonder what the younger son did to atone for his actions, to repair the breach in the family, and to honor his father's love. But we can do more than wonder. We can make our response a reality that delights God, our Father. We can go out to our brothers and sisters whom we have wronged before we feast and enjoy the gracious forgiveness that God has given to us, and we can offer to repair the relationships we have destroyed by our selfishness and greed and thoughtless behavior. Or we can go to those who have returned to God and extend to them a hand of support, of openness, realizing that we too have wronged our Father by acting "as though we have spent our whole lives slaving for God" and self-righteously missing the depth of love that our Father has for all his children. We can ask ourselves if we have been living up to our responsibilities as the elder children of the family. What can we do, with Jesus, to seek reconciliation between our brothers and sisters who refuse to sit down at table and eat together, who refuse to respect all the members of the family, who refuse to confess that we are all sadly in need of clemency, pardon, and some restitution to each other?

What we are called to do in our families we are also called to do on a much wider basis, as Jesus did. Muriel Lester points out what we must be about as children of God:

The job of the peacemaker is to stop war, to purify the world, to get it saved from poverty and riches, to heal the sick, to comfort the sad, to wake up those who have not yet found God. To create joy and beauty wherever you go. To find God in everything and everyone.

Today we need to make sure that we are at any party that God is hosting and that we bring with us anyone God would love to see again. What will God's look of love be like when it is turned on us as we bring them home?

THE THIRD WEEK OF LENT

———— ✢ ————

Sunday of the Third Week of Lent

Exodus 17:3-7
Romans 5:1-2, 5-8
John 4:5-42

Today is a day for remembering the absolute necessity for water in our lives. Many of us in first-world countries take for granted the blessing of water. However the majority of the world still lives or dies depending on the presence or absence of water, and the well is the center of many people's lives. It is the central economic, physical, sociological, and religious reality for them—more precious than gold. Water is life itself.

The reading from Exodus begins with awareness of the lack of water: The people "in their thirst for water, grumbled against Moses, saying, 'Why did you ever make us leave Egypt? Was it just to have us die here of thirst with our children and our livestock?' The people grow bitter and test Moses and God, saying: 'Is the Lord in our midst or not?'" Water is essential for survival, both as human beings and as people belonging to God. The rock of Horeb, where God will be standing when Moses strikes it with his staff of power, will let loose a torrent of water, a flowing stream where all the people can drink and know that God is with them. We too need living waters flowing from the Rock to live with grace and truth as people of God.

The psalm refrain is pointed: "If today you hear his voice, harden not your hearts" (Psalm 95:1-2, 6-9). We are reminded not to act like

B Cycle: Ex 20:1-17; 1 Cor 1:22-25; Jn 2:13-25
C Cycle: Ex 3:1-8, 13-15; 1 Cor 10:1-6, 10-12; Lk 13:1-9

our ancestors in faith, who in the face of hardship want to go back to Egypt. They complain like spoiled children even after God has called them forth into freedom, providing them with food in the desert, leading them out of slavery and into the hope of a land with peace and justice. We are not to revert to being stubborn and hard-hearted, turning away from God at the first sign of trouble in our lives.

Paul's letter to the Romans tells us we have been justified by faith, and we are at peace with God through our Lord Jesus Christ. We stand in grace, hope, and glory; we can boast of this place we dwell in together, for God will not leave us disappointed. Even while we were still sinners, Christ died for us! God deals with us not justly but with an extravagant love that we must learn to trust.

The story of Jesus and the Samaritan woman at the well is a theological conversation that details her conversion and her discipleship. While she is in the town proclaiming the good news the disciples return and Jesus confesses what sustains him: the will of God, the waters of his own Spirit leaping up inside him. The waters of the Spirit are poured into our souls too, and we worship God by drawing others to Jesus.

The woman at the well models for all disciples what must happen to us again and again: we must be faced with the truth during an encounter with Jesus and the Spirit, confess our sinfulness, come to a fuller awareness of who Jesus is and so who God truly is. Then we must acknowledge who Jesus is and leave our water jar at the well, now that we have the fountain of life leaping up within us, and return to our homes and confess who we are—sinners and believers in Jesus—and convert our neighbors by telling them the good news of Jesus.

Jesus challenges the disciples and the woman in the same way—opening with a theological statement to make them think. (The woman seems to do much better with Jesus on a theological and wisdom level than the disciples do. They are a bit slow.) With the woman it is water; with the disciples it is food. Jesus' food is his work. Now the woman sets about the same work after meeting Jesus. Jesus wants the disciples to look and see, as the woman has learned to look and see. The fields ripe for the harvest are the work of the Spirit. The disciples are called to reap the firstfruits of the Spirit's labor. The villagers who heard the woman's testimony believe first because of her faith and the conversion of her life first, but then they go deeper into Jesus, hearing his words and seeing the truth of his person, and they themselves continue the process of harvesting what has been sown by the Spirit. This is the story of the church community, making new believers by the power of the Spirit, the witness of believers, and the conversion of all to a deeper immersion in the waters of life, baptism. It is about initiation into the life of the Spirit.

Today's gospel and the gospels for the next two Sundays will follow a pattern: the individual's growing awareness of who Jesus is and what baptism and belief in Jesus will entail. In each story the entire process of Christian life is revealed. In today's gospel we see the Samaritan woman go from a stranger/enemy to belief in Jesus to a proclaimer of the gospel herself.

John's gospel deals with symbols, large issues, and community beliefs. Most of the individuals are meant to portray the believing community. What happens to the Samaritan woman is what has happened to us and is happening to the catechumens in this season of Lent. We are sinners who encounter Jesus, receive the gift of baptism and the waters of the Spirit springing up within us, and as disciples go back to our own places. We leave our old ways of life behind and together listen to the Word of the Lord and then obey the command to go into the fields and reap the harvest the Spirit has sown in the world. Our own small individual conversions and beliefs, our own small portions of the wisdom and understanding of the Spirit, become powerful when shared with others. Jesus is always more than we know or have experienced. He is savior of the world, and still he is more. In community and in conversion we learn to drink deeper of the Spirit.

This reading can be seen as an examination of conscience for individuals within the community of believers. We can see where we stand in the process of belief, who we think Jesus is, and what we need to do to grow to the next level of understanding and practice of our faith. This next step for all of us is given by the power of the Spirit in the Word, the scriptures, the sacraments, the liturgy, and the community itself. So, as we read the text, we can ask ourselves and our community these questions: With whom have you been at odds? Have you ever thought of Jesus coming to you through your enemy and asking for something basic from you, like a drink of water, or another necessity of life? Have you ever thought that daily encounters with strangers are openings for the Spirit of God to come to you? Who has brought you to recognize the gift of God?

Jesus tells the woman to go and get her husband, and she replies that she has no husband. Jesus tells her she is a sinner, and she accepts that reality.

When a person tells you the truth—that you're a sinner and not what you claim to be or appear to be—what is your reaction? Are you like the woman who acknowledges the truth humbly and so opens the door to change and revelation? Do you see the one who confronts you as a gift of God?

It is not until we admit that we are sinners that we can listen and learn what authentic worship is. The reality of sin gets in the way of worship. We need others and the Spirit to teach us to worship truly. How do we as a community react to our prophets and to the larger church that call us to look at our reluctance to be truthful about our relationships in the world?

Jesus also challenged the disciples. Who has challenged you, corrected you, or changed your idea and practice of authentic worship? When? The quality and extent of our worship changes and matures with the depth and quality of our conversions and confessions.

What constitutes sin for our community? What gods do we worship even as we worship the one true God: materialism, individualism, selfishness, anger, hate, nationalism, self-righteousness, pride, avarice, sloth, contemptuousness, accommodating the world, violence, insensitivity, rote worship?

The woman returns and tells what has happened to her. What kind of word of testimony do you give others so that they come to believe in Jesus? Have you ever told anyone: "He told me everything I ever did—told me I was a sinner and still accepted me, gave me water and entrusted me with his message and work, shared his Father's will with me?"

If there are catechumens in the church today, this is the day they receive the Creed, the key to faith in the community of believers. The prayer that is spoken prior to the recitation of the Creed draws much of this together for all of us:

Lord, we pray to you for these your children, who have now accepted for themselves the loving purpose and the mysteries that you revealed in the life of your Son. As they profess with their lips their belief may they have faith in their hearts and accomplish your will in their lives, We ask this through Christ our Lord, Amen.

This is a day to emphasize the Creed—the speaking aloud the core of our faith and testifying to what we are going to stake our lives on together. These are the words, the wisdom of the Spirit, that we stand on; the Creed is our foundation and source. We are believers that Jesus Christ is the Savior of the world and that we live to draw others to the living water that springs up now in us if we are converted from our sin to the will of God.

There is a story called "Nobiah's Well," a modern African folktale written by Donna W. Guthrie. It is a deceptively simple story of a mother and her children in a village without water. The land has known drought for many years, and the daily task of going to the far-off well to get water and carry it back in a jug on the head is the central work of the entire day for village women. The water is for drinking, cooking, washing, and cleaning, but especially for watering the seeds of the small garden that feeds them. In the story the young son, Nobiah, tends the garden, hoeing and caring for the plants, watching his mother's and the other women's long daily walk and recognizing the preciousness of the water that is their lifeline and survival. This is an adaptation of Guthrie's story:

✢ One day Nobiah's mother is sick and cannot go to the well, so Nobiah is entrusted with the task—a heavy responsibility and an honor. He has become an adult. So he sets off. He walks to the well, appreciating his mother's daily labor, and he waits in line a long time for his turn at the well. Finally he fills his jug and sets off home, thirsty almost immediately. But he does not drink, for they need the water at home: his mother and sisters and the garden patch. It is hot. The sun bakes him, and the sand on his feet burns. He meets creatures along his journey home. First he meets a hedgehog who is very thirsty and pleads for water. Nobiah is kind, and he digs a small hole out with his bare hands and puts a little water in it. The hedgehog drinks it thirstily before it seeps into the sand. The hedgehog goes his way quickly and Nobiah continues his journey, the jug a bit lighter.

Next Nobiah meets a hyena with her cubs. The mother hyena begs for water, and Nobiah thinks of his baby sister. Again he digs a small hole and fills it, and they drink greedily and run off. Nobiah goes on. But again he is met by another creature, a small ant-bear. Used to the cool of the night, he is parched and near death in the noonday sun. This time Nobiah pours the water into his hands, and the ant-bear drinks from the cup of his hands. The small creature is grateful and he speaks: "Thank you, my friend. Your heart is as big and deep as the well that gives this water." Then he lopes off. By this time Nobiah is almost home.

First, he gives his baby sister a drink, then his mother. His mother tells him to take a good drink and then pour the rest of the jug on the garden; it is late in the day and the plants are wilting and in desperate need of water. He takes only a sip, but when he goes to empty the jug there are only a few drops left. His mother is frantic and yells at him—"What have you done?" Meekly Nobiah tells her that he shared his water with the small animals that he met on the way home. She cries in frustration and anger, grabs the jug out of his hands, throws it on the ground, shattering it, and collapses weeping. They have had so little water this day, and the plants are scorched, and she is still sick and unable to go to the well for the water. She scolds him: "How could you have wasted our precious water on those creatures?" Nobiah stands with his head bowed and speaks quietly: "They were as thirsty as all of us are."

It is soon night, and they all go to bed. Nobiah hears his little sister whimpering in her thirst and his mother crying as she tries to sleep and worries about the water and how they are to live tomorrow.

Finally Nobiah falls asleep, but is awakened by a noise, a scratching near his head. It is the hedgehog, calling out: "Nobiah, I am thirsty. Give me something to drink." Nobiah cries softly: "I can't. The jug is broken and there is no water." There is silence for a moment, and then the hedgehog says, "Well, then, dig a well." But Nobiah is so tired that he goes right back to sleep.

The silence doesn't last long before the scratching comes again. This time it is the hyena and her cubs, pleading for another drink. "Go away. I don't have any more water," Nobiah cries, the tears wetting his cheeks. "Well, then, dig a well for us all," says the hyena. But Nobiah is just a little boy and very tired, and he turns over and falls asleep again.

Almost immediate there is more scratching. This time it is the ant-bear, very thirsty, his tongue licking Nobiah's cheeks and tasting the salt tears. Nobiah pushes him away, grumbling that there is no water. He doesn't have any left to give. And the ant-bear too says, "Then dig a well."

This time Nobiah sits up and complains, "How can I dig a well? The sand is deep, the ground is hard, and I have just my hands."

"We'll help," comes the chorus of voices, and they all begin. The ant-bear claws, the hyenas scratch, and the hedgehog burrows. Soon Nobiah is helping. He picks up a shard from the broken pot and digs along with them. He rests often and then carries away the dirt and sand. They dig and dig and dig, but there is only sand and grit.

Nobiah asks: "How deep do we have to go?"

And the ant-bear answers, "As deep as your heart and as wide as your thirst."

But Nobiah is a small boy, and finally he lays down to rest, his head on the ground, and he sleeps long and deep. His friends keep on with the work all night.

The sun is high in the sky when Nobiah wakes up. But the first sound he hears in the morning light is the gurgle of water! He goes to the hole they all had worked on during the night and sees that there is water. Beside the hole is a new jug, with strange markings on it. Nobiah lowers the jar into the deep hole and slowly the jar fills with fresh, clear, cold water. He cries out, waking his little sister and mother, and they come running. Soon they are all screaming in delight and wonder, and all the villagers come running. "Look!" Nobiah's mother cries out, "We have our own well! We do not have ·to go to the far off one now." They rejoice, for now the water is with them. They will be able to quench their thirst and feed their fields.

Nobiah reminds them to share the water with the animals, who are just as thirsty and who gave him the idea for the well and worked so hard to make the gift that they now all share. And so the villagers include the animals and leave water for them. And they take the clay pot and leave it by the well, a symbol to help them remember this truth that Nobiah learned in his giving: When digging a well it must be deep as your heart and as wide as your thirst.

This third Sunday of Lent we come to the well and are reminded of the fountain of water springing up in our midst—the Spirit of God given to us in baptism. We too are asked, How deep is your heart and how wide is your thirst? We gather together around the wellspring and share the source of life: the word and the eucharist. Today we are called to dig into our souls and hearts and let ourselves be seen, sinners and yet disciples, called to salvation and rejoicing. We leave our jugs at the well and return to our places, trusting in the presence of God in our midst. We thirst for the will of God to be done on earth, for the kingdom of peace and justice to come to our towns and villages, and for God to be worshiped in our lives so that the glory of God seeps out into the world, a world that watches to see if we are truly believers in this Jesus, whose heart is deeper and wider than ever we could have hoped.

Monday of the Third Week of Lent

2 Kings 5:1-15
Luke 4:24-30

It is the third week of Lent, the halfway point in our journey. The tension between Jesus and those who stand in opposition to him grows stronger. Jesus himself sets up the confrontations and questions them, and us, on where they stand and to whom they owe allegiance. In this week's readings Jesus is a prophet, delineating good and evil and separating out who is with him and who stands in opposition to the coming of the kingdom into the world. It is a time of choice, of being called to change. We either stand publicly with Jesus, or we do not.

Jesus refers to the story related in 2 Kings. In Syria, there is a man, Naaman, the commander of the king of Aram's army. He is highly respected—and a leper. The Arameans have captured the land of Israel, and a little girl, a child of Israel, becomes a slave in Naaman's household. She tells her master that if he presents himself to the prophet in Samaria, he will be cured of his leprosy. Her faith is unequivocal.

So the king of Aram sends Naaman with a letter to the king of Israel—along with ten silver talents, six thousand gold pieces, and ten festal garments—asking him to cure Naaman of his leprosy.

The king of Israel receives the letter and gifts and tears his garments in despair, thinking that the king of Aram is intent on quarrelling with him. But Elisha, who has followed in Elijah's footsteps and has Elijah's mantle of justice, power of speech, and the power to heal even lepers and raise people from the dead, hears of the king's action and sends word to him, asking why he has acted in despair. He commands him to send Naaman to him so that Naaman and both kings can see that there is a prophet in Israel. This is not just a story about the curing of one individual, but of power and faith in kingdoms among those who rule by God's allowance, whether they know this or not.

Naaman obeys and goes to Elisha's house. There he is told to go and wash seven times in the Jordan River and he will be healed. Naaman is angry. He expected Elisha to cure by some personal gesture. He reasons that the rivers of Damascus are just as effective as the rivers of Israel. And in anger he leaves.

Luckily his servants go after him. They call him father and reason with him, telling him that if the prophet had told him to do something extraordinary he would not have hesitated but would have obeyed. They tell their master that he should obey Elisha the prophet. This reveals a remarkable relationship between servants and master, because Naaman obeys after listening to his servants, and in obeying his flesh becomes again like the flesh of a little child.

Naaman returns with all his servants to the prophet and stands before him and professes his faith directly: "Now I know that there is no God in all the earth, except in Israel." This confession of faith is from an outsider, a Syrian, not one of the chosen people of Israel. It is a story of healing, of obedience to the one who has the word of God in his mouth. It foreshadows what Jesus is trying to do among his own people.

At the very beginning of his gospel Luke presents Jesus as prophet, filled with the Spirit, speaking in the synagogue, and proclaiming that he is the anointed one, come to bring the presence of God to the blind, the lame, the leper, the prisoner, and the lost. He announces to his own people in Nazareth that if they hear the word of God in his mouth and believe it, it will come true in their flesh and in their town.

Then he continues with today's scripture passage. He bluntly reminds them that no prophet in the history of Israel has gained acceptance in his native place. He catalogs the stories: the story of the widow of Zarephath near Sidon, who cared for the prophet Elijah; the story of Naaman, the Syrian leper cured by Elisha the prophet.

Jesus is telling them he is a prophet in the tradition of Elijah and Elisha and that he does not expect them to believe. He does not intend to do what they want—prove to them who he is by their criteria. He is a prophet, and the validity of his message will be shown elsewhere because of their lack of faith and their hard-heartedness. They are indeed children of their ancestors, stubborn and slow to acknowledge the prophets and the message of the prophets to repent and to turn from their sin.

The reaction is the same as Israel afforded Elijah and Elisha: anger and indignation. They rise up, expel him from Nazareth, and lead him to the brow of the hill, intending to hurl him over the edge and kill him. The stage is set. Israel still refuses to listen to the word of God in the mouth of the prophet who challenges them to change and to hear the will of God.

This is the backdrop for the journey to Jerusalem in Luke's gospel. Either we hear the word of God and follow it, realizing that we are part of a faithless generation in need of the prophet's word, or we turn on the prophet and condemn him for accusing us of infidelity and evil behavior. So, today we are accosted by Jesus. As prophet he will work no miracles for our benefit. He will prove nothing to us, and he will not be reduced to currying our favor. He is the prophet of God intent on showing us who we are as sinners who have broken faith with God's covenant. We are called to believe and to acknowledge that God heals our enemies because they are often more open to the Word of God than we are.

We are the children of God, followers of Jesus—or are we? We have been called in baptism to constant conversion, to practice virtue, and to make reparation for our sin and our part in the world's disbelief. The prophet Jesus stands before us and reminds us of our lack of faith, our desire for signs and miracles, our stubbornness in expecting God to act on our behalf, and our refusal to do penance and take responsibility for our part in the evil of the world.

Lanza del Vasto, called Shantidas by his followers, was a disciple of Gandhi and founder of the community of the Ark. He wrote often, as mentioned above, of this need for prophets—for confrontation and conversion for all believers. "Learn that virile charity that has severe words for those who flatter, serene words for those who fight you, warm words for the weary, strong for the suffering, clear for the blind, crushing for the proud, and a bucketful of water and a stick for those who sleep" (*Principles and Precepts of a Return to the Obvi-*

ous). Each of us needs to be "told off," to be forced to see ourselves in a larger context of history and faith. In doing so we are brought up short, convicted. We will either bend and seek forgiveness or stand adamantly in our sin and fight the bearer of the gospel rather than submit to the word of God preached to us. Just because we are the children of the promise does not mean we are faithful children or a light to the nations or hope for our neighbors. Perhaps God is doing marvelous things elsewhere—trying to get us to admit our own faults.

We must be brought up short in our lives, or Jesus will go straight through our midst and walk away from us, as he did from his murderous neighbors in Nazareth. We must be confronted with our weakness, our lack of faith, our sinfulness, or we cannot walk the way with Jesus.

Penny Lernoux, a reporter and writer on the church in Latin and North America, was diagnosed with cancer in her forties, right in the midst of projects and books and a life dedicated to the poor and the telling of the truth. She wrote a letter to friends and colleagues just weeks before her death. In part she said,

> I feel that I'm walking down a new path. It's not physical fear or fear of death, because the courageous poor in Latin America have taught me a theology of life that, through solidarity and our common struggle, transcends death. Rather, it is a sense of helplessness—that I who always wanted to be the champion of the poor am just as helpless—that I, too, must hold out my begging bowl; that I must learn—am learning—the ultimate powerlessness of Christ. It is a cleansing experience. So many things seem less important, or not at all, especially the ambitions.

This week we are called to reassess our priorities, goals, expectations, and lifestyle. Hearing the prophet Jesus, we are to leave our comfortable and controllable space and walk with Jesus to strange places and to find intimacy among strangers in order to meet God, the real God, not our version of who we want God to be. Look! Recall! Remember! Do we heed the prophets? Are we prophets, travelling with Jesus, the prophet of God? Or do we stand against the Word in our midst?

Tuesday of the Third Week of Lent

Daniel 3:25, 34-43
Matthew 18:21-35

This portion of the book of Daniel is a prayer by Azariah (later named Abnego), one of the three young men thrown into a fiery furnace because they were faithful to the commands of God even while they were in exile. This prayer cries out from the heart of the fire, and it is remarkable in its honesty, humility, attentiveness to the honor of God, and awareness of the sinfulness of the whole community. Azariah does not pray for himself but on behalf of the people, with the people, as one of them. He begins with a plea for deliverance from death for the sake of God's name and covenant. It is God's will that comes first, even in the midst of suffering and death. And he prays in memory of those who have been faithful: Abraham, Isaac, Israel, all beloved servants and holy ones to whom promises were given, and to their descendants, who now stand in such dire circumstances.

Azariah lists in sorrow the degree to which they have been reduced—beyond any other nation because of their sins. He links history in the world with a larger vision of good and evil, sin and justice. It is the nation's sins, individually and as a whole, that have brought them to such a pass, without prince, prophet, or place to offer firstfruits. He prays as a prophet and servant of Yahweh, crying out, "Do not let us be put to shame, but deal with us in your kindness and great mercy. Deliver us by your wonders, and bring glory to your name, O Lord."

This is the prayer of those open to the word of God in the prophet's mouth, even amid trials and severe hardship. This is the way the people of Nazareth should have responded. This is the way we are called to respond, acknowledging that we are far from obedient, far from faithful, far from holy. To pray in this fashion would drastically alter our liturgies, personal devotions, and practice as Christians in the world. We would stun the world and call all who witnessed our faith to reassess their own positions in relation to power in the world and the power of God.

Abraham Joshua Heschel, a rabbi and prophet who died in the late 1960s, writes: "Prayer is meaningless unless it is subversive, unless it seeks to overthrow and to ruin the pyramids of callousness, hatred, opportunism, falsehoods. The liturgical movement must become a revolutionary movement seeking to overthrow the forces that continue to destroy the promise, the hope, the vision." The prayer of Azariah meets Heschel's criteria. It is prayer that belongs to people who know they have sinned and know also that God is more merciful and more powerful than evil. This prayer is about finding meaning and strength in the community, even when the community breaks faith with the covenant and goes its own ways. This prayer of Azariah teaches us to pray beyond our individual needs. In *Quest for God* Heschel writes:

> The ability to express what is hidden in the heart is a rare gift, and cannot be counted upon by all.
>
> What, as a rule, makes it possible for us to pray is our ability to affiliate our own minds with the pattern of fixed texts, to unlock our hearts to the words and to surrender to their meanings.
>
> The words stand before us as living entities full of spiritual power, of a power that often surpasses the grasp of our minds. The words are often the givers, and we the recipients. They inspire our minds and awaken our hearts.

As we walk with one another to Jerusalem we must learn to pray differently, to grow into the prayer of prophets, of intercession for others, forgetting ourselves and even our sin before the glory of our God.

This sense of how being before God affects our way in the world is continued even more dramatically in the gospel. Peter stands before Jesus and asks "Lord, when my brother wrongs me, how often must I forgive him? Seven times?" Keep in mind that seven is the number of fullness, of completeness in the Jewish system. And Jesus responds: "No! not seven times; I say, seventy times seven times!" God expects us to forgive all the time, no excuses or exceptions. This is unreasonable, impossibly demanding. So Jesus moves on immediately into a story, a parable of why this is his command.

The reign of God, he says, is like a king who decides to settle accounts with his officials. Immediately one of his officials is brought before him. The man owes him a huge amount. He has no way of paying, so he and his wife and children are condemned to slavery, to be sold along with his property in payment of the debt. This was not an uncommon experience at the time of Jesus. It is not an uncommon experience today either. Statistics say that more than 85 percent of the people living on the streets of the United States today were employed and living in houses only months before. The majority of people in the United States are at best two months away from losing everything if they lose their jobs or suffer catastrophic health problems.

The official prostrates himself before his master and pleads for his life and that of his wife and children. He begs, "My lord, be patient with me, and I will pay you back in full." The master is moved to pity (a characteristic in the gospels), and he lets him go. Even more unbelievably, he writes off his entire debt! The man is free, in the clear. He has the chance to be grateful and to live justly—or more, to imitate the king himself in his dealings.

But, sadly, the man does not appreciate what he has been given. Immediately he goes out and bumps into another servant who owes him a mere fraction of what his own debt had been. And instead of practicing generosity, as the king did, he demands immediate payment. He ignores the man's pleas, which echo his own prayers earlier to the king. He puts him in jail until he can pay back the pittance that he owes, humiliating him and breaking his spirit. The servants are thoroughly shaken and angered by the official's behavior. They go together to the king and tell him what has happened, accusing their colleague before their master.

The master moves swiftly, justly. The official is seized, called accurately "a worthless wretch," ungrateful and insensitive, abusive of power, forgetful of his own sin and how he was dealt with by the king. The king is angry, just and rightly so, as prophets are angry at the way we treat others when God has treated us with kindness and forgiveness. The man is handed over to the torturers until he pays back everything. Jesus ends the story and turns to Peter and the other disciples and says: "My heavenly Father will treat you in exactly the same way unless each of you forgives his brother from his heart."

The story is loaded like a shotgun and aimed straight at us. We are the official found out in our dishonesty and lack of attention to the king's work. We squander what is not ours on our way of life. And, of course, whenever we find ourselves in a predicament we plead for mercy and forgiveness, and God always does forgive us. But we are expected to learn from our experience with God; as we have been forgiven we are to forgive—wholeheartedly, repeatedly, especially when what is owed to us by others is a mere pittance in comparison to what we owe God. And if we don't offer that forgiveness in equal measure, then we will know the justice of God.

This parable reveals the mystery of our Father, who is both incredibly merciful and at the same time just. What tips the scales is our behavior toward one another. We call down God's justice upon ourselves by our stubborn refusal to share God's goodness with others. We are either humble or proud, forgiving or arrogant. There is no middle ground.

Perhaps the most telling part of the story is that our individual behavior either badly shakes up our community or gives it cause to rejoice. We are all forgiven, given back a life in baptism by the mercy and pity of God, and we must hold one another accountable for that gift of forgiveness and salvation. We come before God asking forgiveness whenever we pray Jesus' prayer, the Our Father, and we are thus put in the position of the official who has his entire debt written off. We pray, "Forgive us our debt as we forgive those who are in debt to us."

Eugene LaVerdiere teaches that there are two words in this prayer for debt. The first is a debt that is unpayable, absolutely beyond anything that can be righted. That is the debt that God forgives us in our sinfulness. The second is a debt that is easily repaid, and that is the debts we owe to one another. We all need to follow God's initiative of forgiveness and to obey God's commands with our whole hearts, as Azariah prayed. This is Jesus' way, and no other suits his followers. If the king's audit were begun today, where would we stand with our accounts?

Perhaps before our accounting we need to heed the words of St. Leo the Great:

Anytime is the right time for works of charity, but these days of Lent provide special encouragement. Those who want to be present at the Lord's Passover in holiness of mind and body should seek above all to win this grace, for charity contains all other virtues and covers a multitude of sins. Let us now extend to the poor and those afflicted in different ways a more open-handed generosity, so that God may be thanked with merry voices and the relief of the needy supported by our fasting.

This fasting that St. Leo refers to is not just from food, which becomes bread for the hungry, but it is fasting from grudges, refusals to forgive, and hearts without pity for those who have wronged us or who are in debt to us. What would this Lent be if we, in gratitude for God's forgiveness of us, forgave those who were in debt to us? Would we learn generosity toward those held in bondage by the world's harsh demands and our own insensitivity? What will transpire by Easter day in our hearts and communities?

Wednesday of the Third Week of Lent

Deuteronomy 4:1, 5-9
Matthew 5:17-19

Moses stands before the people and admonishes them prior to their entrance into the promised land. They have sojourned in the desert, an entire generation perishing, and now they are facing their new life in the land to which God has led them. They are told to hear and to observe the Law that they might enter in and take possession of the land of promise. It is in this obedience that they give evidence of their wisdom to the other nations.

These laws are life giving. They are life-lines to God and to the history that was founded in the Exodus and in the desert while God dwelled with the people. Now God's people are to dwell among the nations as light and hope, as the presence of God, witnessing to the power of God in their relationships, contracts, decisions, and ways of life.

Moses gives his last will and testament, pleading with the people not to forget who they are and what God has done for them, not to forget their history. One way of making sure they remember, besides obeying the Law carefully, is to teach their children and their children's children, passing it on through word, example, and communal ritual. This is the greatest blessing that they can offer their children from generation to generation—the will of God inscribed on the tablets of stone, and now inscribed on their hearts and in their lives as the people of the covenant. They are to be a living book for the rest of the nations to read and wonder over, catching glimpses of this God who is so close to them and who shares such wisdom and intelligence with them.

Without the law they are without life, hope, direction, and strength; they are isolated from each other and from God. It is crucial that they learn obedience in this land and do not forget the lessons of the desert: faithfulness, obedience, trust, and heeding the voice of God in their leaders. They have turned from their old ways of living, from slavery, and from settling for less than the promises of God. They must practice remembering, practice putting back together again what is torn apart by sin, disobedience, and forgetfulness of their calling—by treating one another as they were treated in Egypt. They are to be different from the other nations. They are God's portion.

In the gospel text Jesus makes clear that he has not come to abolish the Law and the prophets. He has come instead to fulfill them. Jesus stands by the smallest letter of the Law, and it shall not be done away with. Jesus pleads with his own people, as Moses did, to remember: "Whoever breaks the least significant of these commands and teaches others to do so shall be called least in the kingdom of God. Whoever fulfills and teaches these commands shall be great in the kingdom of God." Jesus is more than Moses, more than the liberator of the people from the slavery of Egypt, more than the prophets, more even than the Law. Jesus is the Spirit of freedom, obedience, wholeness, and justice. Jesus is even more intimate than the God of the covenant in the Law given through Moses to the people. Jesus *is* the Law, and any understanding of Jesus assumes the cherishing of and careful adherence to the Law, which leads to God's Word in human flesh.

Adhering to even the smallest letter of the Law cannot be done alone. This kind of obedience, of holiness, assumes that we live in a community bound to Jesus. This community echoes the people of God in the desert learning to be free, to live in trust daily, practicing hope and relying on the providence of God for even food, water, direction, and survival. If we are to know our God, then we must learn together, travel together, pray together, and support one another. We go home together, or we don't go at all. We are all part of one another. We are called to listen, to hear together, so that we can turn to others and provide affirmation, confirmation, and encouragement. Clarity, steadfastness, obedience, and strength come from unity, from community.

We begin by loving the Law, and then together searching out what the smallest jot and letter of the law demands of us individually and together. Laws both protect the basic values and people of a society and instruct those who adhere to their practice in cherishing those most in need of protection. For instance, "Thou shalt not kill" can be interpreted to apply only to our own family, clan, tribe, or nation. But the smallest letter reminds us that not only are we not to kill *anyone*—friend, neighbor, stranger, wrongdoer, or enemy—but we are to protect those most in need from danger, disease, violence, misuse of power, those caught in the webs of hatred, nationalism, racism, and poverty. We are to resist destruction and violence with nonviolence, with meekness and forgiveness and courage, offering creative and imaginative hope to the powerless. Obeying the least letter of the Law reveals that we are intent on honoring God publicly in all human beings, situations, and nations, intent on letting the Spirit of God define what is to be practiced and taught from one generation to the next. Lived thus, the Law deepens our humanity and extends the power of God into all areas of life. Jesus is intent on the worship of God in full spirit and truth, not just here or there.

Jesus is clear: To break even the least part of the Law reduces one's position in the kingdom of God. Greatness in Jesus' kingdom is based on obedience, on probing deeply into the meaning and intent of the Law as the community of God. Jesus is the new Law, the new standard of obedience. We are to learn to interpret the Law with the Spirit and mind of Jesus and to practice it with Jesus' own fervor and reverence.

How do we learn such obedience? First, we learn it in community, over long periods of time, and we learn it from prophets who have the word of the Lord in their mouth today for our instruction. We learn it in the scriptures, preaching, and in the world around us, which is in sore need because of sin and evil. We learn it the hard way in the effects of *not* obeying the Law, in failing to tend to the values and the people the Law seeks to protect from violence and injustice. We learn it in history and in questions that cut to the bone: How could the Holocaust have happened in nations that claimed to believe in God, in Jesus, in the Trinity? How can smaller holocausts continue in Bosnia, in Rwanda, in the starving nations of Africa, in the escalating violence of our city streets and schools and families, in the terrorism of groups at home and abroad, in one nation set against another, in nations that can contemplate using nuclear weapons? Why do we make these choices and allow them to be made in our name? Why do we allow prejudice, hatred, and viciousness to persist on radio, on TV, in politics? Why do we make economic choices that single out certain groups and beggar them in hopes that others—ourselves—will fare better? Why do we let fear and insecurity and lack of trust control our lives and decision-making? Why do we insist on taking care of ourselves and those we love first, making sure that we have the best of everything? Why do we tear at each other constantly, in small ways such as in gossip after church and in larger ways that affect whole segments of our populations? Sin is the root cause of the world's confusion, destructiveness, and injustices, and sin is at the root of our lives too. John writes in one of his letters: "If we claim to be without sin, we deceive ourselves and the truth is not in us" (1 John 1:8). We cannot save ourselves from this reality of sin. We are, however, already saved through Jesus Christ, who is Lord of all (Romans 7).

Daniel Berrigan writes in *The Nightmare of God*:

> The ecology of the world is ruined, consequent upon moral evil. This is the view of Revelation, in consonance with Genesis itself.
>
> No one is saved in isolation, no part of the universe is destroyed apart from any other; evil in the moral order results in the destruction of the universe.
>
> It is simply unimaginable that one stand alone in the universe, without roots, tentacles, moral vibrations outward; and similarly, no one gets reborn alone.
>
> Sin, properly and biblically understood, cannot be regarded or judged solely on a one-to-one basis. One-to-one is all-to-all. The sins of corporations are corporate sins, a revealing tautology.
>
> Moral evil, property-idolatry, threaten the world's well-being. The Bomb is by no means a chancy event. It was brought to pass by us—but prior to that horror, it exploded within us.

Berrigan's words are frightening, sobering beyond the usual platitudes of what sin is and what its effects are in us and in the world, but they are true. Sin is never just personal failings; sin, according to the whole history and prophetic tradition, applies to the people, the whole people. Isaiah says: "I am a man of unclean lips, and I dwell in the midst of a people of unclean lips" (Isaiah 6:5). What is wrong with the world is wrong with us, and we are all in radical need of transformation, metanoia, both as individuals and in our corporate structures, politics, economics, social strata, churches, and families. No one, nothing is excluded from this exhortation to repent and believe the good news.

We begin of course with God, remembering God and God's ordinances, will, and providence. The Israelites were taken care of in the desert even after they sinned against God, worshiping idols and grumbling and testing God. Daily they were given manna and quail and water. Daily trust, hope, prayer, and acceptance of the goodness of God carried them through the desert.

Julian of Norwich said: "Sin is necessary, but all shall be well. All shall be well, and all manner of thing shall be well." Julian lived in hard times too, during the Black Death, and these words must have startled her as much as they startle us today. She also said: "Our courteous Lord does not want his servants to despair even if they fall frequently and grievously. . . . The more a soul sees this is the courtesy and love of our Lord God, the more he hates to sin." We are counseled to confidence, hope, trust, and turning toward God first, together. In doing so, perhaps we will learn pity and mercy. So, we pray. "Prayer is hope's breathing. When we stop praying, we stop hoping" (Dom Pedro Casaldáliga).

Then we act on our prayer, pragmatically, remembering to whom we belong. In *An Interrupted Life* Etty Hillesum, facing deportation in the Holocaust, writes:

I shall try to help you, God, to stop my strength ebbing away, though I cannot vouch for it in advance. But one thing is becoming increasingly clear to me: that you cannot help us, that we must help you to help ourselves. . . .

There are, it is true, some who, even in this late stage, are putting their vacuum cleaners and silver forks and spoons in safekeeping instead of guarding you, dear God, and there are those who want to put their bodies in safekeeping, but who are nothing more now than a shelter for a thousand fears and bitter feelings. And they say, "I shan't let them get me into their clutches." But they forget that no one is in their clutches who is in your arms.

We begin to cherish the smallest letter of the Law in heeding the prophets, in protecting the Law and those who are desperate for its sheltering care, and "in praying as though everything depended on God and working as though everything depended on us" (John of the Cross). Thus, by God's grace we shall be great one day in the kingdom of God.

Thursday of the Third Week of Lent

Jeremiah 7:23-28
Luke 11:14-23

The message this week is repeated over and over again; it seems that we are deaf and unresponsive, like all those who have been our ancestors in faith. So the Lord says yet again: "Listen to my voice; then I will be your God and you shall be my people. Walk in all the ways that I command you, so that you may prosper." The prophet Jeremiah had a hard task: to admonish and announce destruction to people who would not listen. They refused to hear and persecuted Jeremiah relentlessly, seeking to kill him so that they would not have to listen to his accusations any longer.

Jeremiah's God sounds frustrated trying to reason with unreasonable and stiff-necked people who are not only ungrateful but violent toward the prophets and those who seek to be faithful in the midst of evil and sin. "They walked in the hardness of their evil hearts and turned their backs, not their faces, to me."

God's response is untiringly to send prophets, God's servants, and each group treats them worse than its fathers before. God tells Jeremiah: "When you speak all these words to them, they will not listen to you either; when you call to them, they will not answer you." God laments: "This is the nation which does not listen to the voice of the Lord, its God, or take correction. Faithfulness has disappeared; the word itself is banished from their speech."

The responsorial psalm is that of every matins: "If today you hear his voice, harden not your hearts." God never lets up. The prophets never stop, though we reduce their voices to background chatter and go on about our business, oblivious to God's call for obedience.

✤ Once there was a man who spent years walking the streets of his town, crying out that the anger of God was close, that it was madness to ignore the word of God and not to repent. He cried out for restitution, peace, and justice, but no one listened to him. They thought that he was insane, a religious fanatic. Children pelted him with mud and stones, and adults taunted him. Eventually they just got used to him.

Finally, some good people came out of church one morning and approached him, saying: "Why do you keep preaching this message of doom, of judgment coming and repentance? No one is listening to you. No one is changing."

The man stopped and looked hard at them. Then he answered: "I long ago stopped preaching to you. I now cry out so that I can hear what I need to do. Otherwise I shall be lost, for there is no voice that speaks for God. I keep at this lest I succumb to the madness of violence, selfishness, and routine."

That, in a nutshell, is the message and the life of the prophets of old. They begin in obedience to the word of God in their mouth, and then they become ones who must speak in order to be saved themselves.

There is a saying among storytellers that we are saved by the stories that we tell. Somehow, in the telling, we come to deeper belief and we become the words. We come true in our actions, and we are held accountable by others for the words we speak. As Christians we are saved by the stories we tell—the stories of God coming after God's people in the prophets, then coming after us in Jesus, and now coming after us in one another. We carry the Spirit in earthen vessels, baptized in spirit and in truth.

The gospel finds Jesus, the prophet, casting out a devil that was mute. When the devil is cast forth, the man can speak. Reactions vary. Some are amazed; others are dubious and accuse Jesus of casting out devils by the power and name of Beelzebub, the prince of devils. Still others ignore what is happening and demand a sign from heaven. We can find ourselves in any of these categories, sometimes in more than one at the same time.

Jesus knew their thoughts and confronted them with his response:

"Every kingdom divided against itself is laid waste. Any house torn by dissension falls. If Satan is divided against himself, how can his kingdom last?—since you say it is by Beelzebub that I cast out devils. If I cast out devils by Beelzebub, by whom do your people cast them out? In such case, let them act as your judges. But if it is by the finger of God that I cast out devils, then the reign of God is upon you." (Luke 11:17-20)

Jesus is not about to play word games. While he is in the world he is intent only on the coming of God's reign to all who are open to its power in their lives. He will loose the tongues of the mute and open the ears of the deaf and the eyes of the blind, both physically and religiously, whenever and wherever he can. He brings life, speech, and relationship to people, freeing them from silence that can condemn and destroy and isolate. He will not let those who do not want to follow him attribute what he does to the power of evil. The evil that they see in him they put there themselves, and so he turns their words back on them.

Jesus' use of power announces to whom Jesus belongs; he serves God alone. If his casting out of devils is by the finger of God—the finger of God that wrote the Law on the tablets first given to Moses—then Jesus possesses the power of the Law and of God within him. The reign of God is present in his person, words, and actions. The people must choose either to believe or to oppose God, life or death.

Jesus goes on to say that when a strong man, fully armed, guards his courtyard, his possessions go undisturbed. But when someone stronger overpowers him, that person carries off the arms on which the first man was relying and divides the spoils. Whoever is not with Jesus is against him. The lines of battle are drawn: Either we see the works of God that Jesus performs and come to believe and follow him, or we refuse to believe and serve the reign of all that stands against the reign of God.

The scene between Jesus and the others grows ugly. Individuals and groups are choosing their ground. The refrain is strong still from the psalm: "If today you hear his voice, harden not your hearts." Today. This word is repeated often in Luke's gospel. It carries a sense of immediacy, of the urgency of repenting now, without delay.

Jesus knows our reluctance to stand up publicly for our beliefs, our distaste for the struggles ahead, our shrinking from being associated with him, who is dangerous to all forms of power that do not serve God and those in need. This mute devil is evil that is not mentioned or spoken about publicly, any form of abuse, and long-buried and unacknowledged sin. The most obvious examples include issues of sexual abuse or physical violence. These are not just personal demons, but also consist of long-term, underlying abuses of law, economics, foreign treaties, treatment of other races and nationalities, and the hatreds that are used to justify slaughter and rape and atrocities that have no excuse but evil.

And there are mute acceptances, silent understandings to let the innocent suffer or let another be punished without cause; there are fingers pointed at another's sin so that no one notices our own, even more deadly in consequence.

Today's readings remind us that God will not be mocked. There is a power stronger than any force on earth, and we stand either in the realm of the kingdom of God or in the kingdom of evil. Dietrich Bonhoeffer spoke of this choice:

> The Church confesses that she has taken in vain the name of Jesus Christ, for she has been ashamed of His name before the world and she has not striven forcefully enough against the misuse of this name for an evil purpose. She has stood by while violence and wrong were committed undercover in this name.

We need to repent, but there is another requirement as well: opposition. We are called to act as Jesus did in casting out the devil that made a human being mute. This stance of casting out devils begins small. As Dorothy Day points out: "The significance of our smallest acts! The significance of the little things we leave undone! The protests we do not make, the stands we do not take, we who are living in the world."

Today, let our thoughts be of courage, of casting out the devils that keep people mute, of acknowledging the power of God in our lives and the lives of others. May we find ourselves standing with Christ and not among those who scatter the flock by their refusal to adhere to goodness. May the finger of God touch our lives and the lives of others through us.

or refusal to truly listen + follow wholeheartedly the path of Jesus.

Friday of the Third Week of Lent

Hosea 14:2-10
Mark 12:28-34

This week we hear from many of the major prophets as they entreat the people of Israel to return to God. Hosea is the prophet of faithfulness, of intimacy with God, of love that is offered again and again to those who prostitute themselves with other gods, serving their own desires and wants. Hosea's message is almost too good to be true—come home, all is forgiven. Return to the first and truest love of your life: God.

Hosea reminds us that all we have to do is acknowledge the goodness and compassion of God and remember that it is God alone who can save us, not any alliance that we make with others politically or economically. If only we turn our faces once more to God, then God will heal us and turn his wrath away from us.

God will be like dew for us, and we shall blossom like the lily. Our strength and root will be like the Lebanon cedar, our splendor in God like the olive tree. We will dwell in shade and the fragrance of cedar, raising grain, and our fame will be like the wine of Lebanon. These images are lush with hope and abundance and full of peace. God *wants* to be all these things for us.

But still, there is reproach for those reluctant to listen, and so God speaks again, reminding us that we only bear fruit because of God. This is wisdom. Straight are the paths of the Lord, in them the just walk, but sinners stumble. This is the image we are left with: those who walk upright and freely and those who stumble.

This reading is a description of God and how God loves the chosen people. Yet they turn away and refuse God's care, seeking elsewhere for their happiness and not finding it. They are brought low and left to be attacked by the very nations they sought to make deals with for protection when they refused to rely solely on God. The love of Israel is half-hearted, erratic, and selfish. Israel has forgotten the covenant and the first commandment that God alone is God and worthy of worship, adoration, and attentive devotion.

This is the substance of the scribe's question to Jesus: Which is the first of all the commandments? Of course every Jew would know the answer for he would recite it every morning as part of his prayer and confession of faith. But Jesus answers him. This is the first:

> "Hear, O Israel! The Lord our God is Lord alone!
> Therefore you shall love the Lord your God
> with all your heart,
> with all your soul,
> with all your mind,
> and with all your strength."

This is the second,

> "You shall love your neighbor as yourself."

There is no other commandment greater than these.

Jesus has proclaimed himself a Jew, a loyal son of the prophets, a believer in the covenant and in the God of Israel. He is faithful to the God of his ancestors and the God of the promises.

The scribe compliments him: "Excellent Teacher! you are right in saying, 'He is the One, there is no other than he.' Yet, 'to love him with all our heart, with all our thought and with all our strength, and to love our neighbors as ourselves' is worth more than any burnt offering or sacrifice." The scribe has moved one step further into the insights and teachings of the prophets: the worship of God is consti-tuted not in the ritual elements of the Temple primarily but in a life of love and obedience to the Law. Now it is Jesus who approves the scribe's insight, confirming his words. And Jesus makes a startling announcement to the scribe: "You are not far from the reign of God." After that, no one had the nerve to ask Jesus any more questions!

The scribe had come to understand that the Law led to a sacrifice of heart, mind, soul, and strength—his very life. How close was he to the Kingdom of God? Or even more to the point, how close are we? Worship of God and love of neighbor are so closely aligned that ritu-als are nothing in comparison to how we love our neighbor and our God. But even that doesn't get us into the reign of God.

In the Kingdom of God it is God who asks how we love one an-other. Whom can we say we love with all our heart, soul, mind, and

strength—God, husband, wife, children, parents, kin, friends, lov-
ers, neighbors, strangers, the poor, enemies, those who have wronged
us, those who oppose us, those who ignore us or test us or compete
with us? Where do we sacrifice our life, desires, time, and thoughts
for others? Can we say that our love is as strong as a burnt offering,
totally consumed and given over to another? And who is our neighbor? That perennial question causes us to stumble often on the path
of the Lord.

Oscar Romero, archbishop of San Salvador, was clear about neighbor and God too: "If only we would see that Christ is that person in
need, the tortured, the imprisoned, the assassinated. In every human
figure thrown on our streets with such lack of dignity, we would discover Christ thrown aside . . . which we would gather up tenderly
and kiss." That is love of God and neighbor!

There is an old story told in the Far East that will remind us of the
first law, and the second as well.

✢   Once upon a time a king traveled through the country. One of
     those he encountered was a wise man with scrolls of the Law. He
     gave them to the king as a gift, for he knew that the king loved
     the Law and wanted to be a just and wise ruler. But when the
     king opened the scrolls he found them empty! Disappointed, he
     went back to the wise man and complained: "There is no writing
     on the scroll. How am I to decide what is just and wise?" The
     man replied: "The writing is invisible, like the Law in your heart.
     If you cannot learn to read it, come back in ten years and I will
     write on them for you."

The story points out that we have to search within ourselves for what
is most human, most like God, that which is born of love and integrity. It echoes the wisdom of a very short parable of Nikos Kazanzakis:

✢   A man searches for God, desperate and longing for the divine
     presence. He cries out upon seeing a tree: "Almond tree, speak
     to me of God." And the almond tree blossomed.

We discover this wisdom that is hidden within us by practice on
others, by attending to our neighbor and to the will and dreams of
God—for justice, peace, and compassion for those forsaken and forgotten by the world. This learning is soul-making, and no one can do

it for us, though the experience of another loving us can set us on the path and accompany us for a while. But it takes a lifetime to learn to live with such passion, such sacrifice, and such holiness that our every word, thought, and deed reveals this one truth: "Hear, O Israel! The Lord our God is Lord alone!" It is only by the grace of the Spirit that we can know this God of Jesus and dwell in the reign of God.

Perhaps the prayers of others can start us more surely down the path. This one is by Teilhard de Chardin.

O Lord, lock me up. And fold me in the deepest depths of thine heart. And holding me there, refine me, purify me, rekindle me, set me ablaze and lift me aloft, until I become utterly what thou wouldst have me be. Through the cleansing death of self, in the name of Jesus, the Christ of God. Amen.

Saturday of the Third Week of Lent

Hosea 6:1-6
Luke 18:9-14

The word of God is plaintive and strong. God is reaching out to the chosen people, beloved Ephraim and Judah, who are far from God, caught in their affliction. God is sure that they will realize that although it was God who struck them, it is God too who will heal their wounds.

If we strive to know the Lord, we can be certain that he will come to us like the rain that waters the earth. But God knows Ephraim and Judah—and us. Our piety is like the dew, which early passes away. We are fickle; our faithfulness is short-lived and shallow. So, again and again, God sends the prophets to us to bring us to our senses and make us see that what God wants, the *only* thing that God wants, is love not sacrifice. Ritual, liturgy, devotions, and prayers are all a mockery of God if they are not preceded and followed by love, obedience, faithfulness, and knowledge of God. We must learn to be steadfast, humble, contrite of spirit, and to imitate God in our dealing with others. Nothing else is required. Nothing else will be accepted.

All of this is prelude to Jesus' parable of the Pharisee and the tax collector, addressed to those who believe in their own self-righteousness while holding everyone else in contempt. We are familiar with the story. Two men go up to the Temple to pray. One stands before God with his head unbowed and prays aloud, certain of an audience with the Holy One: "I give you thanks, O God, that I am not like the rest of men—grasping, crooked, adulterous—or even like this tax collector. I fast twice a week. I pay tithes on all I possess." The tax collector, however, kept his distance, not even daring to raise his eyes. He just beat his breast and prayed, "O God, be merciful to me, a sinner."

How do we pray? Do we tell God who we are and how much good we do, expecting God to be impressed, certainly more open to listening to us and granting us what we ask for? Or do we see our true relation to the Holy One? Whatever we do can never be enough. The awareness of God overshadows us and fills us with the awareness of our sinfulness and lack of love. We do not presume to stare God in the face. We are not sure of a privileged position at all. Even though we are the children of God, we are still sinners and in need of mercy and the Spirit, even to pray, even to approach God.

These are the two extremes presented to us. If they were a scale of one to ten, with the tax collector a ten and the Pharisee a one, where would we position ourselves? Where would others who witness our lives place us on the scale? Where would God in divine truthfulness place us? Not easy questions. And Jesus' summary of the parable is clear: "Believe me, this man went home from the temple justified but the other did not. For everyone who exalts himself shall be humbled while he who humbles himself shall be exalted."

In God's reckoning everything is topsy-turvy. We can never be sure of our goodness, which is no more than a mote of dust in someone's eye or a raindrop in a drought. We have a long way to go in order to belong wholly to God. This God, Hosea and Jesus tell us, will heal us and bind up our wounds. We need only turn humbly to God. If we do not, then God will strike us with the force of his words in the mouth of the prophet or rend us and wound us so that we might turn to God in our affliction. Before we even begin to pray, we need to heed the prophet's word and Jesus' parable. They confront us in our pride and puffed-up sense of ourselves as the center of the universe. Perhaps we will be humbled when we least expect it.

This is a good time to look at what we claim to be. In our baptism we made promises, and we will renew them once again at the Easter Vigil, joined by the new catechumens. The ancient phrases are short and somewhat vague. They are couched in the language of rejection rather than the positive tone that calls forth more and more from us. In the Latin American Sacramentary the promises are more direct and can teach us some humility. The first: Do you promise to live forever in the freedom of the children of God? Free as children, bound to Father, Spirit, and Jesus the Christ and one another? Free for the gospel, for justice, for the poor, for the work of peace and hope? Free in the life and death, the cross and resurrection of Jesus? Free, full of possibility, free from slavery, from sin, from all death that is unnecessary and destructive, free for holiness and grace?

The second promise is more detailed than the original version (Do you promise to reject Satan and all his pomps?). It lists a number of things that we must reject. Do you refuse to be mastered by sin? Do you refuse to be held captive by evil? This question is put to us a number of times: Do you refuse to be mastered by the sins of materialism, nationalism, violence, racism, sexism, selfishness and greed, hatred, militarism and war, capitalism and communism, anything that hinders you from following Jesus, anything that hinders the coming of the kingdom of God into the world? The focus is on evils that we contribute to or allow to pervade society.

And the last promise: Do you refuse to live under any sign of power except the sign of the cross? Do you promise to live with humility, gratitude, nonviolence, generosity, forgiveness, mercy, joy? Do you foster a sense of community, a sense of companionship with Jesus and the Spirit and your brothers and sisters?

This is our belief and our covenant. If we look at the promises we have made, where do we stand? Have we been obedient to these promises and to our church community? Is it perhaps time to swallow our pride and move to the back of the church, the back of the group, and cast our eyes on the floor as we realize that we are just like the prophet describes: our piety is like a morning cloud, as dew in the early hours of day. It lasts about that long and is about that insubstantial. At least when we beg to receive mercy as a sinner, we bind ourselves to all those who share our faith and our gratitude for the mercy of God in the gift of Jesus to the world. We return as part of God's people, hoping for healing for our wounds and the wounds we inflict on others. We hope for resurrection on the third day, grace, and the power of the Spirit to sustain us and make us holy.

It is the eve of the fourth Sunday of Lent, a time for us to take a hard look at where we are and how far we've come and what still lies before us. This day can be a threshold, a boundary that we cross, a turning into the path. We can acknowledge how much we stumble and how much we cause others to get lost by our self-righteousness and feigned goodness.

As we are reminded by Diadocus of Paotica, "Baptism revives God's icon and makes it radiant. But to produce his likeness God awaits our cooperation. Then it is that grace starts to fill in this icon with God's likeness." When we go to pray today will we be radiant? Only others will know but that is the way it is meant to be. Diadocus also reminded his followers: "All human beings are created in God's likeness. But to be in God's likeness can be properly said only of those who have lovingly pledged him their will." Today is a time for pledges, for promises renewed and for the surety of God's strength to fulfill our promises.

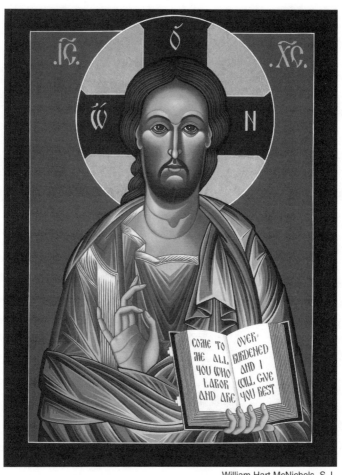

William Hart McNichols, S.J.
St. Andrei Rublev Icons

Christ All Merciful

William Hart McNichols, S.J.
St. Andrei Rublev Icons

The Crucified Lord

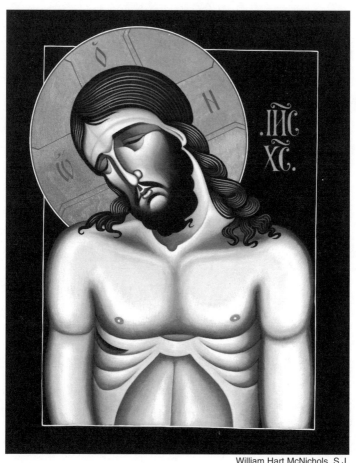

William Hart McNichols, S.J.
St. Andrei Rublev Icons

Jesus Christ Extreme Humility

William Hart McNichols, S.J.
St. Andrei Rublev Icons

The Risen Lord

THE FOURTH WEEK OF LENT

——— ✛ ———

Sunday of the Fourth Week of Lent

1 Samuel 16:1, 6-7, 10-13
Ephesians 5:8-14
John 9:1-41

In the first reading the Lord sends Samuel to find the next king of Israel among the sons of Jesse of Bethlehem. The Lord tells him not to judge from appearances. God does not see as humans do, but rather looks into the heart. This line foreshadows all that is to come, not only the choice of David the shepherd as king, but in Jesus, the crucified and rejected One.

David is brought from the fields and is anointed in the midst of his brothers. From that day on, the Spirit of the Lord rushed upon David. Within the context of God's history there are individuals chosen to serve and obey God and to attend to God's interests in human history. David is one of these people. But he is a faint shadow of the One to come, the One who is the Shepherd of his people, Israel. This image of Jesus as the Good Shepherd is a foundational image of what a believer must come to see in Jesus, the prophet, the disturber of Israel, the teacher, and the One who opens the eyes of the blind to the revelation of God and to the realities of human history.

The responsorial psalm is Psalm 23, with the refrain: "The Lord is my shepherd, there is nothing I shall want." The psalm radiates the

B Cycle: 2 Chr 36:14-17, 19-23; Eph 2:4-10; Jn 3:14-21
C Cycle: Jos 5:9-12; 2 Cor 5:10-21; Lk 15:1-3, 11-32

faithful sense of belonging to God in the midst of evil, sin, and opposition, of being given a place to dwell secure in the house and the
pastures of the Lord—in God's community of Trinity and with the
companionship of disciples in the church. It is the prayer of hope
given individually to each of the catechumens, who will be taught
the gospel story of the man born blind, and to all of us, who together
belong only to God from the moment of our baptism.

The section of Paul's letter to the Ephesians reminds the community of our roots. We once were darkness, but now we are light in the
Lord, and we are to produce every kind of goodness born of that
light: justice and truth, correct judgment, and the courage to condemn the deeds of darkness.

The last line

> "Awake, O sleeper,
> arise from the dead,
> and Christ will give you light"

is addressed to us all. Once we slept unaware of God's presence in the
world, oblivious of the power of the Spirit in the Word-made-Flesh,
but in our baptism we were awakened to resurrection life. Now we
stand attentive and alert, summoned to bring to light what is good
and expose what is evil by the light that is Christ. By our baptism
"we live now no longer for ourselves alone, but we live hidden with
Christ in God," and the work of Christ on earth is entrusted to us.
On this fourth Sunday of Lent we will be put in the position of choosing, like the blind man given sight, whether we walk in darkness and
contribute to the sin of the world or stand with Christ and against
the powers that seek to destroy life.

This long story is not just about the man born blind, who comes to
a deeper awareness of who healed him, who Jesus really is, and what
association with Jesus will entail. It is also the story of every believer
who responds to God's choosing, the outline of each of our lives as
ones who have been forgiven, healed, and given the light of Christ
in baptism. And it is also the story of the disciples' blindness, our
continuing unawareness of the depth of our call in baptism and our
slow, slow growth in the Spirit, in coming to understand who Jesus is
and what it means to be his follower. Finally, it is also the story of
those who choose to reject, to persecute, to destroy Jesus and all who
belong to God in Christ.

This healing story is about seeing and blindness, about good and evil, and about the choices we all make—connected to our baptism and inclusion into the community that lives by the Light. We are called to reveal justice and truth to the world, and we are called also to live with the consequences of making the reality of good and evil known: suffering; rejection by our families, friends, neighbors, leaders, and the world; persecution that is personally directed at us because of our association with Jesus and our proclaimed public belief; and finally death. The week of the cross looms closer with each day of Lent.

Perhaps we should begin with a story. I do not remember where I first heard it, but it troubled me at first, so much that I couldn't tell it. Then it intrigued me, and now it has become a story that I tell again and again, learning from it each time and learning still more from the reactions it engenders in those who listen and hear, who seek to see the story in their minds and hearts. It is a Japanese story about a man born blind.

✛   Once upon a time there was a man who was born blind. He had never known anything else, and so it was part of his nature, incorporated into everything he learned: talking, walking, relations with others, and acquiring the knowledge and skills necessary for life. His blindness did not really bother him, and he made a point of not letting it stop him from doing anything that he wanted to do.

And as he grew older, he grew surer of himself. His house was arranged so that he knew where each piece of furniture and utensil was placed and he got around easily. With time, he knew each street in his village and the paths and places within walking distance: the market, side streets, the temple, and the roads out of town into the forest and fields. He had even mastered traveling to the surrounding villages, knowing the paths over the mountain and back to his own home. His senses were more acute than most, and he felt his way along, using what he smelled, heard, touched, and just sensed as he moved. Being blind didn't bother him as much as it seemed to annoy others or make others uncomfortable.

One day he traveled over the mountain to visit friends on the outskirts of another village. He had been there before; the way was easy and uneventful. The gathering with his friends and others that he met for the first time was one of the best he could remember in a long while. They feasted and talked, sang and told stories, drank and enjoyed each other's company immensely. And slowly, in twos and threes or alone, each headed for home. He was the last to leave. As he lingered at the door of his friend's house to say his thanks and goodbyes and good wishes, his host urged him to take a lantern on his way home since it had grown very dark and there was no moon out. The blind man laughed at his long-time friend. Had he forgotten that the darkness didn't concern him? He would find his way home just fine. There was an awkward silence, and then his host spoke again: "My friend, it wasn't you I was concerned about. The lantern is so that others who do not see well in the dark and are not used to being blind might know you on the path and not stumble into you or be startled or frightened."

The blind man had never thought of anyone else needing his light before and so, humbly, he took the lantern from his friend and headed over the mountain. He cleared the top of the rise and headed down, feeling his way along as he did and savoring the memories of the day and all that they had talked about and shared together, rejoicing in such good company.

And then, all of a sudden someone slammed head on into him, throwing him off the path and sending his lantern flying off away from his grasp. As he groped his way to the path, getting back on his feet again, he spoke into the darkness at the other person. "What is wrong with you? Are you blind? Did you not see my light?"

There was an awkward silence for a moment, and the voice came back: "Forgive me, friend. I saw no lantern. Your light must have gone out."

And so each went his way, the light left lost by the path. It is said that both went home blind.

The story is a parable, like many that Jesus told. Also, like many in the Zen koan tradition, it leaves us bewildered, wondering, and left with fragments of something that intrigues us and disturbs us. It unsettles us as much as being thrown off the path. Many aspects disturb us: the thought that the blind man is used to the darkness and not bothered by his lack or his loss; that he never thought that his ease in the darkness might be a danger to others; or, worse still, that his light had gone out and he was totally unaware of it. The gift given by another more aware was lost. And there is that final line: "It is said that both went home blind." There are, it seems, levels of blindness. We will let the story set and return to the story of the man born blind in John's gospel, a story that deepens the awareness of who Jesus is that was begun in the story of the woman at the well. There are connections to today's other readings as well. David is God's chosen one, and the Spirit rushed upon him. Jesus is God's chosen one, and the Spirit of God has rushed upon him in fullness. We, by baptism, are chosen by God, and the Spirit rushes upon us and opens our eyes to begin to see as God sees. The man born blind is washed, healed, and given sight, and the Spirit rushes upon him.

What follows is a journey that continues to be revealed if we make a commitment to Jesus' person and the will of God. We are already the children of light; we are to see what others do not see in their blindness. But we are also sinners in constant need of God's healing, vision, and conversion to deeper faith and courage. We are presented with a choice. We can be blind in our sin like the Pharisees and scribes, the people who knew the man born blind and who stand around waiting to see what will happen; or we can be healed and given sight, insight, faith, the presence and knowledge of God. If we choose to see, we may be cast out of our old community, as the man born blind is, because he stands up for Jesus and holds fast to the gift of revelation.

John's gospel tells of traditions that do not appear anywhere else, traditions that relate to the sacraments and the liturgical life of the community of believers, especially the process of how one becomes a believer.

In today's reading, Jesus calls for obedience from the man born blind. After obeying, the man can see. Then the man's changes really begin—radical changes in understanding, perception, and lifestyle. They continue until he has lost everything from the past and gained Jesus and the Spirit, hope, salvation and the sight and presence of God forever.

The story begins with a healing and an admonition to change what we think about sin and suffering and blindness—and where evil originates. The disciples and others believed that illness or any kind of suffering was a direct consequence of sin—if not the person's, then his parents' or family's. Jesus, however, boldly pointed out that this suffering was not the result of sin, but the place where God's glory could be revealed, where Jesus' work could be clearly shown. Our weaknesses and pains, sufferings and lacks are the places God desires to heal; they become possibilities that manifest the glory of God's mercy and kindness. Jesus *is* the light of the world, and he cannot bear any darkness that is unnecessary, destructive, or a cause for rejection and isolation. He must and he will bring the light no matter what the cost.

Baptism in the early church was often referred to as illumination, our becoming a light in Christ that will be followed by deeper belief and a commitment to Jesus and the cross, death, and resurrection in our life in community.

All that follows in the gospel, including the death and resurrection of Jesus, is the result of his healing and changing our concept of God, forgiveness, and how to live with and redeem suffering and evil in our midst. Revelation can and does lead to death on the cross. People too often prefer the darkness of ignorance, sin, evil, and injustice. Christians, who are the light of Christ in the world, must be aware of that reality and not ignore the effects of revealing the truth, of siding with the light and doing and being good and holy. The results can be rejection, persecution, loss of place in the world—the way of the cross.

The story of the blind man follows the pattern of other stories. First, his neighbors and the people accustomed to seeing him beg wonder if it is really him. The man assures them, "I'm the one." But they note that he's different. Then he tells his story—that the man called Jesus opened his eyes with mud and sent him to the pool. He obeyed, and now he can see. Simple truth-telling. When asked where Jesus is, he has no idea. He does not know anything except that his old life and person is gone, and he can see!

Second, the people take him to the Pharisees. They question him, and he repeats the story again, making a public confession of belief in what God has done for him in Jesus. The Pharisees respond not with wonder or awe or gratefulness for the man's sight and the power to bring light into the world, but with a theological point about the worthiness of one who can do this sort of thing (as if they ever could!). They use the Law, the sabbath command, to condemn Jesus and call him a sinner. Jesus is now in the same category as the man born blind, in their opinion. Others object, and an argument ensues. The words and actions of Jesus cause dissent and divisions among people! So now they ask the man who he thinks Jesus is. He answers, "A prophet."

His faith is being deepened. He is learning about Jesus even though he still has not seen him, except with his eyes of faith!

This response does not sit well with the Pharisees, or anyone else for that matter. They begin to argue over the man involved. His family acknowledges that he is their son, who was blind from birth, but they will not take responsibility for anything else, or for him.

Meanwhile, the man sees more and more. He refuses to accept the Pharisees' assessment of Jesus as a sinner. He tells his story again and gets bolder (the Spirit is starting to work!), "I have told you once, but you would not listen to me. . . . Why do you want to hear it all over again? Do not tell me you want to become his disciple too?" Now the man is sounding like a teacher and a prophet himself, and the group accuses him of being a disciple of Jesus while they themselves are disciples of Moses. The man defends Jesus' relation to God, but he is ridiculed as "steeped in sin since birth." And he presumes to teach them?! They throw him out of the Temple bodily. Life is starting to get tough, and the man still hasn't even seen Jesus! He has just obeyed him in his need and desperate hope and budding faith.

Then Jesus hears of his expulsion and goes to him (like the lost sheep), and asks, "Do you believe in the Son of Man?" This is a major jump in belief! The Son of Man, the innocent one who silently offers his life as sacrifice to God and then judges with justice on behalf of the poor and the innocent. The man does not recognize Jesus, but he asks, "Who is he, sir, that I may believe in him?" Jesus reveals himself, and the man makes an act of belief and bows down to worship him. He has met and seen and been drawn into the light. He dwells secure now in the house of the Lord.

Jesus then announces,

> "I came into this world to divide it,
> to make the sightless see
> and the seeing blind."

The Pharisees react vehemently: What? You're calling us blind, counting us in with that man born blind, an obvious sinner known publicly? And Jesus responds:

> "If you were blind
> there would be no sin in that.

'But we see,' you say,
and your sin remains."

The Pharisees refuse to look at the light, which reveals them in their sin and darkness; they steadfastly and adamantly reject the truth.

Jesus ends on a dark note: The dividing line is drawn. We are either with Jesus or against him. We either live in the light or dwell in the darkness. We are either made holy in the waters and forgiveness of baptism and live in Jesus' presence, or we are stuck in our sin, blind, refusing to worship God and accept the blind man as our brother. The way to the cross is close. The more we live in the light, the more intolerable those who serve and live in the darkness will find us. The story is a realistic assessment of how the world rejects those who stand in opposition to its evil.

We can ask a question or two of our community in light of the story. Are we the man born blind? the half-blind disciples? the man's family? neighbors? onlookers? Pharisees? Where do we stand in relation to the light, to Jesus? Who do we think he is? Is he a healer/forgiver on an individual level? A prophet who reveals good and evil? is the Word of God in our midst? the Messiah of justice and hope who will convert the nation? the Son of Man, judge of the nations, sacrifice and salvation of sinners? the Light of the World, who reveals the glory of God even in suffering, rejection, and death? Are we in great need of obedience, desperate enough to do what Jesus commands and let him touch us with forgiveness, conversion, and the renewal of our baptismal promises? Can we walk with him in the light, on the way of the cross, which will reveal the glory and kindness of God? At first reading the story appears to be about sin, but it is more about God's work in the world and about our rejoicing that the light reveals God's glory and shows evil for what it is.

Are we the children of light?

Who has opened our eyes to reality and to God in the most unlikely way? Where is Jesus for us? What do we have to say about him? Who excludes us because of what Jesus has done for us? Do we exclude anyone from the mercy of God because of our lack of sight/light? We have seen him speaking to us. How do we bring that presence to others? How do we produce justice, goodness, and truth—the deeds of light? Are we blind and in need of healing and forgiveness? Are we stubborn in our blindness, protesting that we see just fine and know who God is and what God is like? The prayer for the catechumens this day is for all of us:

> Father of mercy, you led the blind man to the kingdom of light through the gift of faith in your Son. Free us from false values that surround us and blind us. Set us firmly in your truth as the children of light forever. Amen.

And now, let's look again at our Japanese story. Are we blind, and have we grown so accustomed to our blindness that we never think of the effect our way of life has on others? Are we a danger to others on the way? Has our light gone out without us even being aware of it? Are we ever the host in the story, who is the only one to think of others, to speak the truth, and to give the gift of light to share in the darkness? Has the light been left unattended on the path after our last collision in the darkness? Is it time to go visit our friends again? In what areas of our life is God wanting to shed light? And do we believe that our failures, sufferings, and lacks are the place that God uses to show forth the divine glory and to bring others to the light? Do we walk in the dark valley and yet fear no evil for God is at our side with rod and staff to give us courage (Psalm 23)?

In *The Cost of Discipleship* Dietrich Bonhoeffer writes:

> To endure the cross is . . . the suffering which is the fruit of an exclusive allegiance to Jesus Christ. When it comes, it is not an accident, but a necessity. . . . If our Christianity has ceased to be serious about discipleship, if we have watered down the gospel into emotional uplift which makes no costly demands . . . then we cannot help regarding the cross as an everyday calamity, as one of the trials and tribulations of life. We have forgotten that the cross means rejection and shame as well as suffering. . . . The cross means sharing the suffering of Christ to the last and the fullest. Only a man thus totally committed in discipleship can experience the meaning of the cross. The cross is laid on every Christian. . . . When Christ calls him, he bids him come and die.

The Light of the world intends to make the sightless see and the seeing blind. If we admit our blindness, then Jesus can spit and mix his saliva with dirt and smear it on the eyes of our soul and send us the Spirit to rush upon us and slowly turn us into the way of the Christian. With Jesus we can begin to make the light that shatters the darkness of the world and is hope in the midst of blind hate, violence, exclusion, and rage. We are the companions of the Light; once we were blind, but now we see.

Monday of the Fourth Week of Lent

Isaiah 65:17-21
John 4:43-54

This week we are immersed deeply in the gospel of John, in a series of readings that show Jesus as the Light of the world, doing the work of the Father. We see also the reactions of those cured, those who are witnesses to his power, those who reject him, and those who seek to kill him. The antagonism builds; there is no way to avoid choosing which side we will stake our life upon. We either witness to Jesus, sent by the Father and empowered by the Spirit, or we sink deeper into our blindness and aid those who seek to kill the Light, siding with the powers of the world of evil and injustice. It is not an easy week. Each reading pushes us closer to the moment when the cross cannot be ignored. It is laid upon us if we stand with Jesus.

The reading from Isaiah is full of light, delight, joy, and everlasting life. A surprising way to begin, and yet it is the inside lining of the shadow that Jesus casts as he moves through the world, even as the world seeks to take his life. It is a creation account, a re-creation story of what God will do.

> "Lo, I am about to create
> new heavens and a new earth.
> The things of the past shall not be remembered
> or come to mind.
> Instead, there shall always be rejoicing and happiness
> in what I create."

This, of course, is resurrection and the world redeemed, saturated with the presence of the risen Lord in our midst. What is about to come to pass in the trial, rejection, and crucifixion of Jesus will break open the doors to a world suffused with exultation and life. The qualities of this life are described in terms of longevity:

> No longer shall there be in it [the world of the new
>   Jerusalem]
>   an infant who lives but a few days,
>   or an old man who does not round out his full
>   lifetime;
> He dies a mere youth who reaches but a hundred years,
>   and he who fails of a hundred shall be thought
>   accursed.

The next description of the Jewish hope is more familiar:

> They shall live in the houses they build,
>   and eat the fruit of the vineyards they plant.

It is the image of the prophets, assuring those who are faithful of enduring peace, justice, and the possibility of rejoicing with their children and grandchildren and great-grandchildren. It promises freedom to worship God with gratitude, offering the firstfruits of vine and field with joy as the people who are the delight of God.

Of course, this is also the description of Jesus' community created and fashioned by his life, death, and resurrection and sustained by the presence of his Spirit among us as first gift to believers. We are to be the oasis, the sheltering place for all who long for a respite from weeping, injustice, and suffering that is the result of others' evil. We begin this fourth week of Lent with the vision and promise of life after death, of life after baptism, of resurrection life that we are invited to share in some portion even now, in the midst of suffering and confrontation with the things of the past and the old earth.

Jesus is traveling from Samaria back to Galilee, back to some of the rougher places of his ministry and preaching, where expectations are high, faith is shallow, and resistance is strong. Some people think they know him and where he came from, but they are blind. Still, he is welcomed by those who had been at the feast in Jerusalem and had seen all that he had done on that occasion.

Jesus goes to Cana, the place of his first sign: the changing of water into wine and the laying of the foundations of his new community. This is the background for the second sign.

At Capernaum there is a royal official whose son is ill. When he hears that Jesus is in Cana, he travels to him, begging for Jesus to cure his child, who is near death. Jesus' response is curt and angry: "Unless you people see signs and wonders, you do not believe." Signs and wonders are for unbelievers, the blind, the hard-hearted, and those who refuse to obey without first seeing. But the faith of the official is startling. He insists, "Sir, come down before my child dies." The royal official addresses him as the Samaritan woman just did, and Jesus tells him: "Return home. Your son will live." The description of this royal official's reaction says it all: "The man put his trust in the word Jesus spoke to him, and started for home." This man is a believer. He has heard the word of God and obeyed it. He now is a follower and disciple of Jesus. He goes home seeing, saved, along with his child.

Even before he gets there, his servants come to him with the news that his boy will live. He asks them at what time the boy had shown improvement, and their answer confirms his obedience and his belief. It was at the same hour on the previous day that Jesus spoke the word. And so the official and his whole household believe. They are now members of the community.

The official's baptism and acceptance of Jesus as Lord parallel in some ways the path of the man born blind. He hears the word, and he obeys. He sets out on his journey and finds out on the way the extent of the power of God in Jesus and the power of the Word spoken. And he extends that belief to others.

This man is a royal official, not a Jew, and he has much to lose by being publicly associated with Jesus. But his family and his servants and those who work with him now know that Jesus is his Lord. Their lives are now lives of gratitude for healing and life. They share in the new creation, in the wine of the kingdom present in the world in the person of Jesus and his community. Jesus' community is open to all; Jesus welcomes anyone who needs, asks, and obeys his word.

Signs and wonders are not sure entrances into Jesus' community of believers or into the kingdom of his Father or into the power of the Spirit. What is sure is belief in and adherence to and response to the word of God. We are commanded to obey without seeing, believing that what God has promised is trustworthy and worth staking our daily life's choices on, especially with others who share that same obedience and hope.

Psalm 30 and its refrain echo this experience of the royal official (all of us who are called to trust the word of the Lord): "I will praise you, Lord, for you have rescued me." This is the psalm of one converted, one saved from sin and death, and from those who seek to destroy goodness on the earth. It is a song of praise from one who is faithful, who has known mourning and who knows the One who turns mourning into dancing. It is a prayer of enduring faithfulness, and it is the prayer of all of us who have been called to give thanks to the Lord our God, who has rescued us.

Perhaps today, as we recommit ourselves to trusting in the word that has been proclaimed to us, we can pray with Thomas Merton his prayer for the road.

My Lord God, I have no idea where I am going. I do not see the road ahead of me. I cannot know for certain where it will end. Nor do I really know myself, and the fact that I think that I am following your will does not mean that I am actually doing so. But I believe that the desire to please you does in fact please you. And I hope that I have that desire in all that I am doing. I hope that I will never do anything apart from that desire. And I know that if I do this you will lead me by the right road though I may know nothing about it. Therefore I will trust you always though I may seem to be lost and in the shadow of death. I will not fear, for you are ever with me, and you will never leave me to face my perils alone. (Thoughts in Solitude)

And perhaps we need to listen closely to the word to find our way, alone and with others. Some things take a lifetime to learn. But we need only remember to listen always, especially in times of distractions, for the voice of Jesus, the Word, guiding us. Today that Voice says: "Return home. You and those you love will live." It is time for us to go home and live this new life shared with us in baptism and in forgiveness and in the word of God.

Feast of St. Joseph
March 19

2 Samuel 7:4-5, 12-14, 16
Romans 4:13, 16-18, 22
Matthew 1:16, 18-21, 24

The first reading takes us back to David, the greatest ancestor of Jesus. Joseph and Mary, both of the house of David, are poor, and yet their house is the royal one. They are descended from the kings of Israel, and the promises made to Israel and to the house of David intimately concern them. The prophet Nathan assured David that Yahweh God would raise up an heir for him and the kingdom would be firm. David understood the promises, as most kings would, only in terms of history, of dynasties and power as the world understands it. But God's word is never just what it appears to be. God's word is layered and grows, having a life of its own once it is spoken aloud in the world of time and space. And so, David's house will be built by a simple, poor, hard-working, hard-dreaming carpenter in the village of Nazareth generations later. His kingdom will indeed endure, but it will be altogether different from any other.

Psalm 88 and its refrain—"The son of David will live forever"—is an act of faith on David's part, relying on the word of God given to him as comfort and hope. And so David sings of the favors of God and of God's faithfulness through all generations. God will be David's rock, father, God, and savior; God will be all that and more for the generations that will follow. This promise is a hinge of the covenant. The favor and kindness of God will be reflected in another man, named Joseph, who will protect God as a child and God's mother and be their rock, safety, refuge on earth.

Paul speaks of the justice that comes from faith and the fact that with faith all is grace. He speaks not of David, but of Abraham, the ancient patriarch, father of all those who would yearn for home and believe in the word of the Lord's covenant. He is father in faith for all nations, but father in the sight of God "who restores the dead to life, and calls into being those things which had not been." All fatherhood is seen in light of God, creator, maker, and source of life, the One who calls into being by the word of his mouth.

Abraham hoped against hope and believed and he became father to descendants more numerous than stars in the sky. Abraham's faith is credited to him as justice, the right relationship with God and so with all others and earth. Justice is *hesed*, loving-kindness as practiced by God toward all that has been made and sustained. Justice is righteousness, holiness, wholeness, enduring peace for all, a state of being that is most human, most like the presence of God, as Trinity, community together. Faith and justice are intimate. The connection to Joseph? Joseph, who lives on a word caught in a dream, in a dark time, in a hard place, is called Joseph the just. He is upright, holy, faithful, hoping against all hope that what he stakes his life on is true. Joseph lives faith and hope that is wildly beyond anything Abraham or David or any prophet before him ever imagined.

The gospel tells us that Jacob was Joseph's father and that Joesph is husband to Mary, of whom Jesus, who is called Messiah, was born. Joseph's relationship to Mary and to Jesus is not bound by blood, marriage, or kinship in any of the usual forms, but by dreams, friendship, and love. Joseph risks adopting the child of God; he is the only human father Jesus will know and come to lean on and imitate as a man. He is husband to Mary, who was more intimate with God than with him—or better, her intimacy with Joseph was based on her knowledge and connection to the Spirit of God.

Joseph's story in the scriptures begins with his engagement to Mary. Before they live together she becomes pregnant by the Holy Spirit. In Luke's account Joseph isn't even mentioned, but in Matthew's story Joseph, learning of Mary's situation and knowing that he is not the father, is caught in a predicament. He is an upright man, but he is not willing to expose her to the Law, so he decides to divorce her quietly. In that one line much is left unsaid. His life as planned is over. His dreams of family, love, tenderness, of a place in the community are gone. Whatever his relationship was with Mary, it was strong enough for him not to follow the Law, which would expose and humiliate her, and perhaps cause her death by ritual stoning or at least force her into exile from the community. Joseph instead decides to divorce her privately. She could go to distant cousins or relatives or become a single parent, a prostitute, a slave in another's household. But at least she and the child would have a chance to survive. This is his intention, probably worked out in agony of soul and spirit, broken in heart and despairing of his own future alone.

And what is he given but a dream. An angel appears to him and says: "Joseph, son of David, have no fear about taking Mary as your wife. It is by the Holy Spirit that she has conceived this child. She is to have a son and you are to name him Jesus because he will save his people from their sins." That's it in a nutshell. A command to live without fear and to do this one thing he had decided not to do. He will have the honor of naming the child Jesus, Joshua, Savior of his people. Clues from the past would have resonated with Joseph's belief: a child born of the Spirit; and the name of Joshua, the companion of Moses, who had brought the people into the promised land, the man who brought down the city of Jericho without any fighting. All this in a dream.

We tend to belittle these dreams as escapes from reality, from hard issues to be faced and decided upon. But dreams in faith are another thing altogether. The book of Genesis tells of another dreamer named Joseph. When his brothers see him coming they mockingly announce: "Behold the dreamer cometh." But it is this Joseph who will rise to power in Egypt and one day feed his brothers and family and save his people and be reconciled with those who sought to kill him. This Joseph and his namesake are well paired. Both believe in the dreams of God for the people and sense that God has always used strange means and circuitous routes.

John Sanford in *Dreams: God's Forgotten Language* reminds us that dreams are one of God's usual-unusual ways of communicating with individuals on behalf of the future of creation. A dream in many of the stories of the Hebrew scriptures imparts knowledge that is sure, so reliable that the dreamer will stake his or her entire life on it, even though unable to explain it to someone else.

Obedience is the only response to such an experience of wisdom and insight. Joseph is visited by the angel and offered an alternative of hope that changes his life, identity, role, and very person forever. He becomes husband to Mary, stepfather to the Savior of his people; it is Joseph who names the Word-made-flesh. He will live without fear in this relationship, saving the child and mother so that we can all be saved by the child grown to be a man.

All we know of Joseph is that he is upright and obedient, but does not follow the Law if it harms another. He heeds dreams, knows his tradition and history, and takes a risk—to live for two other lives.

But those two were more than worth the risk. What knowledge and understanding did Joseph have of Mary and Jesus? What was the quality of love, friendship, and prayer in that household? They shared insecurity, poverty, hatred, violence, oppression, and exile, choosing to settle in backwater towns so that the child would be safe. But they also shared the intimacies of daily life—worship, learning, traditions, meals, gifts, and hope in their God. They lived on the words of angels, who only came in the beginning, and together they worked it out from there. This household was firm and secure; it would last forever, has lasted forever. Their ties were remarkably different than most: belief in God, hope against hope, obedience to the word of God, dreams of salvation and forgiveness of sin, and the presence of a child, God-made-flesh, and the Holy Spirit, holding them together.

We often think of Mary as a disciple because she believed the word of the Lord that was entrusted to her. But Joseph, no less than Mary, is a disciple of the child Jesus for the same reason. His belief was demanding, humbling, and made him a servant no less than his wife. Joseph truly dwelled in the house of the Lord all the days of his life! Jesuit Bill McNichols teaches us this simple prayer:

St. Joseph, in the night you teach a hidden way of retreat in silence, or in obedience to dreams. But by day, you lead us in a prayer, which is simply to watch Mother with Child.

In New Mexico and many places in the Southwest there is a flower called "St. Joseph's staff." (You may know the flower as the hollyhock.) They grow tall and are hardy, blooming with wild, bright, strong flowers, sometimes double blossoms in the height of summer heat and dryness. They stand out, commanding attention and offering beauty in stark contrast to the dusty ground and adobe walls. And they return year after year faithfully, spreading out and growing stronger with time's passage.

Joseph—dreamer, obedient servant of the Holy One, husband of Mary, step-father of Jesus, friend of the just. Joseph—Jesus' human father, protector, and model for being a man. We need to look at Jesus more closely, remembering that he learned much from this man, as he did from his mother. The two of them formed him and taught him how to be Jesus of Nazareth, the carpenter; taught him to pray and nurtured him in the faith of his ancestors; sang with him; fed and clothed him; and loved him into his mission and freely set him on his way. They were Jesus' first companions on the way, his first disciples, his first friends. They shared in a relationship unique in all the world.

Joseph, I'm sure, wouldn't mind adopting a few more of the wandering children of God on earth today. Perhaps, he is only waiting to be asked.

Joseph, husband of Mary, make us dreamers, draw us close to your family and protect us from all harm as we learn to grow up into children that Our Father can rejoice in exceedingly. Help us get home. Amen.

Wednesday of the Fourth Week of Lent

Isaiah 49:8-15
John 5:17-30

Isaiah's announcement details what God will do for us. There is no limit, it seems, to the extent that God will go. The time is one of favor, grace, and spirit, a day of salvation. It is a time to restore the land, allot the desolate their heritages, call out prisoners, show those in darkness the way into the light. God will comfort and show mercy to the afflicted, even remembering infant children with the tenderness of a mother. And even if mothers forget their children, God will not forget. It is a time for rejoicing, for even the mountains to break forth in song for the love that God is lavishing on creation.

This description shows God as intimate, concerned, and without any trace of harshness or shifting moods or lack of kindness. This description of God was known to the leaders and teachers of Israel as well as the God of Moses and the Law. The balance was there, but humans often tend to narrow God to something that is usable for their own agendas. But the tradition is rich, and Jesus is heir to the writings of the prophets and the Law, the history, and the psalms, and Jesus reveals God in depth in his preaching.

In the gospel Jesus says: "My Father is at work until now, and I am at work as well." Their response? They want to kill him! First, they seek to kill him because he works on the sabbath—healing, teaching, touching those who are untouchable. And second, he speaks of God as his own Father, thereby making himself God's equal. Precisely! Israel has known God as Father, as Mother, as full of tender regard, pity, compassion, and strength. Jesus has taken that tradition and appropriated it to himself and to all of Israel, reminding them of the passion of God for the people and the reality that God never forgets them. God is mindful of them always. They are "the apple of their Father's eye; they dwell in the shadow of God's wings and the Father carries them like the eagle to heights." God loves them so much. And they do not want a God like that.

Jesus' response to them is an image of apprenticeship, of son following father, of doing only what he sees God doing. These lines are sometimes referred to as the parable of the Apprentice, the only parable in John's gospel. Jesus describes himself as a follower of God, of his Father: like father, like child, and we are to do and be the same. He tells them they haven't seen anything yet. Greater things are to come. The Father raises from the dead, grants life, and so the Son will do the same.

Jesus knows God, and his work is to show forth God to us, to remind us, as all the prophets did, that God is more than any description, more than words, more than our personal experience, more than what we want or demand that God be. Isaiah's description of God's work and immersion in the pain and troubles of the chosen people must be reckoned with. God is not just the God we want, made in our image. In Jesus we learn all that we can know of God in human terms.

Jesus goes on to tell them—and us—about God. He says:

> "The Father himself judges no one,
> but has assigned all judgment to the Son,
> so that all men may honor the Son
> just as they honor the Father.
> He who refuses to honor the Son
> refuses to honor the Father who sent him."

This image does not seem so startling to us because we have grown familiar with it. But perhaps there is a way of making it very sharp.

Some friends sent me a letter, describing a visit to San Salvador on the third anniversary of the signing of the Peace Accords, technically ending a twelve-year war. They wrote of the beginnings of the long process and the hard road the Salvadorian people have trudged in this decade of horror and terror, killings and disappearances:

> The real beginning of this modern journey can be traced to the death of Padre Rutilio Grande and the newly appointed archbishop's reaction to it. A priest of the diocese gives this account: Four or five priests were standing around on the night of the murder. Bishop Romero walked in. Innocently as a child, he asked, "Tell me, please, what must I do to be a good bishop?" One of the priests said, "It's easy. If you spend seven days a week in San Salvador, you'll spend your time listening to and having tea with the comfortable. So change the recipe. Spend six days a week in the countryside among the *campesinos* and only one day here. Then you'll be a good bishop." Archbishop Romero responded: "Then you can make up my schedule." The next day, in his homily for his friend Rutilio Grande, Bishop Romero said, "He or she who touches one of my priests also touches me!"

Jesus is trying to get us to see that God is that close to us, that to touch one of the people of God is to touch God. This is the incarnation. This is the good news, the message of God in Jesus. It is hope, and it is judgment. It alters all of history for believers. Jesus continues: "I solemnly assure you, an hour is coming, has indeed come, when the dead shall hear the voice of God's Son, and those who have heeded it shall live." The presence of Jesus in the world is a judgment, and how the world responds to Jesus calls down that judgment. This has always been the tradition: salvation for the just and damnation for those who destroy or usurp the power of God. What Jesus is adamant about is this: "I cannot do anything of myself. I judge as I hear, and my judgment is honest because I am not seeking my own will but the will of him who sent me."

Jesus' relationship with the Father is one of listening; his judgment is based on God's perceptions. The work of God is described by Isaiah and repeated in the psalm response: "The Lord is kind and merciful" (Psalm 145). This is the basis of judgment. Do we do the work of the Father as Jesus does? Are we slow to anger? Do we act with great kindness? Are we compassionate toward all? Are we faithful and holy in all our works? Do we lift up all who are falling and raise up all who are bowed down? Are we just in all our ways? Are we near to all who call upon God, especially the poor and the needy, and are we truthful in our prayer? This is the basis of Jesus' judgment of us. This is the work that the Father has entrusted to him, his Son, incarnate Word, human with us.

We will be judged by Jesus on our actions. But we are told in the reading from Isaiah that we are to begin by singing, by rejoicing in God. It is a good place to begin. In Elie Wiesel's *The Oath*, the Rebbe says: "Through song, you climb to the highest palace. From that palace you can influence the universe and its prisons. Song is Jacob's ladder forgotten on earth by the angels. Sing and you shall defeat death; sing and you shall disarm the foe." Let us sing, sing the litany of all those who have done the work of God and gone before us in faith, imitating Jesus, who imitated his Father.

Thursday of the Fourth Week of Lent

Exodus 32:7-14
John 5:31-47

It is the old tale of forgetting, of turning aside and getting lost. Moses goes up the mountain to see God and receive the tablets of the Law. While he is gone, the people grow restless. Factions arise, and some turn to the worship of old idols and encourage the people to go back to their old ways, ignoring their history and their experience of all that God has done for them in bringing them out of slavery. As Moses is coming down from the mountain, God informs him of the people's unfaithfulness and their making of the golden calf. God calls them "a stiff-necked people." And God adds: "Let me alone, then, that my wrath may blaze up against them to consume them. Then I will make of you a great nation."

But Moses pleads with God in behalf of the people, reminding God that they are God's people, for whom God has already done so much. If they are destroyed now, the Egyptians will mock God and say: "With evil intent he brought them out, that he might kill them in the mountains and exterminate them from the face of the earth."

Moses continues, "Let your blazing wrath die down; relent in punishing your people. Remember your servants Abraham, Isaac and Israel, and how you swore to them by your own self, saying 'I will make your descendants as numerous as the stars in the sky'; and that you would give them a land as their perpetual heritage."

Just as Abraham pleaded in behalf of the cities of Sodom and Gomorrah, Moses too pleads for this "stiff-necked" people. He debates with God, using God's own past, promises, and goodness to save the people, who justly deserve judgment, if not destruction. Moses makes God remember! "So the Lord relented in the punishment he had threatened to inflict on his people." God is our model for how to act in this season of "re-lenting." We are not to do what we intend to do, or even to act as others justly deserve, but instead we must practice relenting.

And, of course, there is the other side. We are the stiff-necked ones, the ones who are forgetful of all the intervention of God in our lives, forgetful of our baptismal promises. At the first sign of God's apparent absence, we succumb to our old ways and revert to worshiping idols. Who are our gods—the ones we have made in lieu of the presence of the Holy One? Expediency, materialism, hedonism, individualism, competition, dishonesty, hatred, violence, and the misuse of power, love, money, and reputation. We turn aside from the way that has been pointed out to us by God, who seeks only to set us free and to make us God's own people.

We have adored other images of God and exchanged our glory for images that feed on violence. We too have forgotten who has saved us and all the wondrous deeds that we have seen and been included in: the passion, death, and resurrection of Jesus! We must remember that now we are called to turn back God's wrath from the earth and those who do evil, pleading with God to "re-member" us all again, to return us to the way it was intended to be. Lent is, after all, the season for remembering, for letting the Spirit put us all back together again.

When I was small my Nana would tie a string around my thumb or finger so that whenever I looked at it, I would remember. Perhaps we could tie a string around a finger today so that each time we look at it we will remember the love that God bears for us and once again turn wholeheartedly into the breach between the evil of the world and God. There we stand, praying for ourselves and others who so often choose other ways than those of freedom, community, and hope for a promised land of justice and peace.

The gospel is a stark and honest confrontation between Jesus and the stiff-necked people of his community. Jesus speaks of who he is, what he does and why, and from where his power is derived. At the same time he accuses them very specifically of being unbelievers, because they do not believe in him or the works that he does in their presence. They *are* stiff-necked, unwilling to come to Jesus and so they have never seen God's form, have never heard God's voice and do not have God's word abiding in their hearts. Jesus' assessment of them is devastating: "I know you and you do not have the love of God in your hearts." He ends with the statement that Moses himself will be their accuser, and if they do not believe and obey Moses' words, then they certainly cannot believe what he says to them.

This Jesus of John's gospel is a prophet, greater than any other. He does not witness in his own name, but in the name of the one who sent him: the Father. Just as the prophets before him spoke in the first person, saying, "It is I, Yahweh, who speaks," Jesus speaks and acts in this same tradition. He even tells them to search the scriptures with an open heart and they will see that the scriptures testify on his behalf as well. But they will not. He stings them: "How can people like you believe, when you accept praise from one another yet do not seek the glory that comes from the One [God]?"

This situation between Jesus and those who reject him recalls the time when Moses climbed to the mountain to see God and receive the commandments. The people in the camp quarrelled among themselves, seeking praise and separating off into factions, siding with or against Moses. Instead of seeking the glory of God, they contended for position in the group. They created and made their own gods, easily manipulated and controlled. They followed Moses when it served their best interests and then turned aside when it didn't. Jesus reminds them of John, who testified to the truth of what he was and what he said: "He was the lamp, set aflame and burning bright, and for a while you exulted willingly in his light," and yet Jesus' testimony is greater than John's—it is the testimony of God the Father!

We are to be like John, the lamp set aflame and burning bright to lead others to the Light of God: Jesus. We are called to testify to the Light. To be a witness does not mean engaging in propaganda or stirring up people, but in being a living mystery. It means to live in such a way that our life would not make sense if God did not exist.

We, like our ancestors in faith and many religious people of Jesus' day, are stiff-necked. We refuse to live out our beliefs, to confess with our actions and relationships that Jesus is the One sent by the Father to save us and lead us to freedom. Perhaps this prayer, found on a Norman crucifix, will remind us of whom we have been called and chosen to serve:

> *I am the great sun, but you do not see me.*
> *I am your husband, but you turn away.*
> *I am the captive, but you do not free me.*
> *I am the captain you will not obey.*
>
> *I am the truth, but you will not believe me.*
> *I am the city, where you will not stay.*
> *I am your wife, your child, but you will leave me.*
> *I am the God to whom you will not pray.*
>
> *I am your counsel, but you will not hear me.*
> *I am the lover whom you would betray.*
> *I am the victor, but you do not cheer me.*
> *I am the holy dove whom you will slay.*
>
> *I am your life, but you will not name me.*
> *Seal up your soul with tears and never blame me.*

Friday of the Fourth Week of Lent

Wisdom 2:1, 12-22
John 7:1-2, 10, 25-30

The portion from Wisdom is hard to read because many of us do not recognize evil: its depth, callousness, and conscious intent. Many of us are naive about sin, evil, and evildoers, wanting to believe that we are all basically good and that people don't decide to do evil, they just make mistakes or get carried along on the tide of emotion or by the crowd. But the book of Wisdom portrays those who do evil, those conscious of and intending to harm others for their own benefit. It reminds us of the traditional description of sin: knowledge of sin, intent to do it, and freely carrying it out. In this reading there is intent to harm, and to harm the "just one."

> The wicked said among themselves, thinking not
>   aright:
> "Let us beset the just one, because he is obnoxious to
>   us;
>   he sets himself against our doings,
> Reproaches us for transgressions of the law
>   and charges us with violations of our training.
> He professes to have knowledge of God
>   and styles himself a child of the Lord.
> To us he is the censure of our thoughts;
>   merely to see him is a hardship for us,
> Because his life is not like other men's,
>   and different are his ways.
> He judges us debased;
>   he holds aloof from our paths as from things impure.
> He calls blest the destiny of the just
>   and boasts that God is his Father.
> Let us see whether his words be true;
>   let us find out what will happen to him."

The reasoning and intent are deadly. Awareness of what is being attempted is as clear as a bell rung on a mountain top in the morning air. They have listed their sins in relation to the just one's goodness, and they are crystal clear about his goodness and how it shows them to be sinners and evil. But instead of taking anything that he says to heart, they find him obnoxious because he, by his very being and presence, sets them apart from him. They have power, raw and brutal, and they plan to destroy another who speaks the truth in flesh as well as words. Their rage is triggered by an even deeper awareness of the just one's relation to God; he has knowledge and intimacy, even boasting that God is his Father and that he is the child of God. This is the real crux of the hatred engendered by those who are good. His words reveal the separation of those who do evil from the presence and knowledge of God.

In their lack of knowledge of God, they presuppose a God who acts as they would act. Let us see, they say, if God will defend him and deliver him from the hand of his foes. They are, of course, describing themselves as the foes of the just one and indeed of God. So they decide to revile him and torture him, that "we may have proof of his gentleness and try his patience." These two characteristics of the just are acknowledged as a lived reality, even toward those who are evil.

They have thought this all out ahead of time. "Let us condemn him to a shameful death; for according to his own words, God will take care of him." This is the way the wicked think, but they err, for wickedness and evil blinds them and they do not know God's wisdom or counsel or power. Nothing is as it appears to be in the eye of God. History, evil, destruction, and sin are all redeemable. God alone is everlasting and above all other powers. Holiness and justice are stronger than any hate, deceit, dishonesty, rage, torture, or destruction, stronger even than death itself. Death—the death of the just, the holy, the innocent, and those who seek only to serve God—is buried in the wisdom of God.

Those who do evil cannot see or understand the larger possibilities. They see only what is immediate and present from their own vantage point, and they calculate without counting on God's hidden counsels, which only those who know God can discern. The believer hangs on in hope and faith for a dearer and truer life than the one that evil fashions.

The description, of course, is of Jesus, the Just One, but it is also an apt rendering of what happens to all prophets, those who speak the truth and those who are holy, single-hearted, and single-minded in their obedience and reverence for God and all human beings. True holiness and goodness provoke evil to show its true colors and to be revealed for what it is: an aberration of all that is human. This is wisdom: to know sin, evil, and injustice for what it is and to know God in holiness, innocence, and justice. In John's gospel this is what the Spirit is given for: to prove the world wrong about sin, evil, and injustice and to prove Jesus right, to testify to the Just One's words and life.

Psalm 34 is one of comfort and of resilient hope. It proclaims loudly: "The Lord is near to broken hearts." God, it proclaims, does take sides. God confronts those who do evil so that any remembrance of them may be removed from the earth. When the just cry out, the Lord hears them and rescues them from all their distress. True, "many are the troubles of the just," but in the midst of such trials and hard times we are saved. We are watched over, down to every detail of our bones, and though we may be crushed in body and spirit we will be redeemed if we take refuge in God. This kind of reliance on God is the only route that the just have in a world where evil is threatened by goodness.

These readings and thoughts are setting us up for the inevitable struggle to the death between Jesus and those who oppose him. The gospel begins with the backdrop of intrigue and the climate of hate and killing that is already in motion. Jesus stays within Galilee and does not travel in Judea because some of the Jews are looking for a chance to kill him. Jesus lives in the shadow of hate, conspiracy, and murder. When his disciples go up to Jerusalem for the festival, he goes later, slipping in silently, "as if in secret and not for all to see." Jesus hides himself from the eyes of those who seek to do evil.

But others see and recognize him, remarking, "Is this not the one they want to kill? Here he is speaking in public and they don't say a word to him! Perhaps even the authorities have decided that this is the Messiah. Still, we know where this man is from. When the Messiah comes, no one is supposed to know his origins." Even those who see him are blind. They think they know his origins, so they also discredit him, using their limited information about the scriptures and God. They are intrigued that he is loose and preaching and that no one touches him. They wonder where the authorities stand, since they do not move on him. Yet they are cagey and wary themselves. They do not come to him, listening or believing. They, like those who actively seek to kill him, keep their distance and do not open their hearts to his words or teaching. They stand listening but not hearing, seeing but not believing, and certainly not taking a stand with him. There is evil in what we do and in what we choose not to do.

Jesus knows them well. He is teaching in the Temple, and he cries out:

"So you know me,
and you know my origins?
The truth is, I have not come of myself.
I was sent by One who has the right to send,
and him you do not know.
I know him because it is from him I come:
he sent me."

Jesus declares publicly that he knows God much as the Just One in the book of Wisdom declares that the destiny of the just is blest. Jesus' proclamation, his reminding them of the book of Wisdom's words, engenders the same reaction: "At this they tried to seize him but no one laid a finger on him because his hour had not yet come."

Jesus is the Just One, and his knowledge of God causes those who do not know God as their Father to turn on him. We are left with some blunt questions: Do we know this God of Jesus, who is Father to the just, who confronts evildoers in the bodies and persons of the just and the innocent, and who is near to those with broken hearts? Do we act with evil intent toward others? Do we wait while others suffer unjustly at the hands of evildoers and not stand up for them? Do we think we know God and so stay blind to the presence of the Just One suffering in our midst today?

Listen to the just ones. Listen to Geo Mangakis in a "Letter to Europeans," published in a 1973 Amnesty International Report on Torture:

> I have experienced the fate of a victim. I have seen the torturer's face at close quarters. It was in a worse condition than my own bleeding, livid face. The torturer's was distorted by a kind of twitching that had nothing human about it. . . . It is not an easy thing to torture people. It requires inner participation. In this situation, I turned out to be the lucky one. I was humiliated. I did not humiliate others. . . . At this moment I am deprived of the joy of seeing the children going to school or playing in the park. Whereas they have to look their own children in the face.

Or consider this 1995 banned radio advertisement, again from Amnesty International:

> Listen. Listen. Can you hear it? It's the sound of the
>   hillsides and fields of Rwanda where in their
>   hundreds of thousands the dead lie silent.
> Listen. It's the sound of fear in neighboring Burundi
>   where people are praying that the killing
>   machetes will not come their way.
> Listen. It's the stored up, concentrated silence of
>   prisoners locked away for years for a thing they
>   once thought, or believed, or were.
> Listen. It's the only message there will ever be from
>   the disappeared, snatched by death squads, never
>   to be seen or heard from by their families again.
> Listen. It's the silence of the small room after the
>   torturers have left.

Listen. It's the silence in the councils of great
nations when these difficult subjects are left
unmentioned.
Listen. It's the silence of ordinary, decent people
who think these things have nothing to do with
them, and that they can do nothing to help.
Listen. Deep inside yourself. What do you hear?
Break the silence.

*Listen. The Lord redeems the lives of his servants; no one incurs
guilt who takes refuge in him.* (Psalm 34)

Saturday of the Fourth Week of Lent

*Jeremiah 11:18-20
John 7: 40-53*

As this week draws to a close, we move closer to choosing whether
we are with Jesus or against him. Where do we stand?

Jeremiah is sometimes called the reluctant prophet. He often
sounds like a broken record as he complains of his fate. Harassed by
the king, the princes, the people he preaches to, he himself harasses
God—whining, cajoling, complaining, and getting caught up again
and again in the word that he is driven to profess and prophesy to
those who are adamant in their refusal to hear or to repent. So
Jeremiah knows his own people from experience, their refusal to hear,
their stubbornness and hard-heartedness. He knows that they seek
to kill him, silence him, make his life one long misery if they cannot
stop him altogether: "I knew their plot because the Lord informed
me; at that time you, O Lord, showed me their doings." His knowledge comes from experience, but also from prayer, from the presence
and nearness of the God he serves. And yet he says: "I, like a trusting
lamb led to slaughter, had not realized that they were hatching plots
against me: 'Let us destroy the tree in its vigor; let us cut him off from
the land of the living, so that his name will be spoken no more.'"
Jeremiah's enemies intend to wipe even his memory from the earth.

This is another kind of death, as cruel as killing, because it seeks to invalidate his very life, belief, and hopes.

For all his experience, Jeremiah did not realize the depth of their rage and hatred. Led by God, he moves into the hands of the slaughterers. This is a terrible image, one that will be borrowed and applied to Jesus: the Lamb of God. A goat when led to slaughter cries and struggles, but a lamb is meek, silent, and goes willingly. It is one thing to describe the slaughter of animals, another when the image is transferred to human beings and the conscious intent is to still forever the voice of one who speaks truth.

Jeremiah's prayer is one of anguish, of helplessness in the face of what lies before him, and yet of hope and belief:

> "But you, O Lord of hosts, O just Judge, searcher of
>   mind and heart,
> Let me witness the vengeance you take on them,
>   for to you I have entrusted my cause!"

It is the cry of the innocent, the prophet, the preacher, the truth-teller, the believer who suffers for witnessing to the Kingdom of God.

God does not intervene to stop evildoers, to keep those who serve the kingdom from being slaughtered. But God is the just Judge and will take vengeance on those who do evil. There is a reckoning beyond what appears in history, and Jeremiah wants to witness that vindication. His is the prayer of victims, of those who do not know justice in this life, of those who are caught in the forces of power and deemed either dispensable or problematic.

Psalm 7 is a prayer of trust. Can we begin to speak it?

> Do me justice, O Lord, because I am just,
>   and because of the innocence that is mine.

Can we pray that?

> Let the malice of the wicked come to an end,
>   but sustain the just,
> O searcher of heart and soul, O just God.

We plead with God to be saved from all our pursuers and to be rescued from those who seek to tear us to pieces for speaking the truth, for defending the poor and those without a voice in a world of politics and economic profit, nationalism and racism, old and new hatreds. Can we pray like this? Whom do we defend? In whose behalf do we speak out? When God, the searcher of minds and hearts, looks deep inside us, what is seen? To whom do we belong?

As Jesus continues to preach and teach, the crowd is "sharply divided over him." Some say, "This must be the Prophet. He is the Messiah." Others discuss theological propositions and fundamental interpretations of the scriptures, trying to determine whether he could be the one. Still others are less benign: they want to apprehend him, though no one moves to lay a hand on him. His presence causes dissension. There are those open to hearing the Word, those intent on stopping their ears and staying with their present way of living, and those who are outright hypocrites, evil and intent only on their own place in society.

Jesus' very presence provokes political and military as well as religious reactions, the Temple guards, the priests and the Pharisees are all involved. The guards are questioned as to why they didn't bring him in. After all, he is stirring up the people, disturbing the peace (a definition of a prophet since the time of Elijah). But the guards are disorganized and stunned: "No man ever spoke like that before." They are confounded, at a loss to know what to do with him. They are, at least, honest in their reaction to his teaching. The Pharisees ridicule the guards, accusing them sarcastically of being duped by Jesus. And the guards defend their hate and resistance to Jesus by claiming that no one of the Sanhedrin believes in him, or the Pharisees—only "this lot, that knows nothing about the Law—and they are lost anyway!" There are only two categories, even among them: those who are lost anyway, and themselves, obviously saved no matter what! They have judged in their own fashion, but not as the Searcher of mind and heart judges: justly.

There is just one who makes an attempt to stand up for Jesus: Nicodemus. He once came to Jesus by night, seeking the Light of the world in the darkness and under cover of secrecy. Now he speaks out: "Since when does our law condemn any man without first hearing him and knowing the facts?" And they turn just as viciously on one of their own who dares to oppose them: "Do not tell us you are a Galilean too." Nicodemus is taunted, insulted as stupid, and told: "Look it up. You will not find the Prophet coming from Galilee." They will use limited understanding and fundamental interpretations to discredit Nicodemus, and they do not honor his carefully nuanced question, which seeks to remind them of the nature of their Law, that is, the necessity for hearing the one who is condemned and seeking to know the facts before any making judgment.

But it is the last sentence of the reading that is the most damning: "Then each went off to his own house." They refuse to give Jesus a hearing. They have decided. And so, no one lays hands on Jesus. It is not time. Jesus will decide that moment and freely allow himself to fall into their hands. He is the one full of the Spirit, of power, and of obedience to God, for he is indeed the Messiah.

Day by day the sides are drawn out and individuals choose where they will stand. Some will run from the conflict, leaving Jesus alone with his accusers. Nicodemus has made his one-time attempt to stand up for Jesus and will be silent now, intimidated by the others. Perhaps he begins, like Jeremiah, to see the extent of the plotting and the rage that Jesus' words and presence already have stirred in those threatened by his truthfulness and call to repentance.

Perhaps the real sin of many of those in today's readings—and in today's world—is limiting God to categories that they find understandable and acceptable. They—and we—name God in our own words, in terms amenable to us, rather than letting God be God. Living in relation with the Unknown takes courage, humility, and reverence; an attitude of openness; and awareness of sinfulness and the need for being transformed and made holy. Are we too set in our ways, sure of who God is? Do we only name God with words that we are comfortable with or that reveal what we want God to be for us? Are we intent on making God in our own images? Let us pray these words of prayer by Karl Rahner, which can perhaps open us to the mysteries of the One who sent Jesus into the world:

> What can I say to You, my God? Shall I collect together all the words that praise your holy name? Shall I give You all the names of the world, You the unnameable? Shall I call You God of my life, meaning of my existence, hallowing of my acts, my journey's end, bitterness of my bitter hours, home of my loneliness, You my most treasured happiness? Shall I say: Creator, Sustainer, Pardoner, Near One, Distant One, Incomprehensible One, God both of flowers and stars, God of the gentle wind and of terrible battles, Wisdom, Power, Loyalty and Truthfulness, Eter-

nity and Infinity, You the All-merciful, You the Just One, You Love itself?

Do we limit God, define Jesus, and cramp the Spirit as our ancestors have done? God is truth, and Jesus is the truth of God in a human being. We can lie to ourselves and to others, but not to the Truth. As Friedrich Hebbel once said, "One lie does not cost you one truth, but *the* truth." Today we either hear the words of Jesus with humility, or we go off to our own house, back to our own small bits and pieces of truth. But the time is fast approaching when we must decide publicly where we stand.

We need, like Nicodemus, to make small forays into the fight, not just once but again and again. We must remember the courage of those who stood up for the truth in the midst of silence, conspiracy, and lies, such as Dietrich Bonhoeffer, who said:

We are not Christ, but if we want to be Christians, we must have some share in Christ's largeheartedness by acting with responsibility and in freedom when the hour of danger comes, and by showing a real sympathy that springs, not from fear, but from the liberating and redeeming love of Christ for all who suffer. Mere waiting and looking on is not Christian behavior. The Christian is called to sympathy and action, not in the first place by his own sufferings, but by the sufferings of his brethren, for whose sake Christ suffered.

THE FIFTH WEEK OF LENT

— ✛ —

Sunday of the Fifth Week of Lent

Ezekiel 37:12-14
Romans 8:8-11
John 11:1-45

How do we know God truly? The short reading of Ezekiel is hearten-
ing and precise: God is the one who opens graves and has us rise from
them, who puts the Spirit within us and settles us upon our own land.
This is the promise of the Lord from the very beginning, and God's promises are true. God is life itself, and life consists in having the Spirit of
God within us. We can know we are in the presence of God when death
is shattered and nothing seals up life and the Spirit: nothing!

Psalm 130 is the prayer of one in need, facing death and desperation, yet it is a prayer of confidence in the mercy of God: "With the
Lord there is mercy, and fullness of redemption." There is no sin, no
iniquity, that cannot be forgiven. Our place is to trust in the Lord
"more than sentinels wait for the dawn." All of us must wait together
for the Word of the Lord to be spoken.

These beginning readings are apt introductions to the demanding
story of the raising of Lazarus from the dead and crucial to fleshing
out the theological background of the resurrection. Romans reminds
us that we live in the Spirit of God, for God dwells in us and we
belong wholly to God. Our bodies are dead to sin and our spirits live

B Cycle: Jer 31:31-34; Heb 5:7-9; Jn 12:20-33
C Cycle: Is 43:16-21; Phil 3:8-14; Jn 8:1-11

because of justice. It is this same Spirit, which raised Jesus from the dead, that dwells within us, and we will know the fullness of that resurrection in our own bodies.

But the resurrection is *already* in our bodies, singing in our spirits, words, and lives. This is so basic, and yet many of us act as though we are barely alive. We must live in that Spirit, and not as though we were already in our tombs. What the Father did for Jesus has been done for us in baptism and is a continuing experience for all of us who live in Christ. Like the psalmist of old, we cry out our hope. Out of the depths of sin, suffering, injustice, death, and violence we cry and trust in God for the fullness of life.

Chapter 11 of John is the midpoint and focus of John's entire gospel. Everything leads up to this chapter, and afterward everything is seen in light of the one singular statement of Jesus, who proclaims who he is and what he is about: "I am the resurrection and the life: whoever believes in me, though he should die, will come to life and whoever is alive and believes in me will never die." This is the heart of our belief. Jesus raises Lazarus from the dead publicly so that his disciples and the city can witness to the power of God, to Jesus' relationship with the Father, and what faith does for those who believe. Even death is redeemable in the person of Jesus. There is nothing that is not subject to the power of God in Jesus—not sin, violence, injustice, disbelief, evil, not death itself. All serve the God of life, resurrection, and the Spirit. What happened to Lazarus happens to us first in baptism, confirmation, and eucharist, and then happens in moments throughout all our lives in Christ, and then is fulfilled when we die and come into the resurrection along with all the world.

The long form of this reading is necessary to set up the events of Holy Week. We will all be brought back from the dead—released from the power of sin, evil and death—and given a new life in the Spirit for all to see, one that will bring others to belief in Jesus.

The story begins strangely. Word comes to Jesus that Lazarus is sick unto death, and yet Jesus deliberately delays going to him and lets him die. Jesus announces that what happens to Lazarus, his beloved friend, is to serve God and give glory to God. The gospel states very clearly that Jesus loved Martha and her sister Mary and Lazarus. They are friends and disciples, part of the inner circle of Jesus' community. Then, after two more days, Jesus goes back to Bethany over the protests of the disciples, who know what's waiting for them in nearby Jerusalem: rejection and people who have already tried to stone him to death. They are timid and fearful and unsure. But Jesus tells them that Lazarus is asleep, and that he is going to awaken him. They misunderstand, and so he plainly tells them that Lazarus is dead. It is Thomas who says, resignedly: "Let us go along with him, to die with him." And this is the heart of what these next two weeks are about: Do we understand what we're saying and doing, or not?

They arrive at Bethany, and they hear that Lazarus has been in the tomb for four days already. The word spreads and Martha runs out to meet Jesus on the road. Many people spread the word that Jesus has returned to console Mary and Martha. Martha encounters Jesus and immediately hits him with the words: "Lord, if you had been here, my brother would never have died. Even now, I am sure that God will give you whatever you ask of him." Her address is part faith, part rebuke, part desperation, and part grief. And Jesus responds: "Your brother will rise again." Martha adds, "Yes, on the last day."

Again, we are hearing a theological conversation in the presence of grief and death, loss and mourning. This is a place of proclamation, of teaching, of leading the catechumens and the church to the place of Lazarus's tomb. No one understands the depth of Jesus' power or that Jesus is God. So Jesus announces who he is: "I am the Resurrection and the Life: whoever believes in me, though he should die, will come to life; and whoever is alive and believes in me will never die." This is the whole reason for our baptism, our promises, our commitment to God as church, as the body of Christ. This is our statement of belief, which we grow into every day of our lives and which forms the pattern of our death to sin, our burial in the waters of baptism, and our being raised to life by the Spirit even now. Jesus asks her: "Do you believe this?" (a question directed to the catechumens and to us repeatedly), and she responds with her statement of who Jesus is: Son of God, Messiah, and all that those titles represent.

Then she turns around and goes back to the house to get Mary, telling her: "The Teacher is here, asking for you." Mary encounters Jesus on the path and begins with the same line as Martha: "Lord, if you had been here my brother would not have died." A large crowd accompanies her. Jesus sees her weeping and all those with her, and he is troubled in spirit and moved by the deepest emotions. This is a description of Jesus in the face of death. He asks where Lazarus is, and they say: "Come and see." (Note that these were Jesus' first words to those who followed him and asked him who he was in the first chapter of John.) The reaction of the crowd is mixed: "See how much he loved him." Others are more cynical: "He opened the eyes of the blind. Why could he not have done something to keep him from dying?" And once again, Jesus is troubled in spirit. This description is an allusion to the power of God moving in Jesus as it moved over the water of the Red Sea and as it moves over the waters of baptism. The Spirit troubles us.

They come to the tomb, a cave with a stone across it. Jesus gives a command: Take away the stone. And Martha reacts: "It has been four days now; surely there will be a stench!" Jesus once again has to reassure her and call her again to belief. It is one thing to profess to believe, another altogether to act upon it and to integrate it into our mind and heart. Words are one thing. Staking our life on it is something else.

Martha is told that if she believes she will see the glory of God. The others obey and take away the stone. Jesus prays aloud so that everyone will know what he is doing and where his power comes from—from God who sent him to bring life and to undo death. Then he calls Lazarus forth. Lazarus hears the voice, the Word of God. And even in death, he obeys. He is bound hand and foot, wrapped for burial, and Jesus commands the disciples, "Untie him and let him go free." Lazarus is freed from sin, evil, death, from anything that holds him captive. And it is the community of believers that frees him, facing him in the direction of a new life.

Many who see what Jesus has done put their faith in him. But we know that Jesus' action must have fanned the flames of others' hatred against him. Bringing someone back from the dead—opening graves and releasing the stench—brings people to belief, conversion, and hope, and also turns people against the life of the Spirit.

Jesus' actions are rooted in his single-hearted faith in his Father and what he is in the world for—sent to bring life out of death, resurrection out of despair, loss, and sin. This is the risk and glory of incarnation, of God becoming human and sharing our mortality and his immortality, even as we live as human beings subject to death here on earth. Resurrection life begins here and grows into fullness at our death!

It seems that the closer our relationship to Jesus, the more he may demand of us—letting us suffer and die so that others might come to belief. Association with Jesus and the gift of life in resurrection and intimacy with the voice and Word of the Lord align us so closely with Jesus that people will react the same way to our presence as they do to Jesus' presence. God, who loves us dearly, will not save us from mortal death but, better, from death due to sin, injustice, and evil.

There are many personal questions that the gospel calls us to reflect upon. When did we send for the Lord and he delayed in coming to our aid? How did we feel? What happened? What was our reaction to God's timing in relationship to our need? What kind of expectation do we put on Jesus, especially in times of grief, great need, sadness and suffering? Perhaps the core question is based on Jesus' declaration to Martha: "I am the resurrection and the life: whoever believes in me, even though he should die, will come to life; and whoever is alive and believes in me will never die." *Do we believe this?* Whose death has tested our belief in the resurrection? When has it been hard for us to believe? Did we trust God at that time? Do we trust God with our life now, no matter what is happening in history and in our small part of the world?

Jon Sobrino wrote a letter to his friend Ignacio Ellacuría, who was murdered in El Salvador while Sobrino was away. Written a year after the massacre, Sobrino tries to put into words what Ellacuría's life had meant for him and what it had come to mean for him now. In part, Sobrino writes:

> Ellacu, this is what you've left us, or at least left me. Your exceptional capacities could dazzle, and your limitations could confuse. I think, Ellacu, that neither the one has bedazzled me nor the other obscured what, to me, is the rock-bottom thing you've left me: that there's nothing more essential than the exercise of mercy in behalf of a crucified people, and nothing more humane and humanizing than faith. These are the things I've had in my head for years now. Today on the first anniversary of your martyrdom, I say them. With pain and with joy— but especially, with gratitude. Thanks, Ellacu. For your mercy, and for your faith.

Ignacio Ellacuría, a Jesuit, was one of my first theology teachers. It was a class on Christology, a very small class of only six people. That one semester, four months, exploded every thought and concept that I had of God. It threw me into confusion and opened places in my heart I had long ago closed. Ever since I have listened and studied in light of his questions, passion, and brilliance, his analytical and religious probing mind. When I heard the news that he had been killed by blowing out his brains, specifically because the murderers found his mind so dangerous, something in me died and I felt anger as I had never known before. Over time, with reflection, prayer, and study, he has continued to teach me, bringing some of that faithfulness and mercy that Jon Sobrino speaks about. It is his death that has most profoundly shaken my faith and caused me to ask myself, Do I believe that Jesus is the Resurrection and the Life? Do I believe that all who believe in Jesus, even though they die, will come to life again, and if they are alive that they will never die? His death has made my response less tentative, more bold. I have become more aware of the power of life and the response it can evoke in others: hatred, rage, and the burning desire to kill hope in the flesh and words of believers.

Jesus wept at the death of Lazarus. When have we seen Jesus weep? What makes God weep? What evokes the strongest emotions in Jesus? Are these the same things that evoke our emotions and reactions? Do we believe that Jesus loves us as much as he did Lazarus, Martha, and Mary? Has he wept over us in our tomb? How long have we been in our tombs—four days? Are we more afraid of the stench of opening tombs and exposing the rot in our lives and the world, than of the possibility of the Word of God calling us and others forth into life and wholeness? Where have we seen the glory of God in the midst of death? Why doesn't Jesus stop people from dying? Why doesn't God stop evil, injustice, and sin in the world?

Sometimes the deaths of those who are closest to us both test our faith and give us heart. Our belief says that Jesus stopped death in his own dying. Now our death and the deaths of those we love and cherish give glory to God in the death of Jesus Christ.

We stand with Jesus in his revulsion for death and yet with him in trust as well, as he prays to his Father for life. Jesus' prayer is ours: "Father, I thank you for having heard me. I know that you always hear me but I have said this for the sake of the crowd, that they may believe that you sent me." We believe and go through these last weeks of Lent into Holy Week saying: "If we have died to ourselves in Christ, then we shall rise to new life in him."

On this day, the catechumens are given the prayer of the Our Father. Jesus prays, and we learn how to pray by practice. In today's readings, Jesus prays by waiting, returning, by always turning everything into the glory of God, by letting others hear his own belief in his Father, by questioning Martha and calling her again to stake her actions on her words of belief, by commanding his disciples to help him in the work of bringing forth Lazarus from the tomb, loosing him and all people from that which binds us to death, violence, unnecessary pain, and evil. It is the voice of the Word of the Lord that brings Lazarus forth from the tomb, into the light. We hear that same Word daily in the scriptures and in one another's faith. We are to pray without ceasing, without losing heart, pray always so that the glory of God is revealed in us, as it was in Jesus Christ.

There is an old Jewish story about prayer that has haunted me since I first discovered it. It is one of the stories of the Baal Shem Tov, the Master of the Good Name.

✢ Once upon a time there was a good and faithful rabbi. The day of Yom Kippur came, and all day the rabbi had fasted, done penance, and prayed for his people, his small congregation. That night, the holiest night of the Jewish year, they were all gathered in the synagogue praying, asking for forgiveness and mercy from God, blessed be his Name. The rabbi stood with his back to the people, wrapped tightly in his prayer shawl, and prayed. He prayed as fervently and intensely as he could. He remembered that every synagogue around the world gathered the Jews together on this day and all their prayers were ascending to God, the Holy One.

As he prayed, he begged God for some sign that his prayer on behalf of his people was heard. As soon as he thought it and prayed it, he was taken aback. Why should the Holy One respond to such a prayer, when there were probably many others, hoping for the same thing? And yet, almost instantaneously, he was given an answer to his prayers. For just a moment he heard the voice of God, clear and ringing out like a bell: "Have Tam offer your prayers to me, and I will graciously accept all of you back into my heart, forgiving all things and showering my mercy upon you." And then, just as surely the light, the sense, the sound, was gone. The rabbi stood with his back to the people praying still, and he was alone.

Then he turned and came toward the people. Instead of praying the prayer of intercessions as the ritual demanded, he called out: "Tam! Tam! Where is Tam?" He knew what everyone was thinking—he had been thinking it himself just seconds before. Why Tam? Tam was hardly ever in the synagogue. He was poor, unlettered, and worked so hard that he often missed services. Oh, he was a good-hearted enough soul, but he certainly hadn't amounted to much in the community. The rabbi didn't even know exactly what Tam did for a living. The people were stunned, shocked.

And poor Tam, who was in fact in the synagogue on this holy night, was equally stunned. He was paralyzed and could not move. Why did the rabbi call out his name instead of praying? What terrible thing was about to be visited upon him? But others in the synagogue recognized him, and the rabbi gestured to them to carry Tam forward to the front of the synagogue. Tam stood, silent, with head bowed before the rabbi.

The rabbi spoke loudly and directly to Tam. "I have been praying for mercy and forgiveness for all of us on this night and I have been clearly told by God, blessed be his Name, that we all will be forgiven and taken back into the heart of God if you pray for us, if you give your prayer to God on our behalf."

Tam was speechless. How could he pray? He could not even read the service, the prayers in the book. But the rabbi was insistent. God would only take the community back into his heart and give them a year of blessing, grace, and mercy if Tam prayed for them. He had to pray for them! Finally, Tam agreed. But he looked at the rabbi and said: "I have to go get my prayers."

What? the rabbi thought. You have to go get your prayers? "Then go," he said.

Tam ran down the aisle, pushing people aside. Everyone was in confusion and disarray. But Tam did not live far, just down a side street away from the synagogue's back door. He was back in no time.

Once again there was tumult in the synagogue as Tam returned to the front to stand beside the rabbi and pray on behalf of the community. He stood before them all, and in his hands was a large earthen pitcher. He lifted it high, turned his back on the people, and addressed God. "O Holy One, you know I am not good at praying, but I bring you all I have. This pitcher holds my tears. Late at night, even when I am tired, I sit and try to pray to you. And then I think of my poor wife and children and the fact that they have no clean clothes to wear to services and are ashamed to come to the synagogue, and I cry. And then I think of all the hungry ones, the beggars on the steps of the synagogue and in the streets, in the cold and rain, miserable and so alone, and I cry some more. And then, God, I think of what we do to each other. I think of all the gossip and hate, all the quarrels and wars, and I think of you crying, God, of you looking down on us hurting one another so, and I know that you weep for us always.

God, I cry for you and how we must break your heart and sadden you so. Please, take my tears, accept my prayers, and take all of us back into your heart once again. Give us a blessing and forgive us in your great mercy and kindness."

And Tam took his pitcher and poured his tears over the floor of the synagogue. There was a long silence, and then the rabbi spoke, haltingly: "God has heard Tam, and we are forgiven. We are once again the people of God. Let us live this year with grateful hearts."

The people sang, but they left the synagogue quietly. They vowed never to forget Tam's prayer or his pitcher of tears and to make sure there would be less to cry over in the years to come. They looked at Tam and his family differently, and their neighbors too. Some even reconciled with their enemies. But they all went home thinking of the tears of God.

Today God weeps over the death of a friend, his beloved Lazarus. Perhaps he wept too because of his disciples' faint-heartedness and lack of understanding. Or maybe he wept over Martha and Mary's chiding words: "If only you'd been here," not even allowing him to grieve and mourn his friend's suffering and death. Or did he weep at the hardness of peoples' hearts, looking for something to complain about and find fault with, no matter what he did? Did he weep at death, at sin, at evil, at injustice, and at the prospect of his own death at the hands of religious people sure of God and faith yet so disrespectful of life and human dignity? Did he weep at our lack of passion and lack of belief, ardently desiring that we might come to believe in him as the resurrection and the life?

God weeps today still. There is sin, insensitivity to the terrible destruction of other human beings, physical deaths and killings, unnecessary suffering, famine, economic injustice, and many people who do not rejoice in those who were dead being brought back to life. There are those who plot to kill anyone whose presence brings hope to those who are desperate. There is much to weep over. We, like Jesus, are sent to stand before the tombs and call one another forth with the word of God and to untie and set each other free. We are to encourage one another in faith to live the resurrection life now. We are to stake our lives on the mercy of God and the fullness of redemption, to be the beloved friend of Jesus, like Lazarus, responding to the sound of his voice, even in death. We are to live now, free, for the glory of God revealed in the body of Christ, the church today.

We pray for all those who have died. In faith, we pray:

Lord Jesus, like a shepherd who gathers the lambs to protect them from all harm, you led us to the waters of baptism and shielded us from harm. Now carry us on the path to your kingdom of light where we will find happiness and every tear shall be wiped away. To you be glory, now and forever. Amen.

And we pray for ourselves:

Lord Jesus, by raising Lazarus from the dead you showed that you came that we might have life and have it more abundantly. Through your Spirit, who gives life, fill us with faith, hope, and charity, that we may live with you always in the glory of your resurrection, for you are Lord forever and ever. Amen.

Feast of the Annunciation
March 25

Isaiah 7:10-14
Hebrews 10:4-10
Luke 1:26-38

This feast day seems out of place with Jesus' passion, death, and resurrection. This is the announcement of the Lord, and yet in a truer sense, it is the feast of the incarnation. It is the moment of God's entrance into history and into the world of flesh and blood, birth and death. It is said that we can catch sight of our end in our beginnings. In this moment of a woman's obedience and surrender to the overshadowing of the Spirit, the events that we hear in the scriptures of Lent begin.

The responsorial psalm can refer both to Jesus and to Mary, his mother and disciple, who believed the Word of the Lord that came to her. The response, of course, also belongs to all of us: "Here am I, Lord; I come to do your will." This is the reason for Jesus' being sent into the world: to obey the Father, and to redeem Mary's life and the lives of all those who are called to be disciples of Jesus. We are sent into the world, as the Father sent Jesus, to bear in our flesh and our lives, our histories and communities, the Word of the Lord. Psalm 40 is about the only sacrifice that God wants to receive from us: ears open to obedience and lives that delight in the Law that is in our hearts, a Law that is unrolled in our lives. We are to announce God's justice in the vast assembly and not restrain our lips. We are to speak of God's justice and not keep this knowledge and belief hid in our hearts. We are to be speakers and tellers of the faithfulness of God and make no secret of God's kindness and truth. In all this we imitate the Word of God made flesh in Mary, made flesh now in us by baptism.

The readings go back to the time of King Ahaz and the prophet Isaiah, and the long waiting of the people of Israel for the one who would be the presence of justice, peace, and mercy among them, a presence so sure, so full of light and power that all the nations would know that God dwelled with them, had a sanctuary in their midst. The reading from Isaiah is full of tension and frustration. The Lord speaks to Ahaz: "Ask for a sign from the Lord, your God; let it be deep as the nether world, or high as the sky!" This is a command from God: "Ask!" But Ahaz answers: "I will not ask! I will not tempt the Lord!"

Ahaz refuses not so much out of humility or belief but because he doesn't want Isaiah's advice. He is deeply entrenched in political and military maneuvers and wants the prophet to just disappear out of his life. He is making plans without recourse to God's plans. The historical background is found in 2 Kings 16:5-9, where Syria has entered into an alliance with the northern kingdom of Israel against the southern kingdom of Judah, where Ahaz is king, and together they are laying siege to Jerusalem. Isaiah approaches the king with the offer of a sign: a sign that all will be well and that the future of the kingdom will be assured. And even though Ahaz refuses, Isaiah and God have decided that the sign will be given anyway! "The virgin shall be with child, and bear a son, and shall name him Immanuel." The young woman is Ahaz's wife, and the child born is Hezekiah. God is still with the kingdom, even in the midst of political divisions and war, and God's promises will continue to bear fruit and to grow in meaning and import. On the historical level things didn't work out well for Ahaz; the divided kingdoms fall, though the prophecies continue forward in hope.

The Hebrew word *almah*, meaning "young woman," was translated by the Greek word *parthenos*, meaning "virgin," and the newborn child was called Immanuel, "God with us." The child is given as a sign of the presence of God with a people plagued by trouble. These are Jesus' Davidic ancestors, a mixed lot. But history serves to remind us that the words of the prophet, the word of God uttered in one specific instance, takes on a life of its own and grows to birth a new hope and a new meaning, generations later. Mary's child is "God with us" in ways the prophet Isaiah never imagined. And this child is both Word of God and Lord of all history.

The section from Hebrews continues this process of maturation, of understanding the will of God in the world. First, there was the blood and sacrifice of goats and bulls offered in expiation of sin. These were the original prescriptions of the Law. But the people learned that "God neither desired nor delighted in these offerings." Instead, God wanted "a body that was prepared to do the will of God." This is the fulfillment of the Law, the newer covenant, the will of God: Jesus Christ through the offering of his body sanctifies us once and for all. This is what God wants, only this: that we all live only to do the will of God.

The familiar passage from Luke tells the story of a woman who did the will of God. She said yes, not knowing where the words would take her. Like Abraham, she goes on a journey not knowing where she is going, except that it is the will of God. Her child, to be named Jesus, will be called the Son of the Most High and great will be his dignity. The Lord God will give him the throne of David his father, and his reign will be without end. This child is the Son of God and Mary's son, but he belongs to all the nations, to all who live on promises and the hope of salvation.

There is so little about Mary in the scriptures that we keep coming back to the one thing that we are sure of: she is the servant of God; she obeys and offers her body as sacrifice and God takes delight in that offering. And "it is done to her as God says." The word of God lived in the mouth and the life of the prophet Isaiah and the others, but the Word of God lived in the body and life of Mary. That was her life, more intimate and more demanding than that of any prophet before her. The gospel verse reads: "The Word of God became man and lived among us; and we saw his glory." The glory we see is a child born of a poor woman, a descendant of a once proud nation, of a race of kings. He grew up to be a teacher, healer, and forgiver, a prophet who was murdered in Jerusalem, as the prophets before him were killed. The glory we see is the humility of obedience and trust, of waiting on the Word of the Lord and believing that in the fullness of time all the words of God will come true. The glory we see is a woman whose child is Son of God, Sun of Justice, a human being torn to shreds amid politics, power, and religion, but the sign of the presence of God, the presence of justice and peace with us nevertheless.

The angel announces, asks a favor, receives a whispered yes, and leaves her. The Spirit overshadows her, as the Spirit of God passed over the doors of the Israelites eating the first Passover meal. The blood on the doorposts saved them from death, and the blood of her child crucified and pierced saves us all from death. God is present, not just in signs but as a person, in times of war, nationalism, and hatred, in times of catastrophe and the collapse of faith and the destruction of human beings. And God is present in a woman of steadfast, tough, and enduring grace. In the midst of Lent, God is present in all men and women who plead "Pray for us now and at the hour of our death." We all, with Mary, have found favor with God and in our baptismal promises we whisper again our yes, bearing the word of God in our flesh and in our standing by the cross. For God still wants our obedience in exchange for life, life ever more abundantly.

At the moment of conception God has entered the world, hidden in the darkness and safety of Mary's womb. The promise is coming true. But in the beginning only the angels and this one woman know and rejoice. During Lent, close to the passion of her child, grown to be a dangerous prophet of hope, we are reminded of promises, wild promises with unexpected meanings. What little we know of Mary can perhaps only be spoken of in words of praise, of poetry and song. As Thomas Merton wrote of her in *Ascent to Truth*:

> And far beneath the movement of this silent cataclysm Mary slept in the infinite tranquility of God, and God was a child curled up who slept in her and her veins were flooded with His wisdom which is night, which is starlight, which is silence. And her whole being was embraced in Him whom she embraced and they became tremendous silence.

And we pray simply, borrowing some of the words of Gabriel:

Hail Mary, full of grace, pray for us sinners now. Amen.

Tuesday of the Fifth Week of Lent

Numbers 21:4-9
John 8:21-30

The journey together in faith is hard at times. The Israelites leave Mount Hor and set out on the Red Sea road to bypass the land of Edom. We are told they are "worn out by the journey," and they lose whatever patience they once had. They complain bitterly against Moses and God, whining, "Why have you brought us up from Egypt to die in this desert, where there is no food or water? We are disgusted with this wretched food!" The wretched food they refer to is the manna that God provides for them daily and the quail that fall from the skies. They are ignoring the fact that it is God alone who has intervened constantly in their behalf. They lapse back into a people who have no direction, no meaning, and no sense of identity.

This time the Lord responds and sends saraph serpents that bite them, and many of them die. Then, and only then, do the people come to Moses and confess their sin in complaining against God and against him. They beg Moses to pray for them and to ask God to relent.

God commands Moses to make a saraph, mount it on a pole and to tell the people that those bitten by a serpent should look upon it and they will be healed. Moses obeys and makes a bronze serpent, and the people obey and recover their health.

This is, at root, the ritual of confession. Wrong is done, individually and collectively, and there is a consequence of word and deed. Then there is awareness and an articulation of sin: confession. The penance is to look, to see, to acknowledge the consequences together and begin to recover. Hopefully individuals and communities learn over the course of time and experience not to have to repeat the process too often!

The Israelites were slow to learn, short on patience, and quick to blame others for anything that did not immediately fall into place or make life easier for them. They were ungrateful, dismissing the gifts of God that sustained them, and they were bitter toward Moses and God. It is easy to see in retrospect how patient God was with them, and just as easy to see how stuck they were in their old ways of being slaves to their own immediate needs , even after seeing the power of God at work in their lives and history.

Do we at heart act like them? How mindful are we of God's actions in our lives and communities? Who defends God and stands up for God in our midst? We certainly complain a lot, as individuals, in parishes, religious communities, and churches. We moan and groan about finances, the pope, bishops, priests, deacons, leaders or the lack of them, corruption, lack of integrity, secrecy, mismanagement, and on and on. But as we point the finger at others, are we totally heedless of our own sin? Do we complain against God—who isn't to our liking, who doesn't fall into our categories? It has been said that all our spiritual problems stem from one reality: We are all bitterly angry that we are not God. Whom do we attack in the church and the world, because we can't get at God? Maybe we need to look at the consequences of our lack of gratitude and see what God does for us and who God really is, far beyond our narrow renderings of the Almighty.

Psalm 102 is simple: "O Lord, hear my prayer, and let my cry come to you." It is the cry of sinners, of those who see themselves in right perspective in relation to God, who know that it is God's prerogative to answer as God wills. It is also the prayer of those who see themselves in connection to others, as part of a nation and its history, and remember that God's first priority is listening to, hearing and attending to the prayers of the destitute, the groanings of prisoners and those doomed to die, not people with petty concerns and selfish litanies.

The obvious connection of the two readings is the allusion that Jesus makes in his dialogue with the Pharisees that they will "lift up the Son of Man and they will come to reality that I AM and that I do nothing by myself. I say only what the Father has taught me. The One who sent me is with me. He has not deserted me since I always do what pleases him."

Jesus, unlike the Israelites, knows that God will not desert him and that his Father is always teaching him, as God sought to do in the desert with his slow learners, the Israelites. We are all, it seems, like the Pharisees; we do not grasp what God is trying to do with us and what Jesus is trying to do with us in God.

Jesus begins by stating that he is going away and that they will look for him but will die in their sins. Where he is going they cannot come. Rather than look at what he is saying and examining themselves, those who hear him deflect his words and ask whether he is considering killing himself. Jesus ignores that tack and continues telling them that he belongs to what is above and that the world cannot hold him. And he repeats the deadly announcement: You will die in your sins unless you come to believe that I AM. And they still don't understand! Jesus keeps trying. He says that he only tells the world what his Father has spoken to him. He tells them that he is the Son of Man who will be lifted up, like the serpent in the desert, and if they look and come to know who he is, they will finally see that the One who sent him will not desert him. He is pleasing to God in all things.

John's long discourses are not easy to understand, but small gleanings of insight and meaning, pieces of the mystery, fall into place. Jesus always speaks first of God, a God who breaks boundaries, a God unlike anything any of us have experienced. Jesus' God is the One who stays faithful long after we have gone our own ways and learned sin and collusion with evil, even after we have cluttered our lives with many other small gods that we worship as much or more than God. Even Jesus is more than any one of us can fathom. He is Son of Man, the crucified One, the one lifted up, the consequence of our sin and evil and selfishness. We are no different from the Israelites or the Pharisees. We do not see. We do not understand. We do not know the God of Jesus or the Son of Man. We do not look often enough upon the crucified One or at our own sin, recognizing there the cruelty that we inflict upon one another. If we did, then there would not be such a tolerance for terror and violence among us.

Sheila Cassidy, a British doctor who once worked in Chile, was tortured and imprisoned for caring for a person wounded in a shootout without first asking which side he was on. She has since worked for Amnesty International on behalf of torture victims and now works in hospices for those with incurable and debilitating diseases in southern England. She writes:

> I believe that we have much to learn about Jesus' passion from the sufferings of those more accessible to us and that it is profoundly unhealthy to concentrate upon Jesus' sufferings while ignoring the cruelty and torture which are endemic in our world.

We must look on the ones lifted up, those crucified among us, in order to begin the process of our own recovery, of the health of the human race. God beholds the earth and hears the groans of those in prisons and those doomed to die, and we will know Jesus' God when we do likewise. If we complain, let it be about the misery and destitution of all those who die of starvation, lack of medicine, war, racial tensions, or without ever having had a chance to live. "O Lord, hear my prayer, and let my cry come to you." May our cry be one that acknowledges our sin, our selfish egos, and our lack of knowledge of God.

Wednesday of the Fifth Week of Lent

Daniel 3:14-20, 91-92, 95
John 8:31-42

The readings for the rest of the week get ugly, one building upon the other until Jesus' murder is inevitable. His words, reasoning, quoting of scripture, and intimacy with God enrage them. Jesus, in verbal combat with the Pharisees and others who oppose him, exposes their actions and their motivations and intentions for what they truly are. He is more than a prophet denouncing sin and naming evil. He is the living Word of God, and many turn on him, intent only on silencing him forever.

The first reading is from the book of Daniel. It is the familiar story of three young men in King Nebuchadnezzar's court—Shadrach, Meshach, and Abednego—who refuse to worship the golden statue. Whenever music is played, everyone is supposed to fall down and worship it, or else they will be cast into the furnace and burned alive. The king is arrogance personified: "Who is the God that can deliver you out of my hands?" The three young friends don't even defend themselves before the king. They know whom they serve, and it is not this man, king or no king, who stands before them. He may be able to kill them, but they are not to be deterred from their worship of the true God. They tell the king in no uncertain terms where they stand with their God: "If our God, whom we serve, can save us from the white-hot furnace and from your hands, O king, may he save us! But even if he will not, know, O king, that we will not serve your god or worship the golden statue which you set up."

The reaction of the king is not unexpected: his face turns "livid with utter rage," and he orders the fire to be made seven times hotter than usual. Then men from the army bind the three and cast them into the furnace. But Nebuchadnezzar gets a shock. He sees *four* men, unfettered and unhurt, walking in the fire, and one looks like a son of God. That phrase, "a son of God," can mean an angel or sometimes even the presence of God in the form of a bodily spirit. And so King Nebuchadnezzar falls to his knees and worships the God of the three believers, saying, "Blessed be the God of Shadrach, Meshach, and Abednego, who sent his angel to deliver the servants that trusted in him; they disobeyed the royal command and yielded their bodies rather than serve or worship any god except their own God."

The three exiled servants of Yahweh witness to their God even in captivity, and their faith brings the king to his knees. God intervened and showed forth the divine power by accompanying those who were sorely tried and subjected to the powers of the world. This, of course, shows what God will do for us in Jesus, although he does not interfere but lets history and the dominant powers run their course. God then shatters forever the usual course of history and the patterns of life and death. Jesus is courageous and truthful before those who oppose his God, as were the three men of Daniel's time, and the reaction is the same: rage.

All the readings today are about the nature of God and whose God is God. The psalm is from the book of Daniel. It is a prayer of blessing of God's holy name; the God who looks into the depths and rules above the cherubim and the firmament of heaven; the God who is praiseworthy and glorious above all forever. This is the God that King Nebuchadnezzar never anticipated, relying instead on his own power as the basis of what was mighty and worthy of worship. He worshiped himself and what he had made, forcing and demanding that others do the same, knowing no God.

The gospel reading is addressed to the Jews who believed in Jesus, and so to us: "If you live according to my teaching, you are truly my disciples; then you will know the truth, and the truth will set you free." It is a proclamation of power, of reality from the point of view of God. Even those who believe in Jesus balk at this, because it insinuates that they are not yet free. They argue vehemently back: "We are descendants of Abraham. Never have we been slaves to anyone."

They are sure of their ancestors in faith, relying on their roots, and assuming that they are free.

But Jesus is intent on them seeing themselves as they truly are—on our seeing ourselves as we truly are.

"I give you my assurance,
everyone who lives in sin
is the slave of sin."

This, of course, includes all of us. Jesus contrasts the slave in a household with the legitimate son. The one has no permanent place and the other a place forever. Only if the son frees the slave will he be free. Jesus is well aware that his listeners are of Abraham's stock, but he is also well aware that they are trying to kill him. The two conflict. So he condemns them:

"You are trying to kill me
because my word finds no hearing among you.
I tell what I have seen in the Father's presence;
you do what you have heard from your father."

Their sources of power and freedom are diametrically opposed. They cling to Abraham as their father. But Jesus is teacher, preacher, and prophet, and he uses their own words and reasoning against them. Abraham lived in faith, showed hospitality to the angels and to God when they visited, obeyed God and left his homeland even though he did not know where he was going. He argued with God in behalf of the cities of Sodom and Gomorrah, trying to save even evil people from destruction. If they were children of Abraham, they would act like him. But they don't. They are not children of faith, of life, of covenant, because they are trying to kill Jesus, a man who tells them the truth that he has heard from God. Abraham didn't act as they do! They are livid with rage, blind with hate. They know exactly what Jesus is accusing them of: of being an illegitimate breed!

We can almost feel the deadly stand-off. They act like King Nebuchadnezzar, while Jesus is calm, intent, and unrelenting in his truth-telling. They spit out: "We are no illegitimate breed! We have but one father and that is God himself."

Jesus answers, repeating what he has said so many times before:

"Were God your Father
you would love me,
for I came forth from God, and am here.
I did not come of my own will;
it was he who sent me."

This is the core of Jesus' preaching: if we know God at all, Jesus' words find a hearing in our hearts and we love him, for Jesus alone knows God. Apart from Jesus, none of us knows God. Apart from Jesus, we live in sin, as slaves, and do not know the freedom of the children of God. We do not know Jesus' freedom and power. We do not know the freedom of the three young men willing to die in the fire rather than worship another God than the God of life.

Who is our God? Does the Word of God, Jesus, find a hearing in our hearts? Do we love Jesus? Love is not a feeling that comes and goes, juggled among other things that we serve or love. The love that Jesus speaks about is the willingness to stand truthfully against any power that does not serve the God of Jesus. Do we stand against violence, war, inhumanity, poverty, indignity, injustice, inequality, materialism, individualism, capitalism, nationalism? Do we resist with all our beings, even bodily, as the three friends did, all that is untrue, fabricated, self-serving, political and economically correct?

March 24 is the anniversary of the murder of Archbishop Oscar Romero of El Salvador. He was martyred, shot at the altar after pleading with his people to stop killing one another. His words found no hearing in the hearts of those in power, but they have been honored in the hearts of the poor. His words of April 1, 1979, echo stronger through the years:

Those who, in the biblical phrase, would save their lives—that is, those who don't want to get into problems, who want to stay outside whatever demands our involvement—they will lose their lives.

What a terrible thing to have lived well off, with no suffering, not getting into problems, quite tranquil, quite settled, with good connections—politically, economically, socially—lacking nothing.

To what good? They will lose their lives. . . .

To each one of us Christ is saying: "If you want your life and mission to be fruitful like mine, do like me. Be converted into a seed that lets itself be buried. Let yourself be killed. Do not be afraid. Those who shun suffering will remain alone. No one is more alone than the selfish. But if you give your life out of love for others, as I give mine for all, you will reap a great harvest. You will have the deepest satisfactions. Do not fear death or threats. The Lord goes with you."

It is time to stand with Jesus in opposition to evil. It is time to be truthful and begin to love and worship like the three young men, like Oscar Romero, and like so many thousands of people who have stood up for their belief. This is the only way we will know God, the truthful One, who sent Jesus into the world to save us.

Thursday of the Fifth Week of Lent

Genesis 17:3-9
John 8:51-59

The section from Genesis is the account of God speaking with Abram and making a covenant with him for all time. In the agreement God changes Abram's name, destiny, and his meaning in the world. He becomes Abraham, the father of a host of nations. His offspring will be exceedingly fertile, not only in the biological sense but in the sense of belief and coming to worship with his descendants, for kings will stem from his line and other nations will come to Israel, bringing their homage to God.

God is the initiator of the covenant, its sustainer, the One who lays out the rights and responsibilities on both sides. God will be faithful through all generations and will maintain the covenant throughout all the ages, never to be severed for any reason, and God will give the land in which Abraham is now staying, the whole land of Canaan, as a permanent possession; God will be their God—their only God. In return, only one thing is required on the part of Abraham and all those who follow after him: they must keep the covenant. They must belong to God alone. They must show forth God's glory. The covenant seems to be the focus of the reading, and yet the real

center of the reading is God, who speaks to Abram. It is God's covenant, and Abram prostrates himself before this God who approaches
him and sets in motion the history and religion of Israel.

Psalm 105 tells us more about the God of Abraham and how we
are to live in relation to God. The response is a reminder of God's
part: "The Lord remembers his covenant for ever." We are to learn to
remember God's strength, wondrous deeds, portents, and judgments.
We are to keep in mind that we are descendants of Abraham and the
servants of God, chosen ones, and that we are bound to God for a
thousand generations, at least. We are remembered by God. We are,
literally, held together as individuals and as a people by God. We are
kept alive in the midst of all other histories and nations. We are
present to God always. Our attitude is that of Abraham: prostrate
before God, keeping the covenant, humble, obedient, listening.

Once again Jesus and his contemporaries spar theologically, with
Jesus taking the initiative: "I solemnly assure you, if a man is true to
my word he shall never see death." This line, of course, is enough to
inflame them, and they accuse him of being possessed or insane. They
spit back their reasons: Abraham is dead. The prophets are dead.
And yet you claim that anyone who keeps your word will never know
death. Their deadly insinuation is articulated: "Surely you do not
pretend to be greater than our father Abraham, who died! Or the
prophets, who died! Whom do you make yourself out to be?" This is
the heart of the conflict. Jesus does not pretend to be anything other
than what he is: the child of God, intimate with God because he
listens, obeys, and does only the will of God. He completely fulfills
the covenant given to Abraham. He is one of the descendants of this
faithful friend of God, and he is faithfulness itself, whole and utterly
devoted only to God's ways on earth.

He returns to his refrain: I know God. I glorify only God. "I know
him well, and I keep his word." They do not know God. And Jesus
hits home with an added reference to Abraham: "Your father Abraham
rejoiced that he might see my day. He saw it and was glad!" Jesus'
father is God, not Abraham; Abraham serves God, and so rejoices in
the coming of Jesus, the fulfillment of the covenant.

But the leaders of the Jews insist on not looking deeper into any of
Jesus' words. They interpret them at face value, ignoring their long
history, which clearly shows that the Law, the covenant, and the
word of God in the prophets cannot be reduced to one specific thing

or easily categorized. All of God's utterances have been seeds sown in the hearts of the people of Israel, and in spite of their lack of faithfulness, by the power and mercy of God these seeds keep growing, revealing more and more. But they don't want to hear, and so they object: "You're not yet fifty! How can you have seen Abraham?" They are forgetting that the whole promise to Abraham is about life, about the covenant overruling death and extending Abraham's name, memory, and belief throughout a thousand generations. Abraham *is* alive in those of his descendants who are faithful to keeping the demands of the covenant. They are, on the other hand, dead.

Jesus then forthrightly proclaims: "I solemnly declare it: before Abraham came to be, I AM." This is the name of God given in response to Moses' questioning on the mountain before going to face Pharaoh in Egypt. It proclaims that God is unnameable. Always, God is mystery, unknown, and beyond words. Jesus does not pretend to be anything other than one born of God, living and hidden in God. They deliberately interpret his words wrongly and pick up rocks to throw at him. They intend to stone him to death then and there. But Jesus' time is not yet. Close—but not yet. And so he hid himself and slipped out of the Temple precincts.

Jesus tried to reach their hearts, but there have always been those who, while claiming to be religious, use scripture and tradition for their own agenda. They don't listen but define God in their own terms. Yet God does not serve their ends, their way of death. As Jesus pleaded with them to understand, God is the God of life, life ever more abundantly, life that is stronger than death.

There is a Sufi tale, told by Anthony de Mello and many others, that speaks of learning and discipleship:

✝ Once upon a time many people gathered together in the marketplace to ask questions of the master. Some were seriously interested in the truth and in changing their lives to conform with the power of goodness and life that was the God they sought to know. Many came out of curiosity or were dragged along by friends. Some just found themselves there. Some were intent on invalidating and tripping up the master because they served others and saw the master as a threat to their place in their own groups. And there were the master's own followers, who often didn't understand what was going on until long after the discussions were finished.

That day all the questions seemed to be about death, the grave, and whether one could be sure of a life after death. It was very disconcerting, especially to the master's own disciples, because in response to all the questions the master only laughed. Sometimes softly, a mere chuckle. Sometimes raucously, very undignified. Sometimes with pleasure. Sometimes almost convulsively. Those who asked and those who listened reacted with anger, confusion, a feeling of being insulted. But he spoke no words, just laughed. Finally, the master walked away from them all.

Later that night the disciples prodded him and demanded that he speak about the morning. What had he meant? They were really distraught and perplexed. He looked at them in mock seriousness and spoke: "Have you ever noticed who the people are who keep asking questions about the next life—life after death? It seems that all of them, for one reason or another, have trouble with this one. They always seem to want another life that isn't connected to this one much at all."

This didn't settle the disciples' anxiety, and one sputtered out: "But master, is there a life after death or not? Speak plainly. Say yes or no!" The master did it again: he laughed aloud. Then he asked a question back: "What I want to know," he said, "is whether there is life *before* death?" And he eyed them all: "Are any of you really alive?"

So, in this week before Holy Week, before facing the cross and death, before remembering our baptismal promises and walking with Jesus toward the end of his life before death, that is the question: Are we really alive? Are we alive in Christ?

Friday of the Fifth Week of Lent

Jeremiah 20:10-13
John 10:31-42

The reading from Jeremiah is disheartening, discouraging, and yet it is worded not just with anguish but with conviction and power.

Jeremiah's lot is hard. Others denounce him, whisper against him. Terror surrounds him. Especially plaintive is his realization that even those that he thought were his friends are now on the watch for any misstep. They are waiting to trap him, and then they can take vengeance on him, and their power and their wishes will prevail in the nation. They oppose the prophet and the prophet's God, for Jeremiah has no life except to preach what God orders him to say, no matter the consequences.

But Jeremiah knows the one he serves and knows the faithfulness of his God, who is "like a mighty champion," and he believes that his persecutors will stumble themselves and not triumph over him. But even if they do, in the long run they will fail, because they cannot triumph over the will of God. Ultimately they will be put to shame, "to lasting, unforgettable confusion." And so Jeremiah prays the prayer of the desperate, the needy, the prayer of those who suffer because of their allegiance to God or the poor of God:

> O Lord of hosts, you who test the just,
>   who probe mind and heart,
> Let me witness the vengeance you take on them,
>   for to you I have entrusted my cause.

We have heard this prayer before. It is a universal prayer for judgment, for justice to prevail in spite of those who self-righteously decide on the fate of anyone who resists them, especially anyone who speaks truth and exposes them to the public eye. Jeremiah's prayer ends with praise and song! In the past and even in his own lifetime, God has rescued the poor from the power of the wicked!

The Exodus and the making of the people of Israel began with God hearing that persistent loud cry of the slaves of Egypt. Those in distress, those suffering because of the sin or collusion of others against God, have come to know that Yahweh is with them, accompanying them in the word of the prophets, biding the time to prove God's glory and raise up the lowly who are beaten down.

The psalm response, "In my distress I called upon the Lord, and he heard my voice," is the constant prayer of those who resist evil, who refuse to be mastered by their own weaknesses or the culture and the climate of the times. Often it must have been the prayer of Jesus, certainly in the hours that preceded his own destruction at the hands of his opponents. Psalm 18 describes God: Our God is Lord, our strength, our rock, our fortress, our deliverer, our refuge, our shield, our salvation. And God hears. The voice of the one in distress is the voice to which God is attuned, for that voice tears the heart of God. It witnesses to what is happening on the earth and what is breaking the hopes of God for all creation.

Jesus is about to be stoned. They reach for rocks, and Jesus stands his ground, protesting, making them take responsibility for their actions and the murder they are about to commit. His voice commands their attention: "Many good deeds I have shown you from the Father. For which of these do you stone me?" Jesus teaches, heals, forgives, praises God, cares for the poor, and reaches out to all in need. He stands before them and demands to know for which of these works they are going to stone him.

But they ignore his works and zero in on words. They perceive him to be blaspheming, making himself God. But Jesus won't let them off so easily. He goes back to the scriptures and quotes to them:

> "Is it not written in your law,
> 'I have said, You are gods?'
> If it calls those men gods
> to whom God's word was addressed—
> and Scripture cannot lose its force—
> do you claim that I blasphemed
> when, as he whom the Father consecrated
> and sent into the world,
> I said, 'I am God's Son'?"

Even the prophets were called the sons and daughters of God, having the Spirit of God within them. They were also called the sons and daughters of men, meaning that they were human, made in the image of God, truly faithful people who belonged to the God of the covenant. Jesus is taking that usage and extending it to his particular relationship with God as Father. The words are based on works, on foundations that are true. One is known to belong to another by his or her behavior, association, closeness, not just words; only people of God can do the works of God.

Jesus challenges them: If they cannot put their faith in him, at least they can acknowledge the works that he does and put faith in them. These works have always alerted the people of Israel to the presence of God in their midst. Their Law and covenant repeat them again and again: the poor are protected, the widow and the orphan cared for, the prisoner freed, the alien in their midst honored, the stranger welcomed in the name of God. The quality of life among those in need is a reflection of the shallowness of the faith of the community. And the nation, especially its leaders and priests, its wealthy and elite, are held responsible for their neediness.

The life of the church community is intimately bound to the quality of life of those who are not cherished in society, those deemed expendable. Never, never are God's people to become like their taskmasters and slave-owners, their oppressors in Egypt. The poor in their midst are to be treated with the kindness and respect they owe to God and to their neighbors. This is the covenant. And those who are faithful, those who hear the word of God and put it into practice are the sons and daughters of God, made in the divine image and likeness.

But once again they twist Jesus' words, which convict them of lack of love and belief, of failure to follow the Law. They want the fewest demands possible made on them, even by God.

But we must be careful not to condemn the people of Jesus' time. After all, we have long been privileged to know Jesus and the Father in the power of the Spirit, but what are our works? Where is our faith placed? We are really in no position to think ourselves superior to the people of that time or more holy or more open to the revelation of the Word.

Jesus speaks forcefully: "Put faith in these works, so as to realize what it means that the Father is in me and I in him." And they move on him again, trying to arrest him, but he eludes their grasp. That grasp reveals exactly what they are seeking to do with God: use God to validate their own positions. They lack faith and collapse the words of God into workable statements easily lived with.

So Jesus leaves them and goes back across the Jordan to the place where John had been baptizing earlier. He goes back home, to the place of the Spirit's coming upon him in fullness and the confirmation of the Father's words: "This is my beloved son, my servant, my chosen one. Listen to him." And many come to him. They have listened to him and looked at his works and come to believe in him. We must ask ourselves: Do *our* works reveal the Word of God in our hearts?

As Phil McManus reported in *Fellowship*, a group of poor Mexican women went to the state capital to plead for the release of their husbands. They organized a fast and prayer vigil in the plaza in front of the government palace, then sought a meeting with the officials. The following dialogue took place with the official who received them:

Official: What is this about an action of prayer and fasting? Why do you do these things?

Women: Because we have faith.

Official: You aren't alone; someone is behind you; someone puts these ideas in your head.

Women: You're right about that. We aren't alone. God is with us. God is behind us and puts ideas in our heads. God gives us wisdom.

Official: This is a legal, political matter. Why do you mix God up in it?

Women: Because God is with the poor.

Official: (*who perhaps has read the commentaries of some conservative theologians*) God doesn't make any distinction between the rich and the poor.

Women: (*who surely haven't read Leonardo Boff or other liberation theologians but who have the help that they already spoke of*) If God doesn't distinguish between the rich and the poor, then why does the world do that and treat us worse?

Official: (*running out of patience*) All right, all right, don't start mixing God up in this; I don't want to hear any more of that.

Women: Yes, we understand. For you God doesn't count because you place your trust in money. But we don't have money, and that is why we place our trust in God.

Good works can get us in trouble. Remember Jeremiah. Remember Jesus. Remember the Mexican women and so many other men and women who reveal the God of Jesus. The Father calls them his children and expects—no demands—that they be treated with dignity and respect.

Saturday of the Fifth Week of Lent

Ezekiel 37:21-28
John 11:45-57

This is the last sabbath for Jesus. Who he is and what he has done in the world and the words that he has preached have all set in motion the events of these next eight days. The reading from the book of the prophet Ezekiel is from God's point of view, and it tells of what God will accomplish with the Israelites. The gospel is the view from a more immediate perspective: those in power at the moment. Whether or not they know it, they too are serving God's will. The readings once again look at Yahweh, who has taken the Israelite people from among the nations to which they have been exiled and gathered them together again to bring them home. What God intends is unity, one nation, one land, one prince to lead them, and never again for them to be divided.

God wants the people finally to be true, to leave behind their idols, abominations, and transgressions, their sins of apostasy. God desires that they be cleansed. Always it is the same hope: that they will be obedient. God wants peace, enduring and everlasting peace that overlaps generations, as everlasting as the covenant. Lastly, God wants to dwell with them so that all the nations of the world will know that "It is I, the Lord, who make Israel holy." And all will know this when the sanctuary of God is set up among them forever.

The key word is *sanctuary*, a place of refuge and safety where God embraces them. It had come to mean the Temple in Jerusalem, and even the city itself; for us, it means the inner area around the altar. But God had much more in mind than any building. The sanctuary that will be the dwelling place of God among humankind is the body of Christ, the church that bears his Spirit within. The church is the sacrament of the risen Lord, the sanctuary of God on earth, and a sheltering place for all who are lost. This is the hope of God and the vocation of all who are believers in God's covenant in Jesus.

The recurring image of the good shepherd draws the idea of protection and safety beyond a place of sanctuary and into a person. In Jeremiah 31 the Lord is described as guarding us, as a shepherd guards his flock. Shepherds were hardy and tough souls. They were used to inclement weather and solitude. They were physically capable of fighting off wolves, wild dogs, and robbers. They carried a staff and often had dogs to help them herd the sheep and keep them together. The shepherd took care of all the physical needs of the sheep on a daily basis: food, grass, water, protection. The shepherd with his flock is a strong image of gathering together and coming home.

This image is extended to the people who will come home after exile, streaming in from all the corners of the earth, as the scattered sheep on the hillsides are rounded up and brought in. The people will come shouting, with the harvests of their labors, singing and dancing and making merry, because God, the Shepherd of Israel, "will turn their mourning into joy, and console and gladden them after their sorrows." On this last sabbath there is promise of comfort and of life after suffering and sorrow. It begins now as the net closes in on Jesus.

We are to keep in mind that what happens to Jesus in all his life and death and resurrection is continuing still. In *A Vow of Conversation*, Thomas Merton writes:

> We have to see history as a book that is sealed and opened only by the Passion of Christ. But we prefer to read it from the viewpoint of the Beast. We look at history in terms of hubris and power—in terms of the beast and his values. Christ continues to suffer his passion in the poor, the defenseless, and his Passion destroys the Beast. Those who love power are destroyed together with what they love. Meanwhile, Christ is in agony until the end of time.

Today, we must take time to reflect on Christ's suffering in light of the suffering of the world now—and our part in it. In sermon #62 Bernard of Clairvaux writes:

> Two things console the Church in her exile: the memory of the Passion of Christ in the past and in the future the contempla-

tion of what she both thinks and believes will be her welcome among the saints. . . . [The church's] contemplation is complete because it knows not only what it is to expect, but the source from which it is to come. It is a joyous expectation with no hesitation in it, because it rests on the death of Christ.

The gospel picks up after the account of Jesus raising Lazarus from the dead. It is always disconcerting to realize that Jesus' gift of life to Lazarus did not bring Jesus friends and followers but was the trigger point that brought his enemies to move against him.

As always, the crowd is divided. Some believe, and others go to the Pharisees and report what Jesus has done. The chief priests and the Pharisees call a meeting of the entire Sanhedrin to discuss Jesus and his works. They are concerned with what will happen if he keeps doing these sorts of things. "If we let him go on like this, the whole world will believe in him. Then the Romans will come in and sweep away our sanctuary and our nation."

This fear of losing their place, their Temple, their uneasy collusion with the Romans is the bone of contention. Jesus is putting these things in jeopardy by his presence and his passionate devotion to the will of God, which is light and life in a world of sin and evil. They cannot recognize God acting in history because they have limited God to specific areas of power—the same places where their power operates—and they cannot bear to lose control.

Caiaphas, the high priest that year, speaks up and says: "You have no understanding whatever! Can you not see that it is better for you to have one man die (for the people) than to have the whole nation destroyed?" He, of course, understands nothing either. He sees Jesus as expendable. But for those who believe in God's ways woven in and through the decisions of history, Caiaphas is being used by God to prophesy that Jesus will die for the nation and save them all, in fact save all nations, who will one day, as Ezekiel prophesied, be gathered into one.

So the decision is made to kill Jesus; it is politically expedient, a workable option that solves their immediate problem. The decision is made by the people in power, religious people seeking to protect their strongholds.

Jesus retreats and doesn't move about freely. He goes to Ephraim in the region near the desert, where he stays with his disciples, preparing for what lies ahead. He knows how politics work, how intrigues and plots take on a life of their own, and how violence once set in motion feeds on any anger and source it touches.

It is near the Jewish Passover, and people are streaming into the city, but most are unaware of all that is happening. Many are on the lookout for Jesus. They've heard the rumors and his words, passed from mouth to mouth, and especially they have heard the tales of his raising Lazarus from the dead. Everybody is talking about him and wondering if he'll be at the feast. Word is out that anyone who knows his whereabouts should report it, so that he can be apprehended. He is now a public threat, already convicted, and his fate has been decided. He is to die.

What went on in Jesus' mind and heart in those days before he was arrested, when he was away from the city, aware of what was afoot? Etty Hillesum in her journal, edited after her death in a Nazi concentration camp, wrote on May 18, 1942:

> The threat grows ever greater, and terror increases day to day. I draw prayer round me like a dark protective wall, withdraw inside it as one might into a convent cell and then step outside again, calmer and stronger and more collected again. I can imagine times to come when I shall stay on my knees for days on end waiting until the protective walls are strong enough to prevent my going to pieces altogether, my being lost and utterly devastated.

Today, we too must pray. St. Teresa of Avila left her sisters and the church this prayer:

> *Let nothing disturb you.*
> *Let nothing frighten you.*
> *All things are passing—*
> *God only is changeless,*
> *Patience attains all things*
> *Who has God ceases to want—*
> *God alone suffices.*

HOLY WEEK

—————— ✛ ——————

Passion Sunday/Palm Sunday

From the Procession with Palms: Matthew 21:1-11
Isaiah 50:4-7
Philippians 2:6-11
The Passion Account, Matthew 26:14-27:66

This week, all the catechumens, those who have helped to prepare them for baptism, and all those who believe in Jesus and have
been baptized will be together. We set our faces with Jesus toward
Jerusalem, toward the cross, death, and resurrection. This week we
will be crucified in our hearts and souls, give glory to God with Jesus,
and experience again our baptisms and renew our promises. We will
pass over with Jesus and go through the tomb into the life born of
water and the Spirit.

This is the week of telling the story again and having it come true
in us and our communities. We remember especially the crucified
One, a sign of scandal and hope, a sign of contradiction (1 Corinthians
1:18f.). It is time for us to experience upheaval, wrenching away from
the grasp of the world, and becoming more deeply converted to our
baptismal promises and the explosion of the kingdom of God into
our world. This week the word and the power of the cross must be-

B Cycle: Mk 11:1-10 or Jn 12:12-16; Is 50:4-7; Phil 2:6-11; Mk 14:1-15:47
or Mk 15:1-39
C Cycle: Lk 19:28-40; Is 50:4-7; Phil 2:6-11; Lk 22:14-23:56 or Lk 23:1-49

come part of our flesh and bones so that the world can be injected anew with the Spirit of God.

We begin outside the church—in courtyards, plazas, parking lots, and side streets—for the procession of palms and a short reading from Matthew that sets the stage for our celebration. The rites of Holy Week are familiar to some, strange to others. They are all meant to be celebrated—participated in and absorbed into our very bloodstream and heart. The older sense of the verb *to celebrate* meant "to frequent," "to hold in regard," and that is what we are to practice these days. We are to frequent the company of and honor the Suffering Servant of God, the crucified One, and all those who today wear that mantle of pain laid on them by a world that still experiences violence, despair, and hatred as a usual way of living.

The crowd draws near to Jerusalem, entering Bethphage on the Mount of Olives. They have come to celebrate the feast of freedom, the feast of Passover, the memorial of God drawing the people out of slavery and oppression into hope and an embrace of belonging as God's people. Jesus has come to celebrate with his disciples and friends a last time, and he sends two of the disciples off with instructions to prepare for his arrival and entrance into the city. They are to take an ass that they find tethered and her colt, and if anyone tries to stop them, they are to reply: "The Master needs them." That is how he will come into the city. The prophets will be remembered and their words repeated: "Tell the daughter of Zion, Your king comes to you without display astride an ass, astride a colt, the foal of a beast of burden." Jesus stays close to the earth, close to the poor and the laborer and the slave, those made beasts of burden by the mighty and the haughty.

There are other echoes too. Abigail, for example, rode an ass into David's camp to seek forgiveness and reconciliation for her husband's crimes and to plead for his life. She came humbly, as a sign of peace, knowing that the lives of many depended on her intervention.

So, the disciples lay their cloaks on the animal, and Jesus rides into the city. The people lining the streets on the way to the feast spread their cloaks on the road, and others cut branches from the trees, laying them in his path. These are honors and signs that their hope and their lives have been offered to him. They cry out: "God save the Son of David! Blessed is he who comes in the name of the Lord! God save him from on high!" This is a portion of the Sanctus, which we cry out and sing with the angels and all of creation, acknowledging God. We serve only God, no other power on earth. For the people of Jesus' time, the words expressed a religious and heartfelt hope laced with a nationalism born of long persecution, loss of sovereignty and dignity, heavy taxation, and grinding poverty.

In last week's gospel we read that Jesus was stirred to his very soul. Now it is the city that is stirred to its depths, demanding: "Who is this?" And the answer keeps coming back: "This is the prophet Jesus from Nazareth in Galilee." The depths contain the unknown, the uncontrollable, the dangerous elements, the underside of a city, and they are demanding to know who it is that disturbs, as prophets do just by their presence. The prophet Jesus is the Savior from the north, from the place where revolution is fomented and rebels abound, a place of struggle on the boundaries of Israel. There is excitement, expectation, fear. Plots are already afoot. Jesus knows what he is walking into. His moment of triumph will be painfully short-lived. But he has come to confront Jerusalem—and to stand before each of us and invite us to choose.

We remember that beginning of the week called holy, called passion, by carrying our own palms. These palms will be burned and the ashes for next year's Ash Wednesday will be made from them. The sign of glory and the sign of conversion are made of the same stuff and meet in our flesh and lives. We walk and sing the praises of the One who goes before us. We follow together. It will be a long week for all of us.

Once back in church the first reading is proclaimed from the book of Isaiah. It is a humble description of Jesus and of all those persecuted for the sake of justice and of God's honor. "The Lord God has given me a well-trained tongue, that I might know how to speak to the weary a word that will rouse them." This is not just a word of comfort or consolation, but the rousing word of the good news, the imminent coming of the kingdom breaking into the lives of those who are bent under the weight of evil and the world's inequality and false idols. "And morning after morning he opens my ear that I may hear; And I have not rebelled, have not turned back."

This word teaches how to resist without violence or hatred, how to endure in the face of humankind's inhumanity, and how to rely on a strength that is always offered. Jesus, the Suffering Servant, and the prophets before and after him, the innocent and the just, have "not rebelled, have not turned back, but they have given their bodies to those who beat them and their faces to those who insulted and humiliated them." Their shield, which they grasped and held onto for a dearer life, was God.

"For the Lord God is my help." This is the cry of those who seek to be human rather than to kill or harm others. Even though such a one may die, ultimately there will be no disgrace. But it is hard. Jesus sets his face like flint, knowing that he will not be put to shame and knowing equally that he will be tortured and mocked, reduced to sheer brokenness by other human beings. Through all, he will cling to God. He is our model. St. Paul calls it folly and wisdom, the word and the cross. It is a two-edged sword, a healing balm and grace, a hungry lion, a hammer-shattering rock, and a source of freedom and life, especially for those who are crushed under the heel of hatred and broken by the structures of injustice.

Today is a day of processions, circuses, a band of motley followers who are, along with the holy fools of long ago, meant to keep alive the tradition and belief of the Holy Fool who was stripped naked, cursed, beaten publicly, and forced outside the city and hung on wood in a garbage dump. St. William of Thierry (1085-1148) calls this "holy madness," madness for the sake of love. This is Jesus. This is God, who is so close to the miserable and the wretched of the world: those starving in a world aplenty, those being bombed in Sarejevo, those being hacked to death by neighboring tribes in Africa, those dying slowing of cholera and tainted water and bureaucracy in South America, those on the street in every city, all those outcast from society, culture, and even religion's often narrowly defined boundaries.

Christ, this holy fool, mad with the truth, is part of the ancient tradition of the prophet and the mystic, one who atones for others and refuses to let us keep existing in systems where there is *truly* madness: insensitivity, hostility toward strangers and the poor, and fear of those who are different. The cross cries out loudly that our religion is about uncrucifying the world, about resisting unnecessary pain and humiliation, about standing with those caught in the net of nationalism and ideologies more intent on making their points rather than lifting up people, about true worship. The cross will not tolerate anyone being destroyed while believers spend time and money and effort on buildings, environments, and ways of spirituality.

This week profoundly disturbs the world and is meant to disturb us, break us out of complacency and false pieties. It shatters any sense of self-righteousness we might still entertain in our hearts or practices. God has known this all along and so came to dwell among us, among the most poor and lost of his time.

The ancient psalm with its lament, "My God, my God, why have you abandoned me?," is horrible in its litany of what human beings do to each other and allow others to experience. It is about pain and how to stay human when we fall into the hands of those who consider other lives expendable or mere commodities to be used or destroyed. It is about pain of the body, and worse, pain of the soul caused by the mockery and blasphemy of others calling on God to help us because they won't. The one who is tortured is left with nothing of the past, of material possessions, of dignity.

The only thing remaining is hope, unbridled and unreasonable hope in God: "I will proclaim your name to my brethren; in the midst of the assembly I will praise you." "You who fear the Lord, praise him; all you descendants of Jacob, give glory to him." At the end, what makes us human is the One whom we worship, whom we serve and obey, whom we praise and give glory to, even when lives are tattered or bruised or even taken from us violently. The suffering are reminded that God is not far from them, and God is their aid and help. They, like Jesus, are abandoned to the hands of God when others refuse to help them.

And so the second reading from Philippians reminds us what our attitude must be—like that of Christ. Jesus' message of the breaking in of the reign of God, his companionship with public sinners and those who did not conform to society's norms, and his forgiveness and reconciliation of all have led him to this week when Jesus "emptied himself and took the form of a slave, being born in the likeness of men. He was known to be of human estate, and it was thus that he humbled himself, obediently accepting death, even death on a cross!"

It is this emptying, this obedience, this humbling surrender, that is the source of the glory that is extended to Jesus by God, who will exalt him and bestow on him the name that saves, the name that glorifies God, the name that makes us, with Jesus, the children of God. This name thunders and reverberates in the sea, the sky, under the earth, and in all hearts as all creation proclaims and cries out: "Jesus Christ is Lord!" That is what this week of passion is about. We are called to stand with Jesus and to die with him.

This week is about standing up for our belief. If we believe in Jesus Christ, we believe in the poor and those who suffer the injustices of the world. There is no separation between the two. We must read the passion accounts and hear of the terror and destruction of what was done to God in Jesus with the same horror and dismay that we hear of what is done to others in the world today—what we do, or what we allow to be done in our name, in collusion or without our resisting the deeds.

The backdrop against which we, as believing Christians in the 1990s, must read the passion accounts is not so much the personal experience of Jesus, the prophet of Nazareth in Galilee, but the present and all those who are God's chosen ones, the suffering on the earth. The cross is as much a symbol of life as it is of death. We are marked with this sign, blessed with it, christened with it. We trace it on others' foreheads, hands, and hopefully hearts. This emptying, this obedience, brings life out of the pain, injustice, hatred, and violence. Jesus' pain and ours redeem the world. We have a part in this struggle and the work of the coming of the kingdom into the world.

This week of passion means passion for life, truth, God's honor, the poor, and the reign of goodness in the world. We take up our cross, as Jesus took up his cross, and we take it to the world, to the victims of injustice as a sign of hope and freedom and also to those who do evil in the world as a sign of judgment and justice. "Rejoice and be glad," we are told in Matthew. "Happy are you when people abuse you and persecute you and speak all manner of calumny against you on my account. Rejoice and be glad" (Matthew 5:11-12).

Matthew's account of Jesus' betrayal, trial, and destruction is short. First, the betrayal is arranged for thirty pieces of silver. Then there is the meal, the celebration of Passover, which begins with Jesus' announcement that one of them will betray him. Judas is acknowledged. The meal continues. Bread is broken and shared. Wine is blessed and shared. But Jesus does not eat and drink; he waits for the new wine in the kingdom. And they go out singing to the Mount of Olives. Jesus reminds them that their faith will be shaken, the shepherd will be struck, the sheep scattered, but after he is raised up, he will go to Galilee ahead of them. And Peter brashly boasts of his strength, and Jesus tells him that Peter will disown him before dawn.

And Jesus prays, inviting the others—especially Peter, James, and John—to pray with him. He experiences sorrow and distress, his heart nearly broken with sorrow. He falls before God and prays: "My Father, if it is possible, let this cup pass me by. Still, let it be as you would have it, not as I." Three times. And three times he comes to his friends and they are asleep. He is alone. Then Judas comes into the garden and betrays him with an embrace and kiss. There is a scuffle, fighting, and one of the servants loses an ear. Jesus' words are strong: "Put back your sword where it belongs. Those who use the sword are sooner or later destroyed by it." Jesus resists evil with every bone and fiber of his body and spirit but not with violence, only with the force of truth-telling and his presence. He is taken as a brigand, as a prophet, and he is taken alone.

At the trial with Caiaphas, the high priest, Jesus declares: "Soon you will see the Son of Man seated at the right hand of the Power and coming on the clouds of heaven." He is accused of blasphemy and sentenced to death. He is spit at, hit, and insulted as a prophet, as the Messiah, taunted and held bound. Outside, Peter is vehemently denying that he even knows him. He meets Jesus' eyes for a moment and goes to weep bitterly, disappearing from the story.

Jesus is taken to Pilate, and Judas regrets his action, trying to give back the silver. He confesses his sin but is rejected, and he hangs himself. He too disappears from the story, except as a memory. Jesus, standing before Pilate, is silent. It is the custom to release a prisoner on the feast. The choice: Barabbas, a murderer, or Jesus, the prophet of life? Even Pilate's wife has a dream about Jesus, the holy man, and she exhorts her husband to have nothing to do with his death. Even in dreams Jesus is upsetting. But the crowd cries out for the death penalty: "Crucify him." Pilate is afraid of a riot; the city is packed with people, and he cannot afford that. The crowd becomes a mob. So the responsibility is laid on the people, and Pilate washes his hands of the whole affair. Jesus is handed over to the soldiers and is publicly scourged: his flesh torn by rawhide tipped with metal. Later he is wrapped in a military cloak and crowned with thorns. He is insulted in his pain, tormented, and led to crucifixion.

One man helps Jesus, conscripted into service, a Cyrenian named Simon, who carries his cross. Then he is crucified, his clothes divided among his executioners. Above his head hang the words: "This is Jesus, King of the Jews"—a terrible follow-up to "This is Jesus, the prophet from Nazareth in Galilee." He is taunted by the crowd to show his power, to save himself. But where are his disciples, friends, followers, those whom he cured and forgave? Where are they? Where have they all disappeared to?

Jesus' words "My God, my God, why have you forsaken me?" are words of prayer. The earth reacts violently. The curtain of the Temple is torn in two from top to bottom. There is an earthquake. The soldiers are terrified, and one makes the declaration of faith that belongs to Matthew's community: "Clearly this was the Son of God!" Jesus is dead.

Many women, among them Mary Magdalene, Mary the mother of James and Joseph, and Mary the mother of James and John, come and with Joseph of Arimathea they take the body down, wrap it, and put it in the tomb. Two of the women remain, keeping watch, sitting there, facing the tomb. The tomb is secured by guards because there are some who remember his words about rising. A seal of the Roman government is placed upon the tomb. Jesus disappears into the ground.

The way of Jesus is the way of the cross, which leads to rejection, the experience of injustice, becoming a victim, and finally death. Life is the only gift we have to offer to God in worship and in compassion to one another. This week we gather it up, take it in our hands to offer it, with Jesus and the body of Christ, the church, back to the Father, praying with the power of the Spirit:

> But you, O Lord, be not far from us; O my help, hasten to aid us.
> We will proclaim your name to our brothers and sisters; in the midst
> of the assembly we will praise you: You who fear the Lord, praise
> him; all you descendants of Jesus Christ, give glory to God.

Our attitude must be that of Christ. This week we learn how to empty ourselves as we listen to and tell the story of Jesus. It is a dangerous story, full of risk and resurrection, for those who believe.

Monday of Holy Week

Isaiah 42:1-7
John 12:1-11

This reading from Isaiah is God's account of Jesus, borrowed from times past. Jesus is the servant upheld by God, chosen, the One who pleases God well. God's own spirit is upon him, and he comes to bring justice to the nations. But the way he comes provokes crisis—

> Not crying out, not shouting,
>   not making his voice heard in the street.
> A bruised reed he shall not break,
>   and a smoldering wick he shall not quench,
> Until he establishes justice on the earth;
>   the coastlands will wait for his teaching.

Jesus did not compete with the voices of the world. His path is instead one of tender regard for the weak and the broken, those nearly lost from exhaustion or being ignored, those spent from the struggle and exertion. He is full of care, compassion, tenderness as he heals, strengthens, and nourishes others. He works in the world nonviolently, on the side of the oppressed.

God, the creator and sustainer, has called Jesus for the victory of justice, forming him and setting him as a covenant and a light for all nations. His work is to open the eyes of the blind and bring light to those who live in darkness. His power has been poured into those who have needed the power of God in the face of other powers arrayed against them. It is the work of self-sacrifice, reconciliation, and restoring the broken pieces of people and parts of the world. This reading is a primer in how to fight evil in the world: nonviolently, resisting evil but tending to those who are its victims first, choosing not to harm, even if that means falling into harm's way.

The responsorial psalm and its refrain, "The Lord is my light and my salvation" (Psalm 27), keeps our priorities straight in these last few days of Jesus' mission. We are asked if we live the way Jesus lived. Whom do we fear? Is the Lord our life's refuge? Do we trust God when there is opposition, resistance, and confusion, when we find we have enemies because of our belief in and practice of good news for others? Do we wait for the Lord with courage? Are we stouthearted? Are we waiting for the Lord and aiding his coming in our place and time?

The reading from John is a continuation of Jesus' raising of Lazarus from the dead. Jesus comes to Bethany, Lazarus's village, and he decides to spend his last sabbath meal with Mary, Martha, and Lazarus. The three of them throw a banquet for Jesus and, it seems, Martha sends away her slaves and maid-servants and waits on Jesus and the others herself. She has become a servant-disciple in gratitude for her brother's life and in response to Jesus' call to belief. At table, Mary also shows her gratitude. She takes a pound of costly perfume and anoints Jesus' feet and dries his feet with her hair so that the ointment fills the whole house with its scent.

This is a ritual act with images of incense, anointing, and worship. Kings, prophets, and priests were anointed. Jesus is all of these and more. The prayer of praise and thanksgiving rises and spreads through the house. It is the sabbath meal, the time of remembering God's bringing the people out of Egypt and sojourning with them in the desert. It is a time of deep silence, intimacy, feeding on the spirit of God, and hope among friends who long for the coming of the Spirit of God. There is singing and feasting and communion with one another and God.

But there is division even in Jesus' community. Judas protests that the perfume could have been sold. It would have brought three hundred silver pieces (he'll betray Jesus for just thirty!), and then the money could have been given to the poor. The perfume was worth a whole year's wages. One act of gratitude, of worship, of kindness—lavish by any standards. Jesus' reaction is swift: "Leave her alone. Let her keep it against the day they prepare me for burial. The poor you always have with you, but me you will not always have." It is an oft-quoted verse, but just as often misunderstood.

First, "Leave her alone." Leave alone anyone who cares for another, in public especially, in community, in church. Let people express gratitude, affection, worship, even if their expression seems outrageous, wild, a waste of money. Why? She will need to know that she did something for Jesus; when he is dead and buried she cannot express her love and gratefulness to him. Mary must have heard the rumors. After all, now they want to kill her brother too, because too many believe in Jesus because of what he has done for Lazarus. The cords of the net are being drawn tighter, and her awareness has perhaps made her move beyond her familiar expressions. Jesus is proclaiming that she is performing an act of mercy: preparing him for burial (one of the seven corporal works of mercy).

But it is the last line—"the poor you always have with you"—that has often caused trouble. Some interpret it as meaning that fighting poverty is a losing battle. Or that God must want some people poor. Or that what we do for God is more important than any other work we do. But these interpretations reveal a lack of understanding of who Jesus is and what Jesus has preached and practiced all his life.

His work is healing, comforting, raising from the dead, welcoming strangers, taking care of the needy, forgiving enemies, bringing hope to others. He is, as Thomas Merton writes, "mercy within mercy within mercy." Sometimes this story and particularly this phrase is referred to as John's version of Matthew's sheep and goats parable: "Whatever you do to the least of your brothers and sisters you do to me and whatever you refuse to do for them, you neglect to do for me" (Matthew 25). It is as though Jesus is saying: "I am poor. I am already rejected, plotted against, betrayed by my own. I will be left alone by my friends and those I cherished as my followers. I will be brutally beaten, mangled, cursed, mocked, and murdered. I am as poor as any one you will ever know or meet. She has done me a kindness, been merciful to me now while she could. You will not always have me with you to be in my company and feast with, be familiar with, and so I give you a gift— the poor. They will always be with you, for I am always with them, and whatever you want to do for me, do for them. As grateful as you are, as lavish as you wish to be in response to my love for you, do it for them. If you would think nothing of wasting a year's wages on worship of me in incense, flowers, prayers, whatever, then be that lavish in food, clothes, medicine, dignity, acceptance, even a decent burial if that is what they are in need of." The poor we will always have with us, and that is where we find God most surely, in need, in flesh that struggles to survive in the face of brutality and laws that crush rather than free and lift up.

St. Teresa has a simple prayer that states Jesus' point:

Christ has no body now on earth but yours, no hands but yours, no feet but yours. Yours are the eyes through which he must look out with compassion on the world. Yours are the feet with which he is to go about doing good. Yours are the hands with which he is to bless all others now.

This is John's community. The poor are not to be ignored or left unfed. The honor of God is seen in the same breath as the care of the needy, the works of mercy as prayer rising like incense before God and filling the whole house with its scent. Although there is dissension, smallness of heart, and meanness of spirit in the community, there must also be those who stand up for others, care for the poor, and work against injustice. Taunts and insults cannot be allowed to stand. Those who imitate Judas in being selfish and indignant at the care of others must be confronted and put in their place. The poor are our lifeline with Jesus, our root back into community and into the body of Christ. Even within our communities we must be careful that worship is truthful and intimately connected to the suffering of the body of Christ today.

There is a poem by Bishop Pedro Casaldáliga, bishop of São Felix de Arguaia, Brazil, translated by John Medcalf, which says in part what we need to face this day as we seek to honor God in Jesus, living in communion and solidarity with the poor, and facing the way of the cross as we live.

> Plant your pilgrim footprints like kisses of fiery
>   solidarity upon the flesh of mother Earth.
> Fix your eyes, warm with the sunsets, like oil-lamps
>   crouching in the universal vigil of time.
>
> Cardinals of Rome,
> still my brothers:
> What are we
> if we are not a living Passover?
> What do we celebrate
> if we do not celebrate all the world's blood in each
>   Mass?
> Take not from me the martyrs' blood
> brimming the chalice that nourishes my courage.
> If you remove the supreme blood witness,
> what will be left for the poor of the South?
>
> Cursed be the cross that decorates the wall of an
>   oppressor's bank,
> or that presides behind an unfeeling throne, within a
>   coat-of-arms,
> above an enticing cleavage, before the eyes of fear.
>
> Cursed be the cross thrust by the mighty on the poor,
> in the name of God, perhaps.
> Cursed be the cross that the Church justifies
> —in the name of Christ, perhaps—
> instead of burning in the flames of prophecy.

Cursed be the cross that cannot be the Cross.
Make sure that grace and tenderness fill with new wine
    your earthen vessel.

Or, as a voice from the past, St. Bridget of Ireland, has said it:

I should like a great lake of beer for the King of Kings.
I should like the angels of Heaven to be drinking it
    through time eternal.
I should like excellent meats of belief and pure piety.
I should like flails of penance at my house.
I should like the men of Heaven at my house;
I should like barrels of peace at their disposal;
I should like vessels of charity for distribution;
I should like cheerfulness to be in their drinking.
I should like Jesus to be there among them.
I should like the three Marys of illustrious renown to
    be with us.
I should like the people of heaven, the poor, to be
    gathered around us from all parts.

Very pragmatic, this mixing of worship and the work of the king-dom of God in the world. Whatever thankfulness we owe to God this day, we could give to the poor, knowing that we will be defended by Jesus too: "Leave her alone! Leave him alone! They will get to keep it against the day of my burial."

Tuesday of Holy Week

Isaiah 49:1-6
John 13:21-33, 36-38

These next two days are hard ones. The readings deal with being a prophet of God and with being betrayed by one's friends. The first reading reveals the prophet's agony of spirit, bordering on despair, but clinging to God, hoping that, even in the face of suffering and

death, the will of God will somehow be done. The gospel relates
stories of actual betrayal as experienced within the community, what
goes on between Jesus and Judas, and between Jesus and Simon Peter. (We are left with our own thoughts about how all this affects the
rest of the disciples.)

Isaiah proclaims his vocation:

> Hear me, O coastlands,
>   listen, O distant peoples.
> The Lord called me from birth,
>   from my mother's womb he gave me my name.
> He made me a sharp-edged sword
>   and concealed me in the shadow of his arm.
> He made me a polished arrow,
>   in his quiver he hid me.
> You are my servant, he said to me,
>   Israel, through whom I show my glory.

Prophets belong to no people or nation, because they are sent to
all peoples. Their entire identity, found in their name, is rooted in
God. Even before time, before consciousness, they are bound. Their
lives are to interrupt others' lives, to pierce through shallowness and
superficiality, and to expose ruthlessly what is evil and what is hypocrisy in culture and people, especially religious and political leaders. There is power, force, even a sense of violence in what they are
and what they do. The image of the arrow that cuts through flesh,
down to bone, and the imagery of swiftness are powerful. Once the
arrow is set in motion there is no way to deflect it from its target.
And the aim is always direct and precise, for it comes from God.

We, the people who hear prophetic words, usually respond by seeking the death of the prophet. But in reality it is the prophet who is
the death of us, unless we acknowledge the truth in the accusations
and repent. A prophet is sent for life, for salvation, a last resort by
God to a stiff-necked people.

Isaiah, like all prophets, cries out, "Though I thought I had toiled
in vain, and for nothing, uselessly, spent my strength, yet my reward
is with the Lord, my recompense is with my God." The prophets
dwell alone, isolated from others by the truth and the intensity and
single-heartedness of their focus on God's will. But the prophets' faith
is as strong as their words and message, and they proclaim that they

will be made glorious in the sight of God, for God is their strength! No one and no group can prevail against prophets because no one can prevail against God for long.

Even when the prophet is destroyed, the word is still the arrow of God as it travels through time and history. Its power grows. In Isaiah, the message goes from being one of gathering the scattered believers in the covenant to making that remnant a light to the nations in order that God's saving grace can reach to the ends of the earth. God's word cannot be blunted by our response of killing the messenger. In fact, the prophet's self-sacrifice feeds the thrust of God in history. Isaiah is the suffering servant prophet, the image of Jesus.

The psalms were every Jew's daily prayer, and they were the prayer and mainstay of Jesus' life. As we pray Psalm 71, we can pray it with Jesus in the days of closeness, betrayal, and conscious awareness of the evil building around him:

> "In your justice rescue me, and deliver me;
> incline your ear to me, and save me.
> O my God, rescue me from the hand of the wicked."

This is a prayer filled with confusion yet trust, fear yet hope, awareness of what others can and will do to us and yet belief that God will bear our shame with us and provide strength. We are asked only to give glory to God ceaselessly, as we have been called to do since our births, even in our mother's womb.

John's gospel begins to prepare us for what is to come. Jesus reclines at table, and he grows deeply troubled, giving this testimony: "I tell you solemnly, one of you will betray me." This causes puzzlement, consternation: Whom could Jesus mean? It seems the disciples are so wrapped up in themselves that they are unaware of what is happening. Peter asks John, "the disciple whom Jesus loved," to find out to whom he is referring. There is an intimacy between these two that can be relied upon, and when questioned, Jesus replies with a ritual gesture, common in his day. He takes a bit of food and dips it into the dish and gives it to Judas.

It was a custom among tribes for either host or guest, or one of two close friends, to take a piece of bread or meat and dip it in oil or wine and feed it to the other as a sign of closeness, of kinship. In fact, once a person had eaten at table in a Bedouin's camp and shared food he literally was considered kin for the seventy-two hours that the food shared was in his body, bound even closer than by blood ties. Judas takes the food, and even bound as close as that to Jesus, he intends to betray him.

Jesus speaks directly to him: "Be quick about what you are to do." It is a command, and the others at table have no idea what is transpiring between them. Judas eats the food from the hand of Jesus and goes out. The gospel says simply: "It was night."

Then Jesus once again tries to tell his disciples what has happened: "Now is the Son of Man glorified and God is glorified in him." That is the theological premise. The hour of reckoning, the hour of glory, the hour of the crucifixion is here; in suffering and dying as a human being with graceful endurance and forgiveness God will be glorified. There is to be separation, loss, anguish, death, sadness at being torn apart physically and deeply, at the level of the wound of the heart. "My children, I am not to be with you much longer. You will look for me, but I say to you now: where I am going, you cannot come."

It is Peter who asks, "Where are you going?" Jesus looks at him and says simply: "I am going where you cannot follow me now; later on you shall come after me." Jesus is going to the cross, but also going to his Father, returning home through a breach that is torn in his very flesh, a tear that will rip the Temple curtain asunder and open a door in history's time that will alter everything before and after. And Peter insists that he be able to come with Jesus and that he will, in fact, lay down his life for Jesus, if necessary.

We can almost see Jesus looking at Peter, who does not know himself at all, who is totally unaware of his own weaknesses and unaware of the power of the evil arrayed against Jesus. Ruefully, Jesus says: "You will lay down your life for me, will you? I tell you truly, the cock will not crow before you have three times disowned me!" Peter's "cocksure" attitude is shattered by his statement of utter betrayal, loss of nerve, lies, and fear—all that is within Peter's faltering heart.

The reading ends here, leaving us to deal with our own communities: the Judases, the Peters, and all the other silent, listening, watching witnesses. Perhaps there is one lone figure that is more intimate with Jesus than the others, who knows more of what is happening. Who are we? Where do we stand with Jesus in these few days before his death? Are we closely aligned with him, or are we still unaware of our betrayals, our shallowness? Do we assert our strong egos and confidence in ourselves rather than humbly listening to the Word, who tells us: "Oh, you will lay down your life for me, will you? I tell you truly, the cock will not crow before you have three times disowned me!"

The prophets, Jesus included, are set on a course of fierce honesty that makes them fine teachers. These are the people who are the most threatening to society, to religious structures, and to human beings sure of their own worth. They are the ones who are fluent with justice, their language blunt and direct in hopes of averting disaster. So, Jesus uses his sharp-edged sword, his arrow, on Judas and Peter, but to no avail. Jesus, like John the Baptizer and all the prophets, was honed and formed in desert places prior to entering the cities. Now the time has come for the arrows to be loosed. But Jesus will die as he has lived, as one cut off, driven out, and as one who will not allow God's will to be forgotten or cast aside.

The stage is being set and Jesus knows and is an active part of what is happening, trying to warn Judas, trying to warn Peter and the others what they are facing in the hours ahead. We are being warned too. In 1985 Ryszard Kapuscinski wrote in *Warsaw Diary*: "Evil acts swiftly, violently, and with a sudden crushing force. The good works more closely, requiring time to reveal itself and bear witness. The good often arrives late. We are always on the lookout, always awaiting it."

Today we are called by Jesus to repentance, to intimacy. We are looked at and seen clearly, truthfully. We are all betrayers at heart. We have betrayed God in Jesus, betrayed our baptismal promises, betrayed our faith to the world, betrayed one another in community, betrayed the good news by refusing to forgive others though we expect forgiveness from God repeatedly. We are Peter—brash, blind, trusting in our own strengths, gifts, and knowledge, which are pitifully inadequate. We hear the truth and refuse to take it deep within us, at the same time making sure that we look good and say the right thing in front of others. We are Judas—intent on our own agenda, forcing the hand of God, not understanding the evil of others or of the structures that use individual weakness for their own ends. We are disciples—sitting at table with Jesus, content in our relationship with God, not wanting to hear because we are afraid, reluctant to stand with Jesus among those who stand for justice in the kingdom of God.

Jesus started picking up his cross long before it was laid on him by the soldiers at the time of his execution. Jesus carried the cross of his own friends' betrayals, lies, shallow hearts, misunderstandings of him and inability to love him or know him as Son of Man, Son of the Father, Jesus, prophet.

Today our prayer must be truthful: "Jesus, Lamb of God, you who take away the sins of the world, have mercy on us, for we are sinners." Perhaps we can grow into the awareness that Maryknoll Sister Ita Ford, one of the four American women killed in El Salvador in 1980, showed when she prayed:

> Am I willing to suffer with the people here, the suffering of the powerless, those who feel impotent? Can I say to my neighbors—I have no solutions to the situation, I don't know the answers, but I will walk with you, be with you? Can I let myself be evangelized by this opportunity? Can I look at and accept my own poorness and learn from other poor ones?

It is dark. It is night, but Jesus is still with us.

Wednesday of Holy Week

Isaiah 50:4-9
Matthew 26:14-25

This reading is, in part, the reading from Palm Sunday. It is the description of the Suffering Servant of Yahweh, of Jesus the crucified One. It speaks of extreme humility, humbled even unto death, death that is preceded by spitting, beating, public shame, degradation. But it is about strength and vindication too. The words are bold and forthright, especially if they are spoken in the midst of torture: "He is near who upholds my right; if anyone wishes to oppose me, let us appear together. Who disputes my right? Let him confront me. See, the Lord God is my help." This is the stance of a prophet reminding those who stand in opposition to his word and presence that God is witness to all that is occurring and that God remembers! God will speak in behalf of those who suffer and will uphold the rights of those enslaved, tortured, and killed. It is a courageous stand against the forces of evil even as evil seeks to stop the heart of the one who belongs to God.

Psalm 69 speaks of a closeness, a kinship with God. It expresses an understanding of why God does not intervene to save people in the face of persecution, and it reveals a steadfast sense of faithfulness. Can we pray like this? Have we even stood up for God's will and the poor often enough so that there would be any reason for us to be caught in this predicament of suffering for the honor of God or the cause of justice?

"For your sake I bear insult,
and shame covers my face.
I have become an outcast to my brothers,
a stranger to my mother's sons.
Because zeal for your house consumes me, and the
    insults of those who blaspheme you fall upon me."

Jesus' zeal for his Father's house, the Temple, has caused him to drive the money changers out, but zeal for his Father's house, the community of the covenant, has caused him to side with the ones who have fallen through the cracks of society and religious institutions; to heal and aid those who are ill, despised, and insulted; and to keep company with sinners. His revelation of God contradicts the practice and images of the "religious" ones, and they go after him.

The psalm lists what evil people can do to those who threaten their shallow images of God: They put gall in his food, and in his thirst he is given vinegar to drink. There is no one to comfort him. He is isolated and condemned to suffer and die alone, cursed by human beings, laughed at or ignored by religious people. But the prayer is definitely the prayer of Jesus: "I will praise the name of God in song, and I will glorify him with thanksgiving: 'See, you lowly ones, and be glad; you who seek God, may your hearts be merry! For the Lord hears the poor, and his own who are in bonds he spurns not.'"

This is a prayer of encouragement to others who suffer. And the response praises and acknowledges what must not be forgotten: "Lord, in your great love, answer me." God is love, and it is love that sustains. This prayer takes us beyond our pain into God's heart.

The story is told again of the betrayal of Jesus by Judas. This time the account is from Matthew. We must listen again and let it pierce our hearts. Before the Passover Judas goes to the authorities and asks what they are willing to give him if he hands Jesus over to them. This is a business transaction, a deal. Jesus is a commodity, and money changes hands.

Meanwhile, Jesus is making his own plans for the Passover meal, sending his disciples on ahead into the city to arrange a house for dinner. An anonymous donor lends Jesus his house. And dinner begins. As it grows dark, literally and figuratively, Jesus speaks: "I give you my word, one of you is about to betray me." The rest of the group is distressed and each asks Jesus the same question: "Surely it is not I, Lord?" This is the question each of us must ask of God in the presence of the community this week.

The ritual gesture of dipping in the same dish with Jesus takes place. In this account Jesus adds harsh words: "The Son of Man is departing, as Scripture says of him, but woe to that man by whom the Son of Man is betrayed. Better for him if he had never been born."

Terrible words. And they are not just about Judas. They are about all of us who have betrayed our faith, sometimes in small ways, unaware of the consequences on others and on our own faltering souls, and sometimes in larger ways that have caused others to sin, to lose heart, or to participate with others in violence and evil. When Judas asks, along with the others: "Surely it is not I, Rabbi?" he receives the answer that none of us ever wants to hear or admit to: "It is you who have said it." Even in Jesus' answer there is an open door, a chance to change. Nothing is set. And the gospel stops here. "It is you who have said it." We are sinners. Now what are we going to do?

We must look at ourselves clearly, with the eye of God. We claim to love God. We claim to follow Jesus as Lord on the way of the cross. We claim to belong to the kingdom of God's justice and peace. We claim to resist evil and refuse to be mastered by sin. We claim to live in the freedom of the children of God.

The phrase "love is blind" is often spoken glibly. Perhaps we are attempting to avoid responsibility for what we do to those we claim to love. But, as G. K. Chesterton wrote: "Love is not blind; that is the last thing it is. Love is bound: and the more it is bound the less it is blind." We are bound to God and to one another in God; all that we do affects others. When we sin against God, we sin against one another. We are accountable to the community for what we do personally.

In the same way, what we do or do not do as a community makes us accountable for much of what the world does. The seeds of the world's hatred and violence and lack of belief in God are found in our faithlessness. Instead of being a light to the nations, often we are just another sound in a cacophony.

When I was in Ireland a few years ago I was driving on a back country road and listening to the radio. There had been a short-story writing contest. To make the contest more of a challenge, the story was limited to around thirty words. They were reading some of the entries over the radio, and I was half listening, concentrating more on driving on the correct side of the road and not running into the stone walls that seemed all too close. Then this story was read.

> Welcome home, son!
> Hello, father.
> It is so good to see you. It's been a long time.
> Yes, father, a very long time. It was hard.
> Hard as nails. Hard as wood.
> I know. What was the hardest?
> The kiss, Father, the kiss. (*long pause*)
> Yes. Come in and let me hold you.

I nearly drove off the road. Within seconds I was crying and had to pull over. It hit me hard. I was overwhelmed by the realization that sin is evil and terrible, but some sin is more evil and more terrible: the sin of those who claim to be friends, disciples, companions. My sin, and the sin of the communities I was a part of, the sin of the church were the most devastating of all, like that kiss.

That night, as I sat under a great tree in an old abandoned monastery reading poetry, I came across this line: "Let your heart melt towards me, just as the ice that melts in spring leaves no trace of its chill" (Kokinshu). It was the remedy for the morning's aching pain. And a few days later I was listening to a Buddhist monk in exile from Vietnam speak. A piece I managed to jot down seemed connected as well: "No argument. No reason. No blame. Just understanding which leads to love" (Thich Nhat Hanh).

This is the way God is with all of us. Today, as individual Christians and as the church we pray: "Lord, in your great love, answer us." Today we are all called to be reconciled to one another so that the body of Christ, whole and in communion, can celebrate the Triduum together. All of us, together with the catechumens, are to meet together at the door of the church, forgiven and reconciled, to enter into the mystery of our salvation, belief, and freedom as the children of God.

Officially, today is the last day of Lent. Our journey is complete. Now we go to celebrate Easter. Alexander Schmemann, a great liturgical scholar, writes:

> Even though we are baptized, what we constantly lose and betray is precisely that which we receive at baptism. Therefore, Easter is our return every year to our own baptism, whereas Lent is our preparation for that return—the slow and sustained effort to perform, at the end, our own passage into new life in Christ. . . . Each Lent and Easter are, once again, the rediscovery and the recovery by us of what we were made through our own baptismal death and resurrection.

Mystery now comes over us and we disappear into it, much as Peter, James, and John disappeared into the cloud that overshadowed Jesus at the transfiguration. For our part, we must make sure that all that is evil or half-hearted within us disappears in our desire to walk the way of the cross with Jesus and come home to the Father, to the kingdom, and to the community of those who seek the company of Jesus.

Holy Thursday
Mass of the Lord's Supper

Exodus 12:1-8, 11-14
1 Corinthians 11:23-26
John 13:1-15

Today is often called the feast of friends, the friends of God. But it is also a night of "re-membering," of putting back together the body of Christ, the church, the community of those who gather around the story (the word) and the bread (the flesh and blood) and become what they eat. The Jews begin Passover with the story. The youngest asks the question: Why is this night different from all others?

The ritual of Passover tells the story of terror and death, when the Angel of God passed over the doorways marked with the blood of the sacrificed lamb, and also about the wonder and marvelous works that God did for the chosen people in leading them out of Egypt, away from slavery and repression, through the desert of Sinai, and into the promised land. The ritual ends with the passionate cry: "Next year in Jerusalem!" a blessing and fervent prayer for the fullness of the promises set in motion so long ago.

Remembering is the essence of the ritual. It makes present in history the story and the promises. What God did in ages past for the chosen ones, God will do now for those gathered at table. The story continues in every generation. God waits for us to come.

This is the ritual that the Holy Thursday Mass is based upon, and yet there is more, for Jesus made significant changes in the ritual on the night before he died. We celebrate this night in the shadow of betrayal. It is a bittersweet night of intimacy, gifts given, and love expressed.

The first reading begins with the account of the rite that is to be celebrated as a memorial in the first month of the Jewish calendar. It details the ritual slaying of the lamb, which is to be shared by a family alone or with other households so that the entire lamb is consumed. The lamb is slaughtered during the evening twilight, with the whole assembly of Israel as witness. Those who are to eat together take some of the blood of the lamb and mark their doorposts and the lintel of every house. How they are to eat the meal is specified: the foods are the lamb roasted, unleavened bread, and bitter herbs to remind them of preparation in haste and the bitter, long years of slavery and oppression when they could not worship their God. They eat the meal standing, with their belts and bags around their waists, sandals on their feet, and staff in hand, "like those who are in flight." Because they are. They are in flight from death, from slavery.

This is the Passover of the Lord, because on this night God will go through Egypt and strike down the firstborn, human and beast alike, executing judgment on all the gods of Egypt. This is a night of listening, believing, and clinging to others in fear and hope. It is a night of death that is the prelude to the beginning of life for a whole people. "Seeing the blood, I will pass over you; and no destructive blow will come upon you." The sight of the blood, seeping deep into the wood of the lintels of the doorways, is the mark and sign of salvation. And salvation is about bread, justice, and hope. This day is a memorial feast, a perpetual institution that all generations are commanded to remember, to celebrate the coming of the power of God into the world with freedom and lasting justice for those who cry out for help.

The images of unleavened bread, the lamb of God, and the blood marking those saved are woven through the Christian ritual as well, and yet they are more personal because the bread, the lamb, and the blood are the person and body of Jesus and what we become: the body of Christ in the world, a source of freedom and hope in the midst of terror and death for all who cry out to God.

We remember the dying and the rising of Jesus and on this night, his last meal with his friends, and his gift to them: his own flesh and blood. This memory is steeped in forgiveness, reconciliation, and atonement for the sins of the past, and rebirth. This night is a meal among friends, the sacrifice of the Lamb on the cross, and the resurrection—all braided into one reality. Johannes Metz calls this story the dangerous memory of the passion of Christ. It is dangerous and subversive, because what is seen as judgment and death by some is believed to be salvation and life by others. We must remember this night that the words "body of Christ" describe the eucharist and us, the people of God; we are to become bread for the world with the bread that we share this night.

It is not just the bread that is this rich source of strength and sustenance, it is also the blood. The psalm response sings: "Our blessing-cup is a communion with the blood of Christ" (Psalm 116). This reminds us what we are to do with our lives so that the ritual gestures of our worship are truly expressive of our self-giving. We are to make a return to the Lord for all the good that God has done for us. We are to take up the cup of salvation and call upon the name of the Lord—and we are to drink the cup of wine, blood, suffering, and salvation.

There is an immediate connection between eucharist and death: "Precious in the eyes of the Lord is the death of his faithful ones." All of our deaths are one in the dying of Jesus. All of us are servants, sons and daughters whose bonds have been loosed by our God, and so we offer a sacrifice of thanksgiving, vowing our lives to the Lord in the presence of one another. Our blessing-cup taken and shared proclaims that we trust in the blood that heals and reconciles the aches and wounds of the world caused by sin, evil, injustice, and violent hatred. The blood of Christ is poured into our wounds and we heal, scarred over and mindful of the suffering, but able to understand the pain of those who suffer unjustly and to share in their struggle to be free and whole. St. Paul reminds us: "I have been crucified with Christ. . . . I carry the marks of Jesus branded on my body" (Galatians 2:19; 6:17). In this ritual of eating and drinking with Jesus, we are in Christ, not just repeating his sacrifice and modeling our lives on his, but living in the wounds and heart and very body of Christ, together.

In the short, dense reading from Paul's letter to the Corinthians we are told to remember and to pass on what we have received from the Lord, exactly as we have been given it. The words, actions, and intent are all important. The setting is the night of betrayal. The movement of worship and thanksgiving to God is the offering. The priest takes bread, gives thanks, breaks it apart, and says: "This is my body, which is for you. Do this in remembrance of me." The cup is offered with the words: "This cup is the new covenant in my blood. Do this, whenever you drink it, in remembrance of me."

This is the core of our worship, lives, communities, and sacrifices, the core of our meaning as Christians. In eating the bread and drinking the cup we proclaim the death of the Lord until he comes! In remembering we are saved, the world is saved, the truth is told, the power of death is undone, and love is set loose in the midst of betrayal. There is really no way to explain this short passage; it is learned in living and understood in self-sacrifice, serving others, and remembering all that was taught to us by the words and works of Jesus.

The gospel continues the story. The ritual is based upon the lived experience of Jesus in the world, with his disciples and those who came to believe in him. In John's gospel there is no specific ritual of the breaking of the bread and the sharing of the cup at the Last Supper. Instead, there is another eucharistic ritual, another telling of the story: the ritual of the washing of the feet of the disciples by Jesus. Both rituals are rooted in the same reality. For John's community— and for all the church—getting down on our knees in humble obedience, following Jesus' example of a lifetime of serving and performing those tasks that are needed in the world, is remembering Jesus, putting him back into our communities and uniting us as a holy people belonging to God.

The story is simple. Jesus intends to show his disciples how much he has loved them before he leaves them. He will love them and us to the end, as he passes through the doors of bloody death returning to his Father. So first, he stoops, bending before them, reversing the relationships. He, the master, washes their feet. This is the way to honor God, by honoring one another, and especially those among us in need of healing, care, and tenderness, let alone justice, freedom, and hope of living at long last as human beings.

Jesus comes to Simon Peter. Sometimes we read just the name Simon—his name before he met and encountered Jesus. At other times it is simply Peter—who he is after being converted to Jesus and the kingdom. And at other times, like tonight, it is Simon Peter, where he is of both minds and hearts, acting more as he was before he followed Jesus, yet in the presence of Jesus, who renamed him. He resists: "Lord, are you going to wash my feet?" And Peter is told that he does not understand what Jesus does to him and for him in this gesture of obedience and submission. He resists more forcefully: "You will never wash my feet!" Jesus is patient and yet persistent: "If I don't wash you, you will have no share in my heritage." It is time for Peter to reconsider, and when he does he lunges forward in his typical way: "Not only my feet, but my hands and head as well."

Our society is out of touch with such rituals of hospitality, welcome, service, and honor, and so the depth of what is happening and the reasoning behind Peter's outburst often go unrealized. Washing a person's feet was onerous work. People wore, at most, sandals in a world of heat, loose garbage, and animal droppings. People's feet were crusted, smelly, and repulsive, and even worse if they were diseased or had sores. Even husbands could not demand that their wives wash their feet. It was something that was necessary, but it was done as a courtesy, an honor for a guest arriving in a host's house, or in love, affection, dedication, or service, expressing a relationship of obedience and submission freely given. Sometimes disciples washed their master's feet, an honor that expressed a level of trust and intimacy between the two, but never did the master wash the disciples' feet. Never! This is more than the reversal of fortunes so often spoken of and proclaimed in the good news. This is a reversal of what constitutes worship of God. Submission, obedience, service, bending before others is bending before God, because now, in the mystery of the incarnation, we do indeed bend before God when we serve one another's needs and tend to one another's wounds.

The way the story is told, Judas is mentioned twice: once at the beginning, already intending to hand Jesus over; and again, in his effect on the community: "not all are washed clean." But there is the sense that Judas is present and that he, too, has his feet washed. Jesus bends before him humbly, touching his feet, knowing that he himself will be handled more roughly because of the callousness and treachery of this man he has called his friend. Whom do we refuse to bend before, knowing what they have done, what they intend to do to us? Whom do we resist when they come before us to serve? Whom would we rather not bend before and wash their feet? All must be included in this intimate gesture that takes place around the table of the Lord.

After washing their feet, Jesus reclines once again at the table and asks them: "Do you understand what I just did for you? You address me as 'Teacher' and 'Lord,' and fittingly enough, for that is what I am. But if I washed your feet—I who am your Teacher and Lord—then you must wash each other's feet. What I just did was to give you an example: as I have done, so you must do." This ritual is not just a momentary or one-time experience to impress upon the disciples the depth of the Jesus' love for them. It is a moment that ritualizes and intensifies his entire life and the love that is at the root of all his actions.

This night is about bread and wine, about bodies and blood, about feet and washing, about intimacy and unbounded, unexpected love, about a God who bends before us hoping that one day we will treat each other with the same regard and dignity that he has always lavished upon us. This is what the new covenant is about. This is what worship is about. This is what reality and religion are about. This is what community and love are about.

Some theologians and preachers say that basically Jesus was killed because of the way he ate, whom he ate with, and what he encouraged them to do with one another as sign of their allegiance to him and to the kingdom of his Father.

There is an old story told among Zen teachers.

✝ Once upon a time there was a family, the relatives of a poor sick samurai, who were dying of hunger. They approached Eisai's temple, and the good monk there took the golden halo off the image of the Buddha and gave it to them, telling them to go and sell it and buy food for themselves and find shelter. When others heard about it there was the cry of "Sacrilege!" What reckless and dangerous behavior! What kind of precedent was set for the temples!

But the monk calmly reminded them of the story of the Chinese master Tanka, who burned a wooden image to warm himself. And he preached to them: Buddha's mind is full of love and mercy. If the Buddha had heard the plight of these people, why, he would have cut off a limb if that would have helped them in their pain! What's a halo or anything else that's available in the face of human beings' suffering and need?

We are invited to eat and drink at the table of the Lord, to have our feet washed, to enter the wounds and heart of Christ, to be as his beloved friends. And we are told to do as Jesus did. We must wash each other's feet. Jesus expressed his love in service to the world. Now that is our task.

Good Friday
The Passion of the Lord

Isaiah 52:13-53:12
Hebrews 4:14-16, 5:7-9
John 18:1-19:42

The long portion from Isaiah is a lament, a commentary on the suffering that we can endure at one another's hands. It tells the anguished story of all those tortured, persecuted, and subjected to violence. It is brutal and unrelenting as it seeks to break past our defenses and inertia and touch our belief and hearts.

It is very effective when read by a number of people slowly and solemnly, as one would read the names of the dead in a litany of remembrance. The last portion must be proclaimed with confidence; it is the announcement of belief and faith even in the face of the hideous destruction of a human being. It acknowledges the one who suffers and his undying hope in God in his sufferings, and it proclaims that this kind of suffering redeems and justifies others. In bearing others' guilt Jesus endures death but takes away the sins of many and wins pardon for the offenses of others.

This day is not just about Jesus' suffering and death, a legal but unjust execution. It is about us and our share in his sacrifice in behalf of others. We share in the blessings that result from the suffering of Christ, and we must be sure that we do not contribute to or allow the destruction of others.

We are mortal. We will die, but death does not define us. It is built into the structure of our lives, institutions, and relationships, but what defines us is life, life born of witness to and sharing in the life of Christ. Because Jesus has suffered with us, sharing in our human mortality and our connection to one another, all suffering can be etched in dignity and given the power of God in Jesus.

Commitment to the kingdom of Jesus, to the person of Jesus, invariably places us at the heart of the suffering of the world. Do we choose to ease the suffering and take down human beings from their crosses, resisting those who would destroy others? Or do we stand with those who see violence toward others as a viable strategy? We must choose.

Today we are confronted with the cross. It is held up for us to look at, to bend before and honor and kiss, to share its power to redeem. We are invited to sink into the mystery of a crucified God whose love shares even in the brutality we visit upon one another yet cries out NO! God suffered in Jesus, but God continues to suffer in millions of people caught in the forces of hate. We must confront the cross and Christ in those among us who suffer.

After such a description of evil, we need silence in which to situate ourselves with the victims, with God in Jesus, and to make sure that we are not allied with those who kill or profit from the death and suffering of others. Then, and only then, can we pray "Father, I put my life in your hands." We must remember all those who are forgotten, all those who are broken, all those who fall into the clutches of their enemies and persecutors. We commend ourselves and them to God, vowing with God's help to rescue them, to have courage and hope in the Lord by standing with Jesus, the crucified One, in spirit and in the flesh of others in history. Our ritual and our prayer must proclaim what we intend to do with our energy and power, with our united spirits and the power of God in Jesus, who put his life in the hands of God while the hands of hate nailed him down and marked the wood with his blood.

The letter to the Hebrews tells us our high priest sympathizes with our weakness and was tempted in every way, yet never sinned. We can confidently approach the throne of grace—the cross—to receive mercy and favor and find help in time of need. We are reminded that Christ suffered as we do and yet offered supplications in his agony with tears and loud cries to God. And he was heard, as the cry of the poor and the prophet alike are heard, especially because of his unfailing reverence and obedience to God. We are all human with Jesus, but human now in ways that confound the world and save it. We suffer because we are human and too often because of our sins and the sins of others. The consequences of sin are rampant in the world, affecting us all.

But we are reminded: "Son though he was, he learned obedience from what he suffered; and when perfected, he became the source of eternal salvation for all who obey him." We, the sons and daughters of the Father, the brothers and sisters of the crucified One, learn obedience from our sufferings. Some of us suffer very little, and others suffer terribly, without support or affirmation even from those who claim to share the company of Jesus. Suffering can destroy those without faith, but suffering bound to Jesus can redeem, give dignity to suffering, and restore others to life and holiness. All the pain and suffering of the world are bound in the flesh of Jesus. Once tied to his body and blood, we can disappear into the wounds of Jesus and know that we too "will see the light in the fullness of days."

John's account of the passion of Jesus is different from that of the other writers. It begins with the betrayal in the garden, where Jesus stands before the Roman soldiers and the Jewish Temple police and asks, "Whom are you looking for?" They fall back before him. His power is spiritual, not physical, and certainly not violent. He turns on Peter, who had drawn his sword, and tells him to put it up. He has chosen his way, and violence has no part in it. It is better, holier, to know pain rather than to inflict it on others. And so Jesus is bound and led away.

The trial follows, and Peter betrays Jesus three times vehemently, afraid for his own skin. Jesus is taken to Pilate, for his enemies are seeking the death penalty. Pilate interrogates Jesus, and Jesus is forthright and without subterfuge. When asked if he is a king, Jesus turns the question back on Pilate. And when questioned about his kingdom, he answers: "My kingdom does not belong to this world. If my kingdom were of this world, my subjects would be fighting to save me from being handed over to the Jews. As it is, my kingdom is not here." Jesus is a king, but radically different from anything the kingdoms of the world have ever seen or known. He continues: "It is you who say I am a king. The reason I was born, the reason why I came into the world, is to testify to the truth. Anyone committed to the truth hears my voice." This is the essence of Jesus, his person, work, relation to the Father, place in the world, and place in the realm of the Spirit. Truth. No matter what is done to him, he will speak and be the truth of God. He testifies. He witnesses to God. He is martyred for the truth. He is "disappeared."

Pilate is convinced by the people. He has Jesus scourged, crowned, and mocked by his soldiers. Then he questions Jesus again. This time the issue is power: Pilate's power to kill Jesus or let him live, and Jesus' power to lay down his life and let them kill him. Jesus' explanation is not easy to comprehend: "You would have no power over me whatever unless it were given you from above. That is why he who handed me over to you is guilty of the greater sin." The misuse of power is sin. The use of power to kill, to destroy is a sin. And when that power is misused by those who are connected religiously to Jesus, it is an even greater sin.

Finally Pilate hands Jesus over to be crucified, and crucified as king, between two others. His garments are divided among his executioners, but for his seamless cloak they throw dice.

There are witnesses in John's gospel: his mother, his mother's sister, Mary the wife of Clopas, Mary Magdalene, and John, the disciple that Jesus loved. His mother is given to the disciple and the disciple in turn is handed over to the mother. This is the new family of Jesus. And it is seamless, united, a universal family, symbolized by the inscription, which is written in Hebrew, Latin, and Greek. The relationships are intimate, defying blood or marriage ties. The ties are those of the blood of the cross, sacrifice, and being given to each other for care-taking.

Jesus thirsts and is offered wine with hyssop to drink. When he drinks, he speaks his last words: "It is finished." Then he bows his head and delivers over his spirit. His thirst has been constant all his life: for the will and honor of God, for the truth to be told and given a place of honor in the world, for the kingdom of God to come upon earth, for people who are believers. Now his work is done. His last gift to his father is his spirit, his life, his love: everything.

Immediately the world kicks in and tries to take over. It is the preparation day for the sabbath, and the Jews don't want the bodies left hanging there during the religious prayers and rites. So the legs of the others are broken to hasten their death. Because Jesus is already dead, his side is pierced by a lance and blood and water flow out. The church is born in that gushing forth of blood and water from the side of Jesus. With his last breath the Spirit of God was let loose in the world, free to seep into every corner and crevice of the universe. The resurrection has begun as Jesus' blood seeps into the earth and his breath disappears into the air. Jesus is buried quickly, with haste and no undue attention, wrapped in spices that weighed about a hundred pounds. He is buried in a garden, in a new tomb, and left. Jesus disappears into the earth. Jesus disappears into the arms and heart of his Father. It is done.

We gather to listen to the end, hear the story, kiss the cross, and pray for the entire world. We gather to stand silent before death, sin, and evil and to acknowledge our part in the destruction of Jesus and the continued destruction of human beings and the world that God has created. We stand at the foot of the cross as onlookers, witnesses, disciples—part of the new family of God, crucified, bound to each other in common shared grief and the exhortation to care for one another, especially for those who are broken and in need. We stand in the shadow of the cross, grieving but intent on not allowing this to continue. The cross is our salvation, but it is so much more.

We bear the cross with Christ. We are marked with its sign as saving grace and as belonging to the Son of Man, who was judged, condemned, and murdered. He will come again in glory to judge the living and the dead with justice born of suffering and obedience to God alone. We mark ourselves with the sign of the cross and begin and end our prayers with it. Ezekiel put a mark on the foreheads of all those who sought to honor God and who prayed in anguish over the abominations and sin committed in Jerusalem before the coming of judgment (Ezekiel 9:4). And the book of Revelation tells of the servants of God being sealed on their foreheads before the day of destruction and the coming of judgment (7:3). At our baptisms we are signed with oil, and those who bring us to the fount sign us with the cross, drawing us into the company of Christ.

Death can be tragic, horrible, and even meaningless. Jesus' violent death was expedient, useful, seen as necessary to the powers in control, contrived. He was betrayed, condemned through false witness, and executed according to the capital punishment laws of his days. It was legal; it was unjust.

But death is only meaningless and without redemption when it is separate from the death of Christ. There is more death in those who kill, obeying the powers of the world, than in the death of those who seek to be human and to be truthful. We are commanded to resist death without dignity, without meaning, death that is legal but unnecessary.

But our ways of fighting are as strange as the cross. They are to be the weapons of nonviolent resistance, of communities that offer hope to the victims of injustice, of tender mercies, of offering ourselves as hostage, of working for justice, of living with and choosing the company of the poor and the outcast, and of prayer and love for all, even our enemies. Scratched on the wall of a concentration camp in Germany were these words:

> Lord, remember not only the men and women of good will but all those of ill will. Do not only remember all the suffering they have subjected us to. Remember the fruits we brought forth thanks to this suffering—our comradeship, our loyalty, our humility, our courage and generosity, the greatness of heart that all of this inspired. And when they come to judgment, let all these fruits we have borne be their reward and their forgiveness.

This is the cross. This is Good Friday. This is salvation.

We leave the church in silence. Jesus is dead. It is finished. Now is the time of loss and emptiness, the in-between time of death and resurrection. The seed is in the ground, and with time it will sprout and break forth from the tomb and burst into bloom. For now, though, there is nothing. The presence of God in Jesus has disappeared. Nothing is left, no trace but a stone rolled in front of a tomb, a blood-soaked cross, torn garments, a crown of thorns, and memories. Have we disappeared? What is left of us? What will God have to work on? It seems that resurrection is born most surely of nothingness, of matter that has disappeared into spirit, of flesh that is sacrificed and offered to God. What more do we need to let go of? Perhaps one more story and all that needs to go will disappear.

This is a story from Brazil. It was told by one of my students and friends, Brian O'Sullivan:

✣   Once upon a time there was a poor peasant family that had worked for years scrimping and saving to buy a piece of land of its own. Finally the day came, and they took possession of it. The mother and half a dozen children gathered in the two-room shack that would serve as their house, while the father walked the length and breadth of their land. He paced it out, marking the four corners as boundaries, praying in joy and thanksgiving as he walked. As he rounded the last corner and laid the stone in place he noticed something sticking out from under a bush.

He bent and scratched at the dirt, digging with his hands, and soon unearthed the corpus from a crucifix. It had obviously been in the ground a long time. Its hands and arms were gone, and its feet and legs missing. It was mangled, scratched, cracked, the paint nearly all gone. He picked it up and carried it back in his arms to the house. It was a good size corpus. The crucifix it hung on must have been ten or twelve feet tall. He came in and laid it on the kitchen table.

The family stood around it, looking at it, in an awkward silence. The father explained that he had found it on their land. It was the first thing he had dug out of the ground. What should they do with it? Should they take it to the church and give it to the padre? Should they burn it? Should they bury it again? They all stood and looked at it.

Finally, the youngest spoke: "Father, I have an idea."

"What, my child?"

"Why don't we hang it on the kitchen wall and put a sign underneath it."

"What would you put on the sign?"

And the youngest told them.

There was a long silence. Then the corpus was hung with care on the whitewashed wall of the kitchen and a small sheet of paper was tacked underneath. It read: "Jesus has no arms or legs. Will you lend him yours?"

The memory of Jesus is dangerous, subversive, death-threatening, life-affirming, bursting with hope, and mindful of evil. It is not naive but born of faith and community, the community that stands at the foot of the cross, overshadowed by it, turned toward the tomb, expectant. We leave the church, the tomb, our past behind us, and we go out into the world and wait. Jesus lies in the arms of his Father. His passion is over, passed on to us now. We mourn our loss of his presence among us, but we remember, and we pray:

The tree of the cross has become for us
a plant of endless well-being:
it gives us our nourishment;
we strike root in its roots
and in its branches we spread;
its dew is our joy
and its rustling makes us prolific.

—Anonymous

It is Good Friday.

The Easter Vigil
Easter: The Resurrection of the Lord

Genesis 1:1-2:2

This is the night of storytelling. It begins with gathering around the Easter candle, the light of Christ, to remember our past and where we came from, who we are, and the wonder of God, who has been at work since the beginning of creation. Our roots are all good, very good.

We are bound together, intimately connected, all created by the One who blesses us and tells us to have dominion over the earth as God has dominion over us. It happened as the Word of God, the spirit and breath of God, spoke and it was all very good.

We are made to please God.

Genesis 22:1-18

Our beginning in faith is just as auspicious.

Abraham is called, singled out by God, and put to the test. God wants all that Abraham holds dear, including his beloved son. In anguish and confusion Abraham obeys; he goes to the mountain with Isaac and begins to sacrifice his child. But God is the God of life; there is to be no sacrifice of human beings to God, who is the mystery of all time and life. God wants obedience, surrender, and a life handed over to him alone, trusting that all will be given as needed.

We all begin on that mountain with Abraham, learning to worship truly and hearing the promises of the future echoing in our ears.

Exodus 14:15-15:1

This is the central reading of the vigil: the passing through the Red Sea, with the waters parted by God. The Egyptians in pursuit are caught in the waters of death, while the Israelites are drawn forth into freedom.

The power of God is shown in the Lord's works, in the choice of the children of Israel, and in the waters that redeem and lead to hope and community. The enemies of God, those who imprison, oppress, and destroy others, are judged and in the hands of God. God is on the side of those who pass through the waters.

Isaiah 54:5-14

God seeks intimacy with the beloved people, Israel, as a husband draws near to his beloved wife. There is reconciliation and tenderness in all God's experiences with the chosen people, who are more often than not unfaithful and insensitive to God, refusing to allow God entrance into their hearts.

God's love is enduring. It never leaves us. When we are storm-battered, afflicted, and inconsolable, God approaches to embrace us and establish us with justice and peace where no destruction can come near us again.

Isaiah 55:1-11

This is an announcement: come all who are thirsty, poor, indebted, hungry, and be filled. Come! God will always renew us with life, nation, home, and the glory of God, which will shine throughout us for others to see.

Seek God while God is near, easily found, and seek mercy because God is generous and forgiving. God is not like us. God's thought is not like ours. Yahweh's words come like rain and snow to water the earth, nourishing the seed and yielding the harvest. They do not return to God empty but filled. The divine will is achieved. What

God sends upon the earth will do what it was sent to do. Jesus sent upon the earth will obey God, and life abundant will be brought forth from the seed that is the Word of God.

Baruch 3:9-15, 32-4:4

Hear the commands and know life, even in the midst of exile, dread, and having forsaken the wisdom of God. We can learn prudence, strength, and understanding even when we have walked away from God. We must learn to know wisdom, her treasures and life, her knowledge and light, the mysteries of the universe and stars.

God has traced out this way of understanding and given it to us. Wisdom has appeared on the earth and moved among us. She is the book of law and all who cling to her live. Receive her. What pleases God is known to us. It is given as a gift. Accept it.

Ezekiel 36:16-28

Son of man, I have scattered my people among the nations because they are sinners, defile my Temple, and insult me, and I have judged them. And I have relented because of my Holy Name.

Even when you do not honor me, I remember you and I will act on your behalf and bring you home and I will prove my holiness through you! I will gather you back and sprinkle clean water on you (baptism) and cleanse you and put a new spirit into your stony hearts (confirmation) and I will let you live in the land I gave you and you will be my people (eucharist) and I will be your God.

It is time to come home again.

Romans 6:3-11

With this reading, after the singing of the Gloria and the ringing of the bells and the coming of the light in the church, we are reminded of who we are and what has been done for us in Jesus: "Are you not aware that we who were baptized into Christ Jesus were baptized into his death? Through baptism into his death we were buried with him, so that, just as Christ was raised from the dead by the glory of the Father, we too might live a new life."

We have been crucified; all is destroyed. Our old lives have disappeared, and we are slaves to sin no longer. Death has no power now over Christ and no power over us. "His death was death to sin, once for all; his life is life for God. In the same way, you must consider yourselves dead to sin but alive for God in Christ Jesus." This is the heart of the mystery of Jesus' death and resurrection. We are alive for the glory of God and we live in Christ. We have no life of our own anymore. All of that has disappeared. Our only response for fifty days is Alleluia! Alleluia! Alleluia!

Matthew 28:1-10

Resurrection! It happens in the dark with no witnesses, just the Father bending over the Son and breathing the Spirit back into his flesh. And everything is shattered. The sabbath is over. It is the first day of the week, the eighth day of the week. It is the new creation, and it is just dawning.

Two women come to inspect the tomb: Mary Magdalene and the other Mary. There is an earthquake, and the angel of the Lord descends from heaven. The stone is rolled back, and the angel sits on it. His appearance is a flash of lightning and his garments dazzling as snow. The guards are paralyzed with fear and fall down like dead men. The women are stronger; they stand there, and the angel speaks to them: "Do not be frightened. I know you are looking for Jesus the crucified, but he is not here."

He has been raised, exactly as he promised. "Come and see the spot where he was laid. Then go quickly and tell his disciples: 'He has been raised from the dead and now goes ahead of you to Galilee, where you will see him.' That is the message I have for you."

Matthew's account of the resurrection is very different from the other gospels. There is this angel with the announcement of the end and beginning. There is the violent and physical interruption of the earth, the tomb, and the soldiers, with heaven breaking into history.

The message is proclaimed. It has all the traditional elements of dealing with the power of God: an angel descends, brightness, and the opening words: "Do not be afraid." Resurrection happens when simple grieving people are on their way to inspect the realms of death, seeking the crucified One, Jesus.

But we will not find Jesus in tombs or in any place that is ruled by violence, self-satisfaction, greed, or any institution that deals in death

B Cycle: Mk 16:1-8
C Cycle: Lk 24:1-12

and lies. We find him out in the world, specifically in Galilee, that is, among the poor, the workers, those struggling for a way to survive in an unjust world, our neighbors, believers and unbelievers alike, whom we have known and who have known us always. We will see him there.

Resurrection sends Jesus back into the world, and it sends us back into the world, unafraid now, still seeking the crucified One who is now raised up in glory and hidden in our midst. The women hurry away from the tomb "half-overjoyed, half-fearful," and they go to carry the good news. They are evangelizers carrying the word of life, hope, new creation. There is life after death, the power of evil and violence is broken, light and dazzling possibilities abound. And as they run, there is Jesus standing right in front of them, without any warning. They could have run right into him! Jesus's first word of resurrection is "Peace!" They embrace his feet and do him homage. And he tells them "Do not be afraid! Go and carry the news to my brothers that they are to go to Galilee, where they will see me."

They carry the news and they pass on the story, the words and the command: Go! Go back to your homes and work. Go back to your families and relatives and friends and neighbors and enemies. Go and find God there. Go to the world of commerce, economics, politics. Seek out the poor and those who search for God and go looking with them. That's where he was before. That's where he is now. We touch the feet of the One who has suffered and been crucified and do him homage and obey, returning to those he knelt before and did homage to, honoring them as ones cherished by his Father.

The good news goes first to his brothers and friends. His sisters carry it forth and are told not to be afraid—of anything or anyone! They are to go with peace. Peace is the undeniable presence of the Risen Lord. Peace, not as the world gives, but peace that knows what sin and evil can do, the scars it leaves behind, but also knows the life that is unquenchable within and the Spirit that is irrepressible and indestructible.

This story is ours too. Peace to all of us who have come seeking the crucified One, now risen in glory. We bend and embrace his feet and do him homage. Then we run into the world and spread the good news to our friends, to whom we are bound in baptism and the Spirit. Then we go out into the wider world, to our Galilee, our cities and outskirts of the realms of power, and seek him there. We find him where he is most at home—among the poor and those who struggle for dignity and a life that death cannot tear apart.

Today we proclaim that we believe in the resurrection. What is resurrection? In *Blessed Are You Who Believed*, Carlo Carretto describes resurrection this way:

> When the world seems a defeat for God and you are sick with the disorder, the violence, the terror, the war on the streets; when the earth seems to be chaos, say to yourself, "Jesus died and rose again on purpose to save, and his salvation is already with us."
>
> When your father or your mother, your son or your daughter, your spouse or your friend are on their deathbed, and you are looking at them in the pain of parting, say, "We shall see each other again in the Kingdom; courage . . ."
>
> Every departing missionary is an act of faith in the resurrection.
>
> Every newly-opened leper-hospital is an act of faith in the resurrection.
>
> Every peace treaty is an act of faith in the resurrection.
>
> Every agreed commitment is an act of faith in the resurrection.
>
> When you forgive your enemy
> When you feed the hungry
> When you defend the weak
> you believe in the resurrection.
>
> When you have the courage to marry
> When you welcome the newly-born child
> When you build your home
> you believe in the resurrection.
>
> When you wake at peace in the morning
> When you sing to the rising sun
> When you go to work with joy
> you believe in the resurrection.

Friedrich Nietzsche, a nineteenth-century philosopher, wrote about Christians and Christianity. He praised Christianity as a religion and quoted from the good news. He proclaimed it as hope and promise for the modern world. But he never became a Christian. His answer when questioned about this: "For a group of people who claim to believe in resurrection, none of them looks redeemed!"

The undeniable sign of resurrection is joy, looking redeemed, bringing a sense of hope to others that is tangible and irresistible. It is not shallow but deep, abiding, and enduring. Death cannot break its hold, and suffering and persecution often strengthen it. It brings light and remembers to seek out the stars in the darkest part of night. It is hard-nosed self-sacrifice, knowledgeable of the razor edge of sin, and yet it knows when to sidestep, when to dance, and when to run—and when to stand face to face and stare evil down and take its knife thrust. It is the work of reconciliation, and it abhors violence and insensitivity to others' pain. It knows fear but is not paralyzed or controlled by it. It feeds on the word and trusts in the blood and shares the bread graciously with all. It shoulders the cross and denies itself and turns toward the face of God in all others. It announces the victory of justice and grasps our hand for that victory in our life and wrests us free of the grip of evil and isolation. It thrives in community, and when it is alone it is at home in the larger kingdom of God's realm and the Trinity.

It belongs to all the world and will not honor any one nation or philosophy or group over another, except perhaps those who have no power: the poor. It exalts in the cross and honors those who suffer on behalf of others, closest to the Christ here and now. It hides out, outside the gates, outside the realms of power and institutions, even outside of church, and it hides in mystery and silence. Our lives are proclamations: "We shall not die but live and declare the works of the Lord."

> The stone that the builders rejected has become the
> cornerstone.
> By the Lord has this been done and it is wonderful in
> our eyes. (Psalm 118)

Perhaps a story tells it best. It is a story from Persia, a Muslim tale called "The Two Beggars."

✛ Once upon a time there were two beggars. One day they decided to take their chances and beg from the king himself.

They went straight up to the windows of the palace where he was deciding upon laws and seeing to the upkeep of his land, and they starting crying out. They pleaded and begged, in the name of Allah, the most compassionate one, in the name of mercy, even praising the king himself in hopes of something. Finally, to get rid of them, the king went to the window and had his servants throw them some bread.

Immediately one of the beggars broke into praise of the king, blessing him, singing his praises, and the king smiled. The other, however, ignored the king and broke into song praising Allah for his compassion and mercy and graciousness. The king was annoyed and yelled out at him: "Why do you praise Allah for what I give you? It is I who give to you."

The beggar looked at him and said, "You only give because it was first given to you by Allah to distribute." The king was annoyed, and the two beggars eventually drifted away to eat their bread.

The next day they decided to try again. Back they went and again set up such a din that the king was infuriated. He threw bread and a few coins at them and had them taken from the area. Again, one beggar praised him and the other praised only Allah.

Again the king became angry, and this time he decided to do something about it. He went downstairs to the kitchens and had two loaves of bread made, exactly alike. In one he put a small cache of jewels; in the other, just dough.

The next day the beggars were back, as he suspected they would be, and he was ready. To the beggar who praised him, he gave the loaf with the jewels. To the beggar who praised Allah, he gave the ordinary bread. They left to eat.

On the way to a cooler, quieter spot outside the city, the beggar with the loaf loaded with the jewels noticed his bread was heavy. He thought to himself, This bread must be as hard as a rock. I'll see if this man will trade loaves with me. So, he spoke: "My friend," he said, "this loaf seems very well done, firm, just the way you prefer your bread. Would you like to switch loaves?" And so, they switched loaves of bread.

The beggar who now had the plain loaf of bread made his excuses and went off to eat by himself. The other beggar, the one who praised Allah, took his loaf, as he was wont, to a large tree outside the city, where he often shared his bread with those who hadn't fared as well in their begging ventures. He sat and tore into the bread, giving pieces to others and found the jewels inside! Again he praised Allah profusely and shared the jewels with other beggars.

The next day there was just one beggar at the king's window. When the king looked down he was amazed to find it was the "wrong" beggar, the one to whom he had given jewels hidden in the dough. "What are you doing here? Where is the other beggar? What did you do with the loaf I gave you yesterday?"

The man replied, "I am begging as I always do. I don't know where the other is. He never showed up today. There have been stories of him coming into better times. I gave him the loaf you gave me. It was heavy, lumpy, and I knew it wouldn't taste good. He gladly switched with me."

The king was humbled. The beggar who praised Allah was vindicated. No matter what the king had plotted, Allah had other ideas and had used even his pettiness and meanness, even his arrogance, to change the world's outcomes. And he thought to himself: Perhaps he was right on the other issue as well. Perhaps I only have what I have to give because Allah had given it to me to distribute.

They say there weren't many beggars in the kingdom after a while, and the king was devoted to the praise of Allah.

We are all beggars in the kingdom of God. The praise of God must be ever in our mouths, for the power of God extends and rests deep in history as the cache of jewels hidden in the dough. In the fullness of time all will be laid bare and all will know the power of God that we name resurrection.

The second reading from the Mass for Easter day is about dough, about yeast. We are reminded today to get rid of the old yeast and to make of ourselves fresh dough. We are to disappear now into the dough. Christ our Passover has been sacrificed. We are to celebrate the feast with the new bread of sincerity and truth. Come, let us eat the Body of Christ and take up the cup filled with the wine of salvation and toast the life and death of the Lord with the closing lines of the Easter sequence:

> Christ indeed from death is risen, our new life
> obtaining.

Have mercy, victor King, ever reigning!
Amen. Alleluia

Now, as we begin to live in sincerity and truth, we should remember the words of Daniel Berrigan:

> Sometime in your life, hope that you might see one
> starved man, the look on his face when the bread
> finally arrives.
> Hope that you might have baked it or bought it or
> even kneaded it yourself.
> For that look on his face, for your meeting his eyes
> across a piece of bread, you might be willing to
> lose a lot, or suffer a lot, or die a little, even.

In losing it all we gain life, ever more abundant life. When everything else disappears only Love remains, only God. This is why we tell all the stories. The Word is true. Alleluia.

Works Cited

Amesty International (banned radio advertisement). 1995. In *The Tablet* (July 1).

Bernard of Clairvaux. 1987. *Selected Works*. Trans. Gillian R. Evans. New York: Paulist Press.

Berrigan, Daniel. 1983. *The Nightmare of God*. Portland, OR: Sunburst Press.

Bonhoeffer, Dietrich. 1959. *The Cost of Discipleship*. New York: Macmillan.

Carretto, Carlo. 1983. *Blessed Are You Who Believed*. Maryknoll, NY: Orbis Books.

Guthrie, Donna. 1993. *Nobiah's Well*. Nashville: Ideals Publishing Corporation.

Heschel, Abraham Joshua. 1954. *Man's Quest for God: Studies in Prayer and Symbolism* (also reprinted as *Quest for God*). New York: Charles Scribner's Sons.

Hillesum, Etty. 1983. *An Interrupted Life*. New York: Pantheon Books.

Lanza del Vasto, Joseph Jean. 1974. *Principles and Precepts of a Return to the Obvious*. New York: Schocken Books.

Laverdiere, Eugene. 1994. *Dining in the Kingdom of God: The Origins of the Eucharist According to Luke*. Chicago: Liturgy Training Publications.

Mangakis, Geo. 1973. "Letter to Europeans." *Amnesty International Report on Torture*.

Merton, Thomas. 1958. *Thoughts in Solitude*. New York: Farrar, Straus & Cudahy.

_____. 1988. *A Vow of Conversation: Journals, 1964-1965*. New York: Farrar, Straus, Giroux.

Nouwen, Henri. 1985. *Love in a Fearful Land: A Guatemalan Story*. Notre Dame: Ave Maria Press.

O'Brien, Niall. 1993. *Island of Tears, Island of Hope*. Maryknoll, NY: Orbis Books.

Sanford, John. 1968. *Dreams: God's Forgotten Language*. Philadelphia, Lippincott.

Sloyan, Gerard. 1995. "The Popular Passion Piety of the Catholic West, *Worship* 69, no. 1 (January).

Sobrino, Jon. 1994. *The Principle of Mercy: Taking the Crucified People from the Cross*. Maryknoll, NY: Orbis Books.

Traherne, Thomas. 1950 (reimpression with introduction by John Hayward). *Centuries of Meditations*. London: P. J. & A. E. Dobell.

Van Laan, Nancy. 1989. *Rainbow Crow*. New York: Alfred Knopf. A version for young readers.

Wiesel, Elie. 1973. *The Oath*. New York, Random House.

Wink, Walter. 1992. *Engaging the Powers*. Minneapolis: Fortress Press.